Mindfulness in Good Lives

Mindfulness in Good Lives

Mike W. Martin

LEXINGTON BOOKS
Lanham • Boulder • New York • London

Published by Lexington Books
An imprint of The Rowman & Littlefield Publishing Group, Inc.
4501 Forbes Boulevard, Suite 200, Lanham, Maryland 20706
www.rowman.com

6 Tinworth Street, London SE11 5AL

Copyright © 2020 by The Rowman & Littlefield Publishing Group, Inc.

All rights reserved. No part of this book may be reproduced in any form or by any electronic or mechanical means, including information storage and retrieval systems, without written permission from the publisher, except by a reviewer who may quote passages in a review.

British Library Cataloguing in Publication Information Available

Library of Congress Control Number: 2019951190

ISBN: 978-1-4985-9636-7 (cloth)
ISBN: 978-1-4985-9638-1 (paper)
ISBN: 978-1-4985-9637-4 (electronic)

For Shannon, *my love.*

Contents

Preface	ix
1 Mindfulness Movement	1
Part One: Making Sense of Mindfulness	**11**
2 Attending to What Matters	13
3 Living in the Present	31
4 Ways of Attending	47
5 Thoreau's Wakefulness	63
Part Two: Concepts of Mindfulness	**75**
6 Meditation and Morality	77
7 Mindful Decision Making	95
8 Mindful Valuing and Psychotherapy	111
Part Three: Well-Being	**127**
9 Happiness and Virtues	129
10 Mindful Work in Balanced Lives	147
11 Authenticity and *Seize the Day*	161
12 Mindfulness Movement Critics	175
Bibliography	187
Index	199
About the Author	205

Preface

Live in the moment. I began with this ideal of passion and renewal, of cherishing the moment instead of worrying about the past and future. I reflected on the maxim's undertow of evading responsibility for past wrongdoing and planning for the future, and its neglect of knowledge of the past and hopes for the future in meeting present challenges. There is also its air of triteness—don't we always live in the moment, until it slips into the past and is replaced by a new moment? These reflections led me to refine the ideal: live in the moment, yes, but in light of worthy values that link the present to wider horizons of time and meaning. Thus prepared, I entered the literature on mindfulness, famous for experiencing the here-and-now. I quickly became confused—a good place for a philosopher to get to work.

Exactly what is mindfulness? Why is it valuable, and how does it connect with other values? How does it contribute to good lives? Why do psychologists dominate the literature, and why have they developed such strikingly different concepts of mindfulness? Why have philosophers said so little about mindfulness—or have they said a great deal about it, without using the word? What should we make of the mindfulness movement that so earnestly celebrates mindfulness in everything from mental health to meaningful work, and from spirituality to sports?

In most everyday contexts, mindfulness is paying attention to what matters in light of relevant values. When those values are sound and applied with good judgment, mindfulness is a virtue that helps implement other values. We invoke this virtue, for example, when we say that good drivers are mindful of safety, and good physicians are mindful of the social impacts of prescribing opioids. I apply this everyday concept in making sense of the variety of definitions in the mindfulness literature. I also use it to rethink the dominant paradigm in health psychology of nonjudgmental mindfulness during meditation. My overarching goal is to understand mindfulness as a virtue in good lives. To that end I explore a host of topics at the interface of morality and mental health.

I thank Shannon Snow Martin for her suggestions and, above all, for her love and inspiration. She joins me in thanking Sonia, Nicole, Rafa, Gus, Jesse, and Dylan, for the joy they bring us. Special thanks to Nicole for recommending books with an uncanny sense of when I needed them.

I write in gratitude for my teachers. They include, at the University of California, Irvine, Nuel Belnap (visiting), Jill Buroker, A. I. Melden, Stanley Munsat, Nelson Pike, Gerasimos Santas, David Smith, William Ulrich, and Peter Woodruff; at the University of Utah, Peter Appleby, David Bennett, Mendel Cohen, Fred Hagen, Richard Henson, Bruce Landesman, Sterling M. McMurrin, John Rawls (visiting), Waldemer P. Read, T. M. Reed, Max Rogers, Bangs Tapscott, William Whisner, and Peter Windt; and at Bountiful High School, Mrs. Whitaker and Dr. Max Harward.

Chapter One

Mindfulness Movement

Mindfulness is celebrated everywhere—especially in health psychology and spiritual practices, but also in the arts, business, consumerism, eating, education, environmentalism, sports, and using digital devices.[1] Psychologists are mainly responsible for launching this mindfulness movement, and they remain its primary cheerleaders. Some of them proclaim a "mindfulness revolution"[2] and declare mindfulness "the essence of well-being and happiness."[3] One distinguished researcher claims that "virtually all our problems—personal, interpersonal, professional, and societal—either directly or indirectly stem from mindlessness."[4] Another therapist prescribes "the mindfulness solution" for most everyday problems.[5] Journalists, too, report "a popular obsession with mindfulness as the secret to health and happiness."[6] "Mindfulness" is no longer just a fancy word for paying attention. It now names a cluster of wide-ranging skills, practices, attitudes and habits, and even a virtue. To be sure, mindfulness has always been a key virtue in Asian religions, especially Buddhism where it is step seven in the Eightfold Path to Enlightenment.[7] It is somewhat less clear which virtue is being celebrated in psychology and popular culture.

What should we make of this mindfulness movement, including the "current popularity of mindfulness practices"[8] and the wide-ranging advocacy of mindfulness as a tool in or even a feature of good lives? Is it a superficial fad and an outgrowth of a narcissistic society? Is it one more indication that psychological and therapeutic outlooks are replacing morality in our society? Or does it herald something important for integrating moral and therapeutic understanding? It is some of all these things.

The call to be more mindful is certainly a response to contemporary life, with its increasing complexity, fragmentation, and stress. Under the heading of mindfulness, health psychologists have developed an array of therapies and tools to help us cope with these challenges. Many of the therapies, especially those connected with meditation, enter popular culture through self-help books and media. That is not surprising. But it is remarkable that mindfulness has acquired a spiritual, even magical quality, no doubt owing in part to its connections with Asian religions. I will emphasize the ordinariness of mindfulness. Nevertheless, I agree that the mindfulness movement highlights something important. It highlights the importance of paying attention to what matters, in light of values.

I have four interwoven aims, each centered on how mindfulness connects with values. First, I try to make sense of the striking variety of concepts of mindfulness in terms of how they relate to values in different contexts. Second, I argue that health psychologists who study mindfulness invariably presuppose moral values that should be made transparent. Third, I comment along the way on the promise and perils of the mindfulness movement. Fourth, my overarching aim is to understand mindfulness as a virtue in good lives—as an excellence that helps implement sound values.

What is mindfulness? In popular culture the word has an air of profundity, a whiff of preciousness, and redolent vagueness. Different thinkers have ample leeway to stipulate definitions suitable for their purposes, and those purposes vary widely. I too develop a definition useful for my purposes, the first of which is to make sense of the diversity of mindfulness concepts and conceptions. Or rather, I develop a trio of definitions: value-based mindfulness, personal-mindfulness, and virtue-mindfulness.

Value-based mindfulness is paying attention to what matters, where mattering is understood in terms of values relevant to a situation (or in general). It is paying heed to important matters, bearing in mind significant truths and evidence, noticing crucial details, exercising vigilance and foresight, and responding appropriately and responsibly to a situation. Value-based mindfulness branches in two directions, depending on the reference point in specifying relevant values. *Personal-mindfulness* is paying attention to what matters in light of one's personal values, whatever they may be, for example compassion or cruelty, generosity or greed, justice or oppression. *Virtue-mindfulness* is paying attention to what matters in light of sound values—those which are permissible or defensible, rather than immoral, irrational, or unhealthy. Virtue-mindfulness is manifested by a school-bus driver maneuvering safely on a dangerous road, an athlete skillfully competing during a game, a business manager integrating conflicting considerations in making responsible decisions, and each of us in pursuing a good life.

Value-based mindfulness, personal-mindfulness, and virtue-mindfulness are all skeletal concepts until fleshed out with relevant values. Nevertheless, this trio of concepts helps us clarify and connect the mélange of meanings in religion, popular culture, psychology, and elsewhere. It forms the hub of a wheel to which diverse definitions attach as spokes. Most obvious, conceptions of virtue-mindfulness are familiar in spiritual writings, and arguably all religions develop practices of mindfulness associated with their values. In particular, Buddhist concepts of *right-mindfulness* tether mindfulness to values such as compassion, kindness, truthfulness, and peace. I discuss Buddhism more than other religions, not because I am a Buddhist (I am not), but because Buddhist values frequently blend with psychological themes in popular writings on mindfulness. Such a blend is found, for example, in Shamash Alidina's *Mindfulness for Dummies*: "Mindfulness means paying attention on purpose, in the present moment, infused with qualities like kindness, curiosity and acceptance."[9]

Far more than religious concepts, psychological concepts of mindfulness are my focus. I do not attempt a comprehensive survey of psychological concepts. Instead I select a few influential thinkers for close study: Jon Kabat-Zinn, Ellen J. Langer, Albert Ellis, and (more briefly) positive psychologists such as Mihaly Csikszentmihalyi and Martin E. P. Seligman. I argue that psychological concepts of mindfulness repeatedly presuppose moral values that should be made transparent. The concealment takes place in many ways. For example, psychologists conceal moral values under expansive definitions of mental health as "mental well-being," an expression that easily camouflages moral well-being. Recent positive psychologists conceal value assumptions under their eponymous term "positive"—although, to their credit, positive psychologists are far more open in discussing moral values than most psychologists. And psychologists disguise value assumptions under key terms used in defining mindfulness. These terms include "attention" and "awareness," which in the mindfulness literature imply consciousness of noteworthy things, not willy-nilly darts of consciousness. It is also true of being attentive and aware "in the moment," an expression sometimes used to sever connections of values to wider horizons of time and meaning. But above all, value assumptions are concealed by the word "nonjudgmental," the most slippery word in the mindfulness lexicon.

"Nonjudgmental" is the operative term in many psychologists' definitions of mindfulness. Most famously, Jon Kabat-Zinn defines mindfulness "the awareness that arises from paying attention on purpose, in the present moment, and nonjudgmentally."[10] His concept is enormously influential in generating new therapies for stress, anxiety, depression, and a host of other ailments. In addition, it permeates popular culture, to the point where it is sometimes reflected in dictionary entries for "mindfulness," for example in *Merriam-Webster's Collegiate Dictionary*: "the practice of maintaining a nonjudgmental state of heightened or complete awareness of one's thoughts, emotions, or experiences on a moment-to-moment basis."[11] The word "nonjudgmental" is used ambiguously in the mindfulness literature, in ways that conceal values. It might mean everything from avoiding unduly negative judgments (its ordinary meaning) to avoiding all negative judgments. Or it might mean suspending all value judgments (during meditation), or suspending only undiscriminating judgments. These shifting meanings blur or eclipse values in understanding mindfulness, or so I argue.

The therapeutic emphasis on nonjudgmental generates what Eric Harrison calls "one huge contradiction" in mindfulness studies: "The Buddha understood mindfulness (*sati*) as the function of discriminating attention. The very purpose of attention is to refine our capacity for accurate judgment and decision-making in all matters, big and small. So how did 'mindfulness' become so widely used in a sense that is virtually the opposite: a state of nonjudgmental acceptance?"[12] The answer centers in part on Kabat-Zinn's influence. But Harrison's question and concern also bears on the wider mindfulness movement. Is the shift from value-based mindfulness to value-suspending mindfulness worrisome, perhaps ominous? Is it yet another sign that moral values are at risk in our society, as illustrated by reducing them to feelings? Indeed, one writer stipulates that "paying attention to our feelings is the very definition of mindfulness."[13] The elemental connection of mindfulness to values, and ultimately to sound values, is obscured or lost altogether.

I understand the mindfulness movement as part of a broader therapeutic trend in ethics: the tendency to approach moral matters in terms of mental health, as understood by psychologists and psychiatrists. The therapeutic trend in ethics sometimes seeks to replace morality with therapeutic outlooks.[14] At its best, however, the trend integrates moral and therapeutic outlooks in beneficial ways. In this spirit, we can integrate value-based mindfulness with the temporary value-suspending mindfulness that occurs during much meditation. We can do so, I argue, by showing that Kabat-Zinn's value-suspending mindfulness (as I call it) is a tool embedded in a context rich in values.

My overarching aim is to understand mindfulness as a virtue in good lives—lives that are morally decent as well as healthy, meaningful, happy, and fulfilling. As a virtue, mindfulness helps implement the kaleidoscope of sound values that enter into good lives. It is not a magic elixir. Nor is it separable from the plethora of additional values that guide good lives. But it deserves to be counted as a virtue when it is attached to sound values. Virtue-mindfulness is the activity or disposition to attend to what matters in our situation, where what matters is specified in terms of sound values. It is bearing in mind what is genuinely important in a good life—taking it into account on appropriate occasions and with good judgment.

No book could explore mindfulness in all areas of good lives, for mindfulness helps implement the kaleidoscope of values that enter into the kaleidoscope of good lives. I select topics such as work and happiness that concern the interface of morality and mental health, and are of equal interest in philosophy and psychology. Along the way I connect mindfulness to a host of additional topics, including aesthetic appreciation, creativity, education, sports psychology, and coping with illness. I also comment on the mindfulness movement. Overall, on the negative side, I object to the movement's tendency to embrace the subjectivism about values that already permeates culture, in particular the tendency to downplay moral reasoning and rational reflection on values. On the positive side, I find a wealth of serious thought and conscientious practices, amid the movement's welter of ideas and practices.

Finally, in discussing mindfulness as a virtue in good lives I widen the terrain. Mindfulness is not the privileged turf of scientists and therapists who embrace it as a term of art. I discuss humanists such as Goethe and Thoreau who explore mindfulness without using the word. I also compare and contrast key therapists to philosophers who discuss mindfulness without relying on the word. To highlight the tacit value assumptions of psychologists, and to illustrate how those assumptions might be made more explicit, I link psychologists with philosophers who made moral values salient in discussing mindfulness, often under other names. In particular I pair Kabat-Zinn with the Buddha, Langer with John Dewey, Ellis with Epictetus and other stoics, and positive psychologists with virtue ethicists. Although many philosophers could have been selected, I choose thinkers whose interests are close to those of the psychologists.

Here is an overview. Part One (chapters 2–5) develops the concepts of value-based mindfulness, personal-mindfulness, and virtue-mindfulness. Part Two (chapters 6–8) explores three concepts of mindfulness prominent among psychologists: what I call value-suspending mindfulness during meditation, flexibility-mindfulness in making decisions, and mindful valuing as a tool and aim of cognitive therapy. Part Three (chapters 9–11) applies psychological and philosophical studies of mindfulness to happiness, work, and authenticity, thereby illustrating how mindfulness contributes to good lives. The concluding chapter 12 illustrates how critics of the mindfulness movement also make controversial value judgments about "true mindfulness."

Chapter 2. In everyday language, "mindful" and "mindfulness" have myriad meanings, but one theme stands out: paying attention to what matters in a situation, in light of relevant values. In this way, most everyday mindfulness is value-based, as it was long before psychologists began to develop technical definitions of mindfulness during the 1970s. Personal-mindfulness is attending to what matters to individuals in light of their de facto values. Virtue-mindfulness is attending to what matters in light of sound values—that is, permissible values that are not immoral, irrational, or unhealthy. I emphasize that concepts and conceptions of mindfulness need not rely on the words "mindful," "mindfully," and "mindfulness," thereby inviting bridge-building between contemporary psychology and classical philosophical discussions of attending to what matters in good lives. I also affirm a pluralistic value perspective on the values that guide mindfulness.

Chapter 3. Most writers on mindfulness highlight attention and awareness in and to our *present* situation. I do so as well, but I underscore that what matters in the present is generally connected to what matters in the future and past. Moreover, the present situation is vague and elastic. It might be a moment, day, season, or stage of life. In addition, typically the present concerns time as experienced (subjective time) more than time specified by clocks and calendars (objective time). Either way, the present might be understood with two contrasting emphases: (a) as isolated and insulated from the past and future, or (b) as linked to the past and future. Temporarily insulating the present can be useful in increasing enjoyment and personal control. Linking the present to wider horizons of time and values, however, is essential in pursuing goals, and even to maintaining perspective on present difficulties. Knowing when to adopt one emphasis or the other, when to shift between them, and when to employ them in tandem are important skills.

Chapter 4. The attention involved in mindfulness is not a univocal activity or state. It is misleading to call it a "mental muscle," as is frequently done in popular writing. Instead, it can involve a host of mental skills, including remembrance and foresight, observation and inference, self-control and responsibility. Attention by itself has many modes. They include general awareness, selective attention, concentrated focus, open monitoring, agent-attention of participants versus spectator attention, self-reflection versus outward attention, rapid and automatic attention versus slow and reflective attention, and (in normative terms) skillful versus unskillful attention. Values enter into understanding all these modes of mindful attention.

Chapter 5. Value perspectives on mindfulness attempt to specify when and why mindfulness is itself a value or virtue. They go hand in glove with general value perspectives on good lives. Henry David Thoreau's value perspective in *Walden* is a good illustration. Thoreau is frequently cited in the mindfulness literature even though he doesn't rely on the words "mindful" and "mindfulness," instead preferring terms such as "awake" and "wakefulness." He takes up a variety of contemporary moral themes, including authenticity, respect for moral diversity, simplicity, attunement to nature, happiness, and the overlap of morality and mental health. At the same time, his value perspective is controversial and illustrates how conceptions of virtue-mindfulness invariably elicit disagreement.

Chapter 6. Today mindfulness is most often associated with meditation, whether for therapeutic, spiritual, or skill-enhancing purposes. But mindfulness is no more reducible to meditation than physical fitness is reducible to calisthenics. Health professionals who study meditation, strongly influenced by Jon Kabat-Zinn, typically understand mindfulness as value-suspending (at least during meditation). Yet Kabat-Zinn extensively invokes value judgments in connection with mindfulness when he writes for popular audiences. The moral assumptions of health psychologists need to be more transparent, for when they are, value-suspending mindfulness connects to virtue-mindfulness such as found in Buddhism, a spiritual orientation that greatly influenced Kabat-Zinn.

Chapter 7. Ellen J. Langer developed a concept of mindfulness in making decisions and solving problems. Her concept, which I call *flexibility-mindfulness*, is reasoning based on flexibility, inventiveness, and openness to new information and viewpoints.[15] I interpret her flexibility-mindfulness as an anemic version of virtue-mindfulness, one centered on the values of inventiveness and openness to new information and ideas. In addition, she presupposes an array of values in discussing particular examples and psychological experiments. Yet she tends to reduce values to personal preferences and social conventions, ultimately sliding toward a concept of personal-mindfulness. Many of her themes are pursued with greater clarity and consistency within a framework of virtue-mindfulness, such as John Dewey's conception of intelligent problem solving.

Chapter 8. Mindful valuing is paying attention to what matters concerning valuing itself, where valuing is embedded in value judgments (evaluations), emotions and attitudes (whose core are value beliefs), desires and choices (that implement values), and reviewing and revising value judgments (in more rational or reasonable directions). Mindful valuing has particular importance in cognitive behavioral therapy, as I illustrate with Albert Ellis's pioneering Rational Emotive Behavior Therapy, and the more recent Acceptance and Commitment Therapy. Ellis celebrated the values of rationality, health, and happiness, using them to critique conventional morality that is heavily blame oriented. In contrast, the classical stoics explicitly tether mindful valuing to morality, although they too caution against excessive guilt, shame, and blame.

Chapter 9. Philosophers have a long-standing interest in happiness—what it is, how best to pursue it, and its significance in good lives. Yet it is positive psychologists who currently dominate studies of happiness and its ingredients. More a general emphasis than a set of techniques, positive psychology explores the positive side of human experience, character, and organizations. In particular, positive psychologists illuminate how mindfulness contributes to meaningful relationships and activities, to enjoyment and savoring, and to happiness. I connect their studies to my view of happiness as loving one's life, valuing it in ways shown in ample enjoyments and a robust sense of meaning. I also discuss the paradox of happiness—to get happiness forget it—as a general strategy in mindful pursuits of happiness.

Chapter 10. Mindfulness practices are used as a tool for workers, managers, and leaders. In these contexts, it is usually understood as value-suspending mindfulness during meditation, but other psychological understandings may enter as well. In the background, I suggest, is the everyday idea of mindfulness as attending to what matters (concerning work), in light of values. When those values are sound and implemented with good judgment, mindfulness is a virtue. It becomes a broader virtue when work is connected with professions, consumerism, philanthropy, income, and wealth. Mindfulness is less a new managerial tool than a familiar excellence governing good work—work that is ethical and excellent.

Chapter 11. Gurus celebrate mindfulness as an ideology and a quick fix for problems. Saul Bellow cautions against such abuses in his comic, poignant, and cautionary tale, *Seize the Day*, a novella that connects with many of my themes. Specifically, the novella provides a case study in how mindfulness is not a stand-alone value. Mindfulness is a virtue only when tied to sound values, ultimately to a value perspective on good lives that illuminates what should matter in the present. Value perspectives typically include responsibilities undertaken in the past and extending into the future. Without such temporal and normative perspective, living in the present can be a recipe for self-indulgence, irresponsibility, and exploitation by gurus of mindfulness. Authentic self-expression in the present embodies sound values, where authenticity is understood as a hybrid of self-honesty, autonomy, and self-respect.

Chapter 12. The mindfulness movement has drawn criticism, including from internal critics who participate in the movement. In different ways, internal critics charge that the movement distorts and betrays "true mindfulness," by introducing superficial versions of mindfulness. Buddhists see the movement as diluting the true meaning of mindfulness and using it to increase self-absorption and material attachments. Even some psychologists, most notably Thomas Joiner in *Mindlessness: The Corruption of Mindfulness in a Culture of Narcissism*, worry that genuine mindfulness has degenerated into shallow and sham substitutes. Although I am sympathetic to some of these criticisms, I argue that critics' appeals to true mindfulness could benefit from greater clarity about the themes I explore throughout my book.

NOTES

1. For a sampling of interests in mindfulness, see Barry Boyce, ed., *The Mindfulness Revolution: Leading Psychologists, Scientists, Artists, and Meditation Teachers on the Power of Mindfulness in Daily Life* (Boston, MA: Shambhala, 2011). On connecting mindfulness to all aspects of daily life, see Laurie J. Cameron, *The Mindful Day: Practical Ways to Find Focus, Calm, and Joy from Morning to Evening* (Washington, DC: National Geographic, 2018).

2. Michael A. West, "The Practice of Meditation," in Michael A. West, ed., *The Psychology of Meditation: Research and Practice* (New York: Oxford University Press, 2016), 3–25, at 15.

3. Christell T. Ngnoumen and Ellen J. Langer, "Mindfulness: The Essence of Well-Being and Happiness," in Itai Ivtzan and Tim Lomas, eds., *Mindfulness in Positive Psychology: The Science of Meditation and Well-Being* (New York: Routledge, 2016), 97–107, at 99.

4. Ellen J. Langer, *Mindfulness*, 25th Anniversary Edition (Boston, MA: Da Capo Press, 2014), xiii.

5. See Ronald D. Siegel, *The Mindfulness Solution: Everyday Practices for Everyday Problems* (New York: The Guilford Press, 2010).

6. Kate Pickert, "The Art of Being Present," *Time*: Special Edition on *The Science of Happiness* (New York: Time Books, 2016), 71–79, at 72.

7. Bhikku Bodhi, *The Noble Eightfold Path: Way to the End of Suffering* (Onalaska, WA: BPS Pariyatti Editions, 1994).

8. Gay Watson gives the former characterization of the mindfulness movement in *Attention: Beyond Mindfulness* (London: Reaktion Books, 2017), 54.

9. Shamash Alidina, *Mindfulness for Dummies*, 2nd ed. (Chichester, UK: John Wiley and Sons, 2015), 7.

10. Jon Kabat-Zinn, *Meditation Is Not What You Think: Mindfulness and Why It Is So Important* (New York: Hachette Books, 2018), xxxiv.

11. *Merriam-Webster's Collegiate Dictionary*, 11th ed. Chauncey A. Goodrich (Springfield, MA: Merriam-Webster, 2014).

12. Eric Harrison, *The Foundations of Mindfulness: How to Cultivate Attention, Good Judgment, and Tranquility* (New York: The Experiment, 2017), 12–13.

13. Leah Weiss, *How We Work: Live Your Purpose, Reclaim Your Sanity, and Embrace the Daily Grind* (New York: HarperCollins, 2018), 2.

14. See Mike W. Martin, *From Morality to Mental Health: Virtue and Vice in a Therapeutic Culture* (New York: Oxford University Press, 2006).

15. Langer, *Mindfulness*, 64.

Part One

Making Sense of Mindfulness

Chapter Two

Attending to What Matters

At the 2017 Academy Awards ceremony, Warren Beatty and Faye Dunaway announced *La La Land* as the winner of the Oscar for Best Picture. In fact *Moonlight* had won.[1] The blunder—the misexecution of a ceremonial announcement—was not due to mindlessness on the part of Beatty and Dunaway.[2] Perhaps an ideally mindful agent would have immediately identified the error. But Beatty did sense that something was amiss because the card he read from wasn't formatted in the way he anticipated. Quite simply, he and Dunaway were handed the wrong card and envelope by an employee of PricewaterhouseCoopers, the accounting firm entrusted with keeping the winners secret until the appropriate moment during the ceremony. It was that employee who failed to perform his task mindfully. Carelessly, he held two envelopes, the correct one and a duplicate of another envelope used earlier to award the Best Actress Award to Emma Stone for her role in *La La Land*. Inattentive, he mixed up the envelopes and handed the wrong one to Beatty and Dunaway. Confused and distracted, he and another employee then failed to correct the mistake promptly, even though they knew the actual winner, having been required to memorize all the winners prior to the ceremony.

Mindful employees would have been more alert and taken greater care to ensure the actual winner was announced. The correct announcement mattered in light of relevant values—including the values of truthfulness and fairness, accuracy in recognizing achievement in film, excellence in a television program having cultural importance, conscientiousness in carrying out responsibilities, and self-interested values such as doing their job and being respected rather than ridiculed. The PricewaterhouseCoopers employees were no doubt paying attention to something, but they were not paying attention to what *mattered* in their situation. They did not attend to the right (urgent) things, at the right (correct) time, in the right (appropriate) manner, and in accord with the right (relevant) values.

In the predominant everyday sense, mindfulness is value-centered—value-based, value-infused, value-guided. In this chapter I clarify and provide the rationale for a trio of concepts of mindfulness that underscore this value-centeredness:

1. Value-based mindfulness: paying attention to what matters in the present situation in light of relevant values.
2. Personal-mindfulness: paying attention to what matters in our situation in light of our values.
3. Virtue-mindfulness: paying attention to what matters in the present situation in light of sound values, that is, permissible values that rule out immorality, irrationality, and unhealthiness.

MINDFULNESS AND OTHER VALUES

Mindfulness sparkles with meanings. It can mean attentiveness, heedfulness, vigilance, bearing in mind significant truths, remembering to do important things, and conscientiously implementing values. These multiple meanings shadow the word with a penumbra of ambiguity and vagueness. Bhikkhu Bodhi suggests "the word 'mindfulness' is itself so vague and elastic that it serves almost as a cipher into which we can read virtually anything we want."[3] His suggestion is hyperbole designed to make a key point: Different thinkers with different aims may assign strikingly different meanings to the word.

Those meanings are frequently honorific, especially when thinkers stipulate definitions of "true mindfulness"—the real thing as opposed to ersatz versions. In this vein, thinkers might claim to identify an essential or primary meaning, sometimes proposing necessary and sufficient features that precisely define it. We should be suspicious of essentialist definitions, and cautious about honorific definitions. As I see the conceptual landscape, different thinkers embrace the words "mindful" and "mindfulness" with different interests and aims. In doing so they reshape or refine everyday meanings for purposes that might be therapeutic or psychological, spiritual or moral, commercial or academic, or any number of other things.[4] The resulting maze of meanings is not unified by a simple essence, although various meanings may have similarities, what Ludwig Wittgenstein called family resemblances.[5] The maze can be confusing and disorienting in ways expressed by another metaphor from Wittgenstein: "Language is a labyrinth of paths. You approach from *one* side and know your way about; you approach the same place from another side and no longer know your way about."[6]

I too develop definitions that serve my aims, which are fourfold. First, I seek to discover some order in the maze of meanings of mindfulness. In doing so I identify conceptual connections where they exist and build bridges where there are gaps, emphasizing that mindfulness involves values that guide attention. Second, I argue that psychologists, who currently dominate mindfulness studies, frequently presuppose moral values, especially under the heading of *mental health*. Those values need to be more transparent. Third, I sometimes offer cultural comments about the promise and peril of the mindfulness movement. Finally, and most important, I explore mindfulness as a virtue in good lives, selecting topics at the interface of mental health and morality, psychology and moral philosophy. With these purposes in mind, I clarify a concept of mindfulness, or trio of concepts, which remains close to ordinary language, is flexible enough to illuminate more specialized concepts, and highlights the role of values in understanding mindfulness in good lives.

According to one dictionary, to be mindful is to be carefully attentive.[7] *Carefully* suggests that more is involved than simple consciousness or observation. It hints that we pay attention to what is noteworthy in light of relevant values, as well as taking note of important details. Furthermore, in some contexts mindfulness suggests perceptiveness in noticing what is *most* important. It also suggests *conscientiously* taking into account what matters, and doing so in *reasonable* ways in our thinking, feeling, and conduct. Typically it implies *caring* about relevant values so as to implement them. The attention involved in mindfulness is not simply looking or listening in a certain direction, or squinting to bring an object into focus. Nor is the attention a generic "mental muscle," contrary to a recurring metaphor in popular discussions of mindfulness.[8] All such mental maneuvers and capacities need to be tethered to values in order for concepts of mindfulness to gain a foothold.

Here are some additional examples of how mindfulness is rooted in values that guide attention. Mindful drivers pay attention to speed, traffic signs, stoplights, lane indicators, other vehicles, bicyclists, pedestrians, and laws, as well as to their destination. Mindful travelers remain alert to what is new or otherwise interesting on their trips, in a spirit of exploration or adventure. Students are mindful when they concentrate on assigned readings, listen attentively to lectures, seek to understand, and perhaps try to be creative. Mindful engineers attend to costs, quality, safety, aesthetics, schedules, and the wider social implications of their technological projects.[9] Musicians are mindful in practicing regularly and in heeding standards of artistic excellence when they perform. Mindful athletes are attuned to what it takes to win, and to do their best in competitions. Advertisers are "mindful of trends" in order to know what their audience is interested in.[10] Consumers are mindful of their finances when making purchases, in order to minimize debt and increase savings, and they respect the environment by recycling. Responsible philanthropists bring "self-restraint and mindfulness to giving that affects the lives of their fellow citizens," paying heed to both the good and possibly harmful aspects of their gifts.[11] As for millionaires, "while the popular perception of millionaires is that they are more ostentatious than frugal, recent research shows that single-digit millionaires, at least, are generally far more mindful about how they save, spend and invest their money."[12]

In these examples "mindful" is an adjective applied to groups of individuals, such as drivers. In addition, "mindful" can be an adjective modifying activities, as in "mindful driving," or an adverb as in "driving mindfully." And it can morph into a verb, as when we urge a friend to mind the sharp curve in the road ahead. Furthermore, the things we are mindful of vary enormously, and they can be specified in different ways. They might be general types of considerations that demand due care, such as the costs, quality, and dangers to which engineers attend. Or they might be specific risks in daily activities, such as walking in a dangerous neighborhood. Judith Freeman says that she lived in a dorm at Macalester College while her toddler recovered from a heart operation, and she found students eager to play with her child: "Everyone understood the need to be very watchful and careful with him. It would be disastrous if he should receive a blow to his chest. They understood this and they were mindful."[13] Again, we are mindful of social and moral rules. James A. Michener describes an African tribe, the Xhosa, who consider it permissible for boys and girls past puberty to "play at night . . . always mindful that there must not be any babies."[14] Again, we can also be mindful of gifts and benefits from the past. Michener says that he and his wife were motivated to donate millions of dollars to the arts because they were "mindful of the contributions" they had received from others.[15] And we can be mindful of opportunities and challenges in the future: "Mindful of midterm elections, Republicans are divided on how to proceed."[16]

The Oxford English Dictionary (OED) provides additional illustrations of how mindfulness is rooted in values.

"What is man, that thou art mindful of him?"

"[Although] he was very mindful of all other things, he never would remember any injury done unto him."

"We beseech you be mindful that the twenty-ninth of May be kept for a thanksgiving."

"In all their actions to be ever mindful of the last day."

"He had always been mindful of his health even in his pleasures."

"Mindful of the fastidious ways of his friend."

"Guinevere, not mindful of his face, desired his name."

"The monks were always mindful to establish themselves where there was water close at hand."[17]

These sentences are decontextualized, so that the values indicating what matters remain in the background. It is clear enough, however, that the relevant values are such things as human dignity, self-respect, survival, friendship, love, shared thanksgiving, devotion to God, and social standing. The backgrounding of values is also commonplace in contemporary discourse, and I argue in part two that it is equally commonplace in psychological studies of mindfulness. To emphasize, mindfulness centers on attending to what matters *in light of* values, as distinct from attending to values themselves. Sometimes, of course values can be what matters and should be attended to—for example, in confronting ethical dilemmas, studying philosophical ethics, or in fostering mindful valuing during cognitive therapy. But whether in the background or foreground, values provide the framework for understanding the *senses* of "mindfulness," the *references* to things we should be mindful of, and the *assessments* of persons and actions as mindful.

WORDS, CONCEPTS, CONCEPTIONS

Mottos also illustrate how mindfulness is tethered to values.[18] Thus, "Mind your manners" applies on social occasions where courtesy and etiquette are important. "Mind the gap" reminds passengers to avoid injury by paying attention to the break between the platform and train. "Mind your own business" enjoins respect for others' privacy, although sometimes we should risk intrusiveness because we are mindful of a friend's needs. We can even be mindful of a motto or admonition: "Mindful of the rabbinic sage Hillel the Elder's admonition, 'If not now, when?' I have decided to make some changes."[19] Mindfulness mottos need not actually use the word "mindful." For example, "Take time to smell the roses" recommends mindfulness in the form of savoring the beautiful little things in life. "Keep your eye on the prize" offers advice to be mindful of your long-term goals. "Keep calm and carry on" advocates focusing mindfully on tasks at hand and avoiding panic, which was singularly important during the bombing of Britain during World War II, when the motto became popular.

The last observation, that mindfulness mottos need not use the word "mindful," can be generalized. Mindfulness is sometimes discussed without actually using the word. As Gilbert Ryle notes, many additional English words indicate minding or heeding: "noticing, taking care, attending, applying one's mind, concentrating, putting one's heart into something, thinking what one is doing, alertness, interest, intentness, studying and trying."[20] This observation has considerable importance. It reminds us that the literature on mindfulness is much wider than the writings by psychologists or Buddhists who have adopted the word for their purposes. It enters into identifying important thinkers who might discuss mindfulness without relying on the word, including thinkers I discuss. For example, Henry David Thoreau explores mindfulness using words like "awake," "wakefulness," and "awakening" (chapter 5); John Dewey contributes to understanding mindful problem solving under the rubric of "intelligence" (chapter 7); Epictetus and Marcus Aurelius discuss mindfulness as moral vigilance (chapter 8); and Saul Bellow discusses mindfulness under the rubrics of seizing the day and living in the moment (chapter 11).

In general, there is a distinction between *words* (elements of language), *concepts* (ideas), and *conceptions* (perspectives, especially value perspectives). Concepts are not reducible to the words used to express them in a particular language. After all, the same concept can be conveyed with different words in different languages. The English words "mindful" and "mindfulness" gained currency during a particular place and time, namely in England during the fourteenth and fifteenth centuries. But concepts of mindfulness were developed much earlier, sometimes in connection with particular value conceptions that guided how the concepts were applied.

For example, the Buddha developed a conception of mindfulness in the sixth century BCE, and for millennia his conception has been interpreted, refined, and modified by his followers. Buddhist words for mindfulness—such as *sati* (in Pali) and *smrti* (in Sanskrit)—were translated into English as "mindfulness," however, only in the late nineteenth century.[21] How did the British scholar T. W. Rhys Davids determine in 1881 that "mindfulness" was an apt translation of *sati*? Drawing on his mastery of English and classical Asian languages, he examined contexts where *sati* was used—including linguistic, literary, historical, and cultural contexts. Other scholars might disagree with Davids' translation, and point to other nuances in all the words and languages involved. Such technicalities arise in all translating, and mindfulness raises no special issues. The key point is that concepts of mindfulness are involved in all discussions of paying attention in light of values, regardless of whether the word "mindfulness" is employed.

MINDFULNESS AS A VIRTUE

Any mention of values invites familiar questions. Which values? Whose values? Are the values defensible, properly understood, and intelligently applied? When these questions are left open, I speak of *value-based mindfulness*: paying attention to what matters, in light of values, either in a situation or in general. Beyond this starting point, two reference points are elemental:

the values a particular person holds at a given time, and the values that are reasonable or at least permissible. *Personal-mindfulness* is attending to what matters to individuals in light of *their* values, whatever those values happen to be. In contrast, *virtue-mindfulness*—mindfulness as a virtue—is attending to what matters in light of relevant *sound* values, that is, permissible values that are not immoral, irrational, or unhealthy.

Personal-mindfulness and virtue-mindfulness are not incompatible, of course. They overlap insofar as individuals hold sound values. Nevertheless, the distinction has a basis in everyday speech. Thus, when individuals act attentively in applying perverse values, for example, racism or misogyny, we might say they are mindful in implementing their values (personal-mindfulness). More likely, however, we say they are (morally) mindless, for they are not paying attention to what matters in light of sound values (virtue-mindfulness). The PricewaterhouseCoopers employees failed to be mindful in both ways: they failed to act on their values, and they failed to implement sound values.

Virtue-mindfulness is not a stand-alone virtue. Especially in moral contexts it is what Michael Slote calls a *dependent virtue*: it depends for its worth (or full worth) on other virtues and goods with which it is allied—or alloyed.[22] Value-dependency is a feature of many virtues. For example, conscientiousness, courage, and humility are full-blown virtues when they implement responsibilities and ideals, and they are fully admirable only when accompanied by decency and respect. The conscientiousness of a Nazi officer, the courage of a fanatical terrorist, and the religious humility of an abusive parent are not admirable. At least, they are not entirely admirable, and there is a case for saying they use good to serve evil. Likewise, the mindfulness of thieves and terrorists in carrying out immoral activities is not a virtue. Mindfulness is a virtue insofar as it implements sound values—that is, understanding, appreciating, and acting on values that enter into a good life. Regardless of whether moral or nonmoral values enter into specifying what matters and should be attended to, virtue-mindfulness requires some degree of good judgment about what is important in the situation, or in a good life.

Virtue-mindfulness is an aspect of practical wisdom in living a good life.[23] It is intelligent and caring attunement to the variety of values that enter into a good life—including moral and many additional types of values. "Practical wisdom" perhaps sounds a bit lofty, but it indicates something crucial. It underscores the reasonable integration and balancing of myriad values that is crucial in good lives. It invites questions about which values are sound, and which values and attitudes are unhealthy, immoral, or otherwise unjustifiable. And it invites questions about which moral values are mandatory (e.g., justice), worthwhile but optional (e.g., romantic love), an expression of a particular individual's authenticity (e.g., in caring for a family's collection of antiques or perhaps netsuke[24]).

We might disagree about who is being virtue-mindful on a particular occasion because we disagree about the relevant facts, because we disagree about the soundness of the values being used, or because we disagree about how best to balance sound values that come into conflict. In climate-change debates, for example, is the lobbyist for the coal industry mindful of what matters, or is it the environmental activist? Both are mindful of what matters to them, in light of their values. But are they equally mindful of what is genuinely important, or most important, in light of sound values? In general, how would a responsible person and government reasonably balance and integrate the relevant concerns in dealing with climate change? Our answers to such questions reflect our value perspectives. Needless to say, we frequently disagree about which values and value perspectives are reasonable. We disagree even more about how best to apply and balance sound values. Conceptions of mindfulness reflect such disagreements.

Usually I discuss the mindfulness of individuals. There is also such a thing as group mindfulness, as shown in tendencies of thought and conduct shared by many individuals. As just noted, we speak of political groups as being mindful or mindless. Again, creative teams of scientists may share a fine-tuned mindfulness of previous contributions relevant to their disciplines.[25] And physicians, as a group, might be mindful of the standards that govern their work. In addition, critics might identify how organizations and societies are collectively mind*less*, that is, lacking in virtue-mindfulness. In *Road from Coorain*, Jill Ker Conway depicts her gradual mid-twentieth-century awakening to and growing mindfulness about the patriarchal and colonialist aspects of her native Australian society, even though she was reluctant "to join my radical friends in railing against a heedless [or mindless] society."[26] And as recently as 2017, when the #MeToo Movement brought greater awareness, American society as a whole was often mindless about sexual harassment and assault from people having power over subordinates. Both Conway and the #MeToo movement call for societies to be more mindful of feminist values of equality, fairness, and decency.

Psychologists usually emphasize the immediate situation—living in the here-and-now—and I will do so as well. Of course many things might be important in our immediate situation (let alone in general). Does virtue-mindfulness imply awareness of and good judgment about all of them, or only the most important thing? And does it require integrating sound values in the most reasonable or desirable way in the situation? Usually we don't raise such questions. We simply take for granted that mindfulness can be a matter of degree. It can target some important things but not others, and does not entail completely successful outcomes. Multitasking might enable us to cope with several important things, exercising good judgment in juggling and integrating them. For example, during a discussion with a student, a teacher might be attuned to the course material, how the student is doing in the class, the student's nervousness about a personal matter, and the teacher's own family problems. There are limits to how much we can juggle. Sometimes multitasking while trying to focus on everything important is counterproductive. Moreover, usually we assume that mindfulness can be accompanied by varying degrees of reasonableness and good judgment in integrating multiple values and concerns.

Occasionally, however, we ratchet up the standard. We insist that mindfulness implies attending to the *most* important thing(s) in a situation, as discerned by exercising good judgment, and integrating values in the most reasonable manner. For example, the word "mindful" might imply high importance in moral matters, as in "He was very mindful of respecting boundaries and never strayed from the principles he lived by."[27] Again, moral dilemmas are occasions requiring contextually established orders of importance among conflicting moral values. For example, we have responsibilities to care for a sick family member and also to be at work to complete an urgent project, and the two can conflict. We attend to both concerns but we are mindful in setting priorities. Of course there is frequently room for reasonable disagreements about how priorities should be set. Calls to be mindful can themselves provide conflicting advice: "Focus on your career" versus "Be mindful of your family above all." In any case, the distinction between important and most important needs to be drawn contextually. And contexts may serve to both clarify and complicate how we understand mindfulness.

Disagreements about virtue-mindfulness are no more unusual than disagreements about other virtues. Linguistic and moral ambiguities surround most virtue words, indeed all value terms that have evolved in different cultures and regarding various controversies. For example, "equality" has a host of meanings, as in speaking of equal moral dignity, equal rights, equal opportunity for a fulfilling life, equal pay for the same work, equal outcomes in terms of income or wealth, etc.[28] These meanings are sometimes in tension, for example equal opportunity in education may lead to wide gaps between rich and poor (unless mitigated through progressive taxation) and thereby erode equal opportunities for future generations. Again, "freedom" can refer to basic liberties and rights, freedom from poverty and disease, autonomy in the form of rational self-mastery and development of one's talents, etc. And virtues such as love, justice, and authenticity can be understood in strikingly different ways by different thinkers and traditions. A first step in any serious discussion of values is to sort out such ambiguities. A second step is to indicate why a particular meaning is appropriate in a given context and for a particular purpose. A third step might be to reconnect the various meanings by identifying where they complement and enrich each other in good lives, uniting them while taking into account their possible tensions. I do all these things with respect to mindfulness.

Finally, I understand the *virtue* in "virtue-mindfulness" expansively. For one thing, words for virtues can refer to a habit or general trait of persons, but also to specific acts, activities, and states of mind. The same is true of most virtues. Thus, we speak of honest, fair, and generous persons, and also of honest, fair, and generous actions and attitudes. This dual application of virtue terms raises an interesting question. When virtue terms are applied to actions, must the actions reflect the trait of the agent? For example, are honest actions always a manifestation of honest persons, that is, of persons who are generally honest? Aristotle stipulated that: "virtuous acts are not done in a just or temperate way merely because they have a certain quality, but only if the agent also acts in a certain state, viz. (1) if he knows what he is doing, (2) if he chooses it, and chooses it for its own sake, and (3) if he does it from a fixed and permanent disposition of character." I disagree.[29] If virtuous acts required acting from "a fixed and permanent disposition" there would be little virtue in the world, perhaps none. Psychologists have documented that few of us are virtuous in Aristotle's sense, even though most of us are able to display courage, self-control, honesty, and mindfulness in many situations.[30]

For another thing, virtue-mindfulness implements both moral and nonmoral excellences. When moral virtue is involved, the excellences are such things as implementing moral responsibilities, respect for human beings, honesty, fairness, gratitude, and caring about animals and other life. But in addition, virtue-mindfulness implements values of rationality, professional skill, beauty and aesthetic sensitivities, health, athletic ability, talents in cooking and sewing, etc. This wide sense of "virtue" has an etymological and historical basis. Thus, the Greek word for "virtue" is *arête*, which translates as either virtue or excellence. Even Aristotle divided virtues into moral and intellectual virtues, although other ethicists expand moral virtues to include intellectual virtues.[31] In any case, readers who object to my expansive usage of "virtue-mindfulness" can replace it with terms such as "sound-value-mindfulness," "excellence-mindfulness," or "normative-mindfulness."

VARIETY OF VALUES

The last point bears emphasis: the values in good lives include moral values but also other types of values. Ideally, good lives are morally decent, happy, healthy, authentic, fulfilling, and each of these general headings connects with a multitude of more specific values. Here are a few general comments about how I understand these general headings (postponing authenticity to later chapters).

Values include general norms, individual ideals, desirable traits of character, and all forms of good and excellence. They also include personal acts and experiences of *valuing*: bestowing value on things, and responding to the value they already have—whether the value is positive, negative, or neutral. Values include things important in their own right, such as defensible ideals of justice, honesty, and compassion. They also include things to which we give value by valuing them—by desiring and caring about them, for example our friends, family, home, car, hobbies, sports, and other events that attract our interest or preferences.[32] Value responses can be explicit evaluative judgments, or they can be implicit in emotions, attitudes, commitments, and actions based on value judgments. As Robert Solomon writes, "the heart of every emotion is its value judgments, its appraisals of gain and loss, its indictments of offenses and its praise of virtue."[33] Thus, hope contains a positive evaluation of possibilities; anger and resentment are built on negative evaluations of perceived injury or injustice; and joy contains a sweeping affirmation of everything (in our field of attention) as wondrous.

Meaningful lives have inherent value. They are also rich in particular values that generate a *sense of meaning*—a sense of coherence and intelligibility in light of values. The expression "sense of meaning" is ambiguous. It can refer to subjective meaning, which is the conviction that our lives are intelligible (make sense) in light of our values. Or it can refer to objective meaning, which refers to making sense in terms of sound and defensible values.

Self-fulfillment also combines subjective and objective aspects, and can be understood in objective terms or as a subjective sense of meaning.[34] Its subjective aspects consist in unfolding our strongest needs, desires, and aspirations. Its objective aspects consist of unfolding our most valuable potentials, including moral potentials and development of our talents. It can be viewed as both a process and outcome, and measured over a lifespan or along the way.

Morality includes ideals and good character traits centered on self-respect and respect for other persons, as shown for example in justice and love. It also includes compassion for sentient animals who suffer, and appreciation of additional forms of life and the natural environment—an attitude Albert Schweitzer called "reverence for life."[35] In formal terms, morality includes mandatory values that comprise basic moral decency incumbent on everyone, such as respect for human rights. It includes obligations and duties of various kinds, most of which are prima facie rather than absolute—that is, they can have permissible exceptions when they come into conflict with other important values that override or balance them. Still other moral values concern desirable though optional forms of goodness. For example, ideals concerning love might include affirming love-filled marriages while rejecting any notion that marriage is obligatory for everyone. And there are many degrees of supererogatory generosity, courage, and kindness.

Some philosophers use the term "ethical" to encompass all types of values that enter into good lives, not just moral values.[36] I avoid that usage because to my ear "ethical" and "moral" are too close in connotation to warrant it. I appreciate the intent of the contrast, however, which is to underscore that a wide variety of values enter into good lives, not only moral values. To that end, as indicated above, I employ the word "virtue" in its wide sense of excellence. Thus, when I speak of virtue-mindfulness I intend paying attention to what matters in light of all kinds of sound values that might be relevant to a situation.

Sound values are permissible values, those which are not immoral, not unhealthy, and not irrational. They include vastly more than onerous duties. Indeed, they include simple preferences insofar as they contribute to good lives—lives that are happy as well as morally decent. The contribution of many preferences is minor but not to be dismissed as insignificant in thinking about mindfulness. For example, I like milk chocolate mixed with almonds. I am mindful of places to purchase it inexpensively, and I take advantage of free samples at See's Candy. I also try to be mindful of my strong tendency to overindulge, so I never take home a full box of chocolates. I make no claims that other people ought to share my preference, and I know that people with food allergies or diabetes ought to avoid acting on it. I pursue my preference in a value-based, personal-mindfulness way. Assuming I do not overeat, steal, or compulsively pursue my preference, my personal-mindfulness might in some small way enter into a good life for me.

I am an ethical pluralist, who affirms the kaleidoscope of good persons and good lives.[37] Ethical pluralism is not ethical relativism, in the crass version that reduces values to whatever a society or group happens to believe about good lives. Nor should ethical pluralism be equated with ethical subjectivism, which reduces values to individual feelings, desires, and attitudes. Some beliefs about moral matters are false, even despicable, and some lives are monstrous.[38] Ethical pluralism leaves much room for *reasoning* about moral issues—for good and sound reasoning. Ethical pluralism, minus crass versions of ethical relativism and ethical subjectivism, is conveyed with the maxim "Let a thousand flowers bloom, but keep killing weeds," where the weeds are wrongheaded and misguided moral outlooks.[39] Discriminating between the flowers and weeds demands moral skills developed throughout a lifetime. All lives are subject to moral appraisal, but the appraisal should be nuanced and humane. Emphatically, moral assessment is not reducible to parochial, harsh, blame-and-punishment outlooks. Psychologists rightly warn us against such blinkered views of morality. Unfortunately, they also fail to leave sufficient room for moral reasoning (as discussed in part two).

As for *health*, I favor holistic definitions, as do most psychologists. The most famous one is promulgated by the World Health Organization (WHO): "Health is a state of complete physical, mental and social well-being, not merely the absence of disease or infirmity."[40] The WHO definition is idealized. Thus, "complete well-being" could easily be interpreted as requiring perfect physical functioning, maximum happiness, morally ideal socially functioning, and in other ways encompass all dimensions of good lives. Expansive definitions of mental health make it easy for health psychologists to embed and conceal moral values as part of mental well-being. Nevertheless, I agree that health has physical, mental, and social dimensions, in degrees needed for effective (if not ideal) functioning. I also agree that mental health and morality overlap, interact, and interweave. Well-being is as much a matter of health as morality, and the two overlap and intertwine.

Finally, different types of mindfulness can be distinguished according to the types of values used to specify what matters. Thus, *moral mindfulness* is paying attention to what matters in light of moral values, both in our immediate situation and in general, as those values are implemented with caring and good judgment. *Health mindfulness* is responsiveness to what matters in terms of health. *Spiritual mindfulness* is attunement to the values of religious communities or personal spirituality. *Environmental mindfulness* is attunement to justified values concerning the natural environment. *Enlightened cherishing* might suggest attunement to aesthetic, historical, and cultural values.[41] And *mindful work* includes attunement to values that make work excellent, ethical, and meaningful. I am interested in all these types of mindfulness, but I emphasize the interplay of morality and mental health.

MINDFULNESS AS MULTIFACETED

Having emphasized the core idea of mindfulness as value-based, I conclude by noting that mindfulness has additional elements or aspects. Here are some of them, with the value-based core listed alongside the others.

1. *Value-Based*. Mindfulness is paying attention to what matters in light of values. Values—of myriad kinds—guide, infuse, and otherwise shape attention, object selection, and purposes in attending carefully. For example, to pay attention might imply giving something its due, in a caring or appropriate manner; again, it might suggest appreciating something based on discerning its worth, beyond simply cognitively apprehending it. And to be mindful of our responsibilities is to act on them with caring and good judgment, or at least seriously try to.
2. *Context-Dependent*. What matters, and hence should be attended to, depends on the context. The context, or situation, can be specified in

terms of activities, relationships, roles, or interests. It can be specified as detailed or nuanced circumstances, or more general types of occasions, such as mindfulness while driving or meditating.

3. *Object-Attached*. Mindfulness is paying attention *to* things, for example focusing on relevant persons, physical objects, advice, feelings, truths, thoughts, tenets, our roles, and what we are doing (such as managing the winners cards at the Oscars). Objects might be specified as individual items, such as being mindful of the hazardous bend in the road ahead; or as types of things, such as being mindful of crime when walking in high-crime neighborhoods; or as wider categories, such as being mindful of the moral aspects of your work.

4. *Purpose-Oriented*. Mindfulness is typically attending with a purpose in mind, such as performing one's job well, solving a problem, learning a new language, reading a book, studying a new discipline, meditating in order to relax, appreciating paintings in a museum, and setting goals.[42]

5. *Modes of Attention*. We can attend by using different faculties, such as sight, hearing, touch, taste, smell, and kinesthesia. We also attend by using different mental capacities, including cognitive (judgment, discernment), affective (emotions, caring), and volitional (desire, action, reaction, self-control). Paying attention to what matters is not a static mental static, nor passive observation. Instead it is a dynamic activity of coping effectively in response to a situation, and often to a problem contained in a situation. We might attend by focusing on one or a few things (such as handing the right card at the right time to the presenters at the Academy Awards), focusing on one thing while monitoring something else (as in taking an exam while monitoring the time, or meditating by concentrating on our breathing while acknowledging thoughts that drift through consciousness), or attending as a spectator rather than a participant (as in watching a tennis match). In some contexts, calls to pay attention carry a tone of caution and wariness (where danger is involved), delight and appreciation (where good things are involved), taking care (of a person or in performing an entrusted task), and remembering (to implement important truths and values in relevant circumstances).

6. *Present-Oriented*. Mindfulness involves sensitivity to time (and timing), for example handing the card to the Oscar presenters at the right moment. Again, to be mindful of family birthdays is to remember them, make timely preparations for celebrating them, and if possible attending parties as scheduled. We can be mindful of things in the past and future, and we can be mindful as a habit or tendency. I give some emphasis to mindfulness to the immediate situation, however, in order to stay close to the literature on mindfulness and because attunement

to the present is generally essential in good lives. Even so, what matters in the present situation typically requires taking into account the past and future. Moreover, exactly how the present is specified can vary widely in accord with our interests and purposes, which include our needs to sometimes isolate and buffer the present from the past and future, and other times to connect them.

These six elements are connected. Mindfulness is paying attention, in various modes, to things that matter, given our purposes and in light of relevant values, at appropriate times (especially in the present situation). They are connected as well in that values play a role in understanding all of them, which will be clear throughout the remainder of this book. Taken together the elements suggest some of the complexity of mindfulness. They also indicate that mindfulness is literally *mind-full*. Even when it involves narrow focus on some things while disregarding or downplaying others, it can draw on skills of cognition, emotion, valuing, willing, memory, foresight, etc.

Moreover, the different aspects of mindfulness, each of which is multifaceted, help explain the variety of concepts of mindfulness. For example, thinkers interested in therapeutic meditation might emphasize attention to and awareness of particular sorts of object, such as immediate bodily activities like breathing, and momentary feelings and thoughts. Thinkers interested in mindful work or creative decision making might accent modes of attention focused outwardly on tasks and downplay attending to the self. And thinkers having particular value commitments might highlight selected values in understanding what matters and should be borne in mind.

Finally, the multiple elements of mindfulness help explain the various connotations of *mindlessness*, which include: careless, heedless, senseless; distracted, inattentive; forgetful, absentminded; negligent, neglectful; foolish, stupid, dumb, devoid of thought; clumsy, awkward, frazzled; insensitive, indiscrete, inconsiderate, thoughtless, tactless, poor mannered; imprudent, injudicious, rash; indifferent, callous; lacking full alertness, thorough deliberation, keen attention, heightened awareness (and using similar scalar concepts). As these connotations suggest, the word "mindless" is usually pejorative and disparaging, as in speaking of mindless violence. Occasionally "mindless" is neutral, however. For example, it might indicate the absence of mental exertion in a context where such exertion is not required or even desirable. Mary Gordon reports that when writer's anxiety erupts she quiets her soul by playing music and copying quotes that interest her: "I enjoy the music and the rhythm of the mindless copying."[43] She immediately qualifies her remark, however: "Or not entirely mindless; I'm luxuriating in the movement of the words which are, blessedly, not mine. I'm taking pleasure in the slow and rapid movements of my pen, leaving its black marks on the whiteness of the paper."

In sum, value-based mindfulness is paying attention to what matters, in light of values relevant to the present situation. Personal-mindfulness means the values are the de facto values of an individual. Virtue-mindfulness means the values are sound (permissible or desirable) in the sense of not immoral, irrational, or unhealthy. This trio of concepts is rooted in ordinary language and experience, but I do not claim they provide *the* correct definition of mindfulness. Different concepts of mindfulness can be useful for different purposes. One of my purposes is to explore the variety of concepts of mindfulness, and for that purpose my trio of working definitions is helpful. More important, the centrality of values in understanding mindfulness proves especially useful in exploring mindfulness in good lives, as well as psychologists' and philosophers' contribution to that exploration. Mindfulness is multifaceted and polymorphous. In the next chapter I discuss its value connection with living in the present, and in chapter 4 I say more about different ways of attending.

NOTES

1. Rebecca Shapiro, "Oscars Ballot Counters: We Blew It, Warren Beatty Given Wrong Envelope," https://www.huffingtonpost.com. Accessed February 27, 2017.

2. "Misexecution" is J. L. Austin's term for the type of error involved. See J. L. Austin, *How to Do Things with Words*, 2nd ed., ed. J. O. Urmson and Marina Sbisá (Cambridge, MA: Harvard University Press, 1975), 17–18, 35–38.

3. Bhikkhu Bodhi, "What Does Mindfulness Really Mean? A Canonical Perspective," in Mark G. Williams and Jon Kabat-Zinn, eds., *Mindfulness: Diverse Perspectives on Its Meaning, Origins and Applications* (New York: Routledge, 2013), 19–39, at 22. See also Virginia Heffernan, "The Muddied Meaning of 'Mindfulness,'" *New York Times Magazine* (April 14, 2015). https://www.nytimes.com/2015/04/19/magazine/the-muddied-meaning-of-mindfulness.html. Accessed June 25, 2017.

4. See for example Robert Meikyo Rosenbaum and Barry Magid, "Introduction," in Robert Meikro Rosenbaum and Barry Magid, eds., *What's Wrong with Mindfulness (and What Isn't): Zen Perspectives* (Somerville, MA: Wisdom Publications, 2016), 1–10, at 5.

5. Ludwig Wittgenstein, *Philosophical Investigations*, 3rd ed., trans. G. E. M. Anscombe (New York: Macmillan Company, 1958[1953]), 32, Remark 67.

6. Wittgenstein, *Philosophical Investigations*, 82, Remark 203.

7. Entry for "mindful" in *The Random House Dictionary: Classic Edition*, ed. Stuart Berg Flexner (New York: Random House, 1983).

8. For example, see Kate Pickert, "The Art of Being Present," *Time*: Special Edition, *The Science of Happiness* (New York: Time Books, 2016), 71–79, at 74; and Rick Hanson, with Forrest Hanson, *Resilient: How to Grow an Unshakable Core of Calm, Strength, and Happiness* (New York: Harmony Books, 2018), 25.

9. See Mike W. Martin and Roland Schinzinger, *Ethics in Engineering*, 4th ed. (Boston, MA: McGraw-Hill, 2005).

10. Kathleen Rooney, *Lillian Boxfish Takes a Walk* (New York: Picador, 2018), 59.

11. See David Callahan, "The Mindful Philanthropist," in *The Givers: Wealth, Power, and Philanthropy in a New Gilded Age* (New York: Alfred A. Knopf, 2017), 305.

12. Paul Sullivan, "Frugal When They Don't Have to Be," *New York Times* (June 6, 2015), B-5.

13. Judith Freeman, *The Latter Days: A Memoir* (New York: Anchor Books, 2016), 287.

14. James A. Michener, *The Covenant* (New York: Random House, 1980), 235.

15. James A. Michener, *The World Is My Home: A Memoir* (New York: Random House, 1992), 474.
16. Jonathan Martin, "Mindful of Midterm Elections, Republicans Are Divided on How to Proceed," *New York Times* (March 29, 2017), A-20.
17. Selected from the entry for "mindful" in *The Compact Edition of the Oxford English Dictionary* (New York: Oxford University Press, 1971), with the spelling updated.
18. On the importance of mottos in guiding and motivating, see Mike W. Martin, *Of Mottos and Morals: Simple Words for Complex Virtues* (Lanham, MD: Rowman & Littlefield Publishers, 2013).
19. Mark Oppenheimer, "Tweet Fatigue," *Los Angeles Times* (June 6, 2017), A-11.
20. Gilbert Ryle, *The Concept of Mind* (New York: Barnes and Noble, 1949), 136.
21. Rupert Gethin, "On Some Definitions of Mindfulness," in J. Mark G. Williams and Jon Kabat-Zinn, eds., *Mindfulness: Diverse Perspectives on Its Meaning, Origins and Applications*, (New York: Routledge, 2013), 263–279, at 263.
22. Michael Slote, *Goods and Virtues* (Oxford: Clarendon Press, 1983), 61–63. Deirdre N. McCloskey develops the metaphors of alloyed and allied virtues throughout *The Bourgeois Virtues: Ethics for an Age of Commerce* (Chicago, IL: University of Chicago Press, 2006), especially 171, 249–250, 281–282.
23. Valerie Tiberius provides an illuminating exploration of practical wisdom in *The Reflective Life: Living Wisely with Our Limits* (New York: Oxford University Press, 2008).
24. See Edmund De Waal, *The Hare With Amber Eyes* (New York: Farrar, Strauss and Giroux, 2010).
25. See, for example, Yrjö Engeström and David Middleton, "Introduction: Studying Work as Mindful Practice," in *Cognition and Communication Work*, ed. Yrjö Engeström and David Middleton (New York: Cambridge University Press, 1998); Vera John-Steiner, *Creative Collaboration* (New York: Oxford University Press, 2000); and Walter Isaacson, *The Innovators* (New York: Simon and Schuster, 2014).
26. Jill Ker Conway, *The Road from Coorain* (New York: Vintage Books, 1989), 233.
27. Padma Lakshmi, *Love, Loss, and What We Ate* (New York: HarperCollins, 2016), 193.
28. An example of philosophically astute exploration of moral ambiguities surrounding equality is Harry Frankfurt, "Equality as a Moral Ideal," in Harry G. Frankfurt, *The Importance of What We Care About* (New York: Cambridge University Press, 1988), 134–158.
29. Aristotle, *Nicomachean Ethics*, revised ed., trans. J. A. K. Thomson and H. Tredennick (Harmondsworth, UK: Penguin, 1976), 97 (II.4, 1105a28–1105a33).
30. See John M. Doris, *Lack of Character: Personality and Moral Behavior* (New York: Cambridge University Press, 2002).
31. See Linda Trinkaus Zagzebski, *Virtues of the Mind: An Inquiry into the Nature of Virtue and Ethical Foundations of Knowledge* (New York: Cambridge University Press, 1996).
32. See Harry G. Frankfurt, *The Importance of What We Care About* (New York: Cambridge University Press, 1988), 92–93.
33. Robert C. Solomon, *The Passions: The Myth and Nature of Human Emotion* (Notre Dame, IN: University of Notre Dame Press, 1983).
34. See Alan Gewirth, *Self-Fulfillment* (Princeton, NJ: Princeton University Press, 1998). See also Joel Feinberg, "Absurd Self-Fulfillment," in Joel Feinberg, *Freedom and Fulfillment: Philosophical Essays* (Princeton, NJ: Princeton University Press, 1992), 297–330.
35. I give my interpretation of Schweitzer's ethics in *Albert Schweitzer's Reverence for Life: Ethical Idealism and Self-Realization* (Aldersthot, UK: Ashgate Publishing, 2007); republished by Routledge in 2017.
36. Bernard Williams draws something like this distinction (which I avoid), although he also gives a pejorative, blame-oriented meaning to "morality," in *Ethics and the Limits of Philosophy* (Cambridge, MA: Harvard University Press, 1985). In addition, Williams is a virtue ethicist who uses "virtue" to include both moral and non-moral types of excellence (a view I share).
37. See Mike W. Martin, *Everyday Morality: An Introduction to Applied Ethics*, fourth ed. (Belmont, CA: Thomson, 2007), 52–62.

38. On moral objectivity see T. M. Scanlon, *What We Owe to Each Other* (Cambridge, MA: Harvard University Press, 1998); and Thomas Nagel, *Mind and Cosmos* (New York: Oxford University Press, 2012).

39. Jeffrey Stout, *Ethics After Babel: The Languages of Morals and Their Discontents* (Princeton, NJ: Princeton University Press, 2001), 98.

40. "Preamble to the Constitution of the World Health Organization," *Official Record of the World Health Organization*, vol. 2 (Geneva: World Health Organization, 1946), 100.

41. See Harry S. Broudy, *Enlightened Cherishing: An Essay on Aesthetic Education* (Urbana: University of Illinois Press, 1994).

42. Eric Harrison highlights purposes and values in mindfulness in his illuminating book, *The Foundations of Mindfulness: How to Cultivate Attention, Good Judgement, and Tranquility* (New York: The Experiement, 2017), 8, 101–112.

43. Mary Gordon, "Putting Pen to Paper, but Not Just Any Pen or Just Any Paper," in John Damton, ed., *Writers on Writing* (New York: Henry Holt and Company, 2001), 78–83, at 82.

Chapter Three

Living in the Present

Live in the moment; be present; forget the past; stop fretting about the future; it's the journey, not the destination; one day at a time; seize the day; be here now.[1] Such maxims may serve as lighthearted invitations to have a bit of fun (go for the gusto), relax and enjoy (smell the roses), or stop procrastinating (no time like the present). In the mindfulness literature, however, they are voiced earnestly as strategies in good lives, and tactics to increase calm, confidence, control, and commitment. What does it mean to live in the present? It is not something we always do, by definition, assuming we are alive at this time. Instead, the concept of value-based mindfulness provides a clue: To live in the present is to attend to what matters in our immediate situation, in light of values. All types of values are involved, but in this chapter I accent aesthetic values. In addition, much turns on how the present is understood, defined, measured, and framed in relation to the past and future in light of values.

SELF-EXPRESSION AND APPRECIATION

Brenda Ueland's *If You Want to Write* is about living as much as writing. Her theme is *choosing* to live as much as possible in the present—as an ideal to which we aspire, rather than something we can always achieve. In her view, to live in the present is to live spiritually, in ways that combine self-expression with appreciation.

Self-expression, in Ueland's sense, is akin to what I call personal-mindfulness, with an added emphasis on focusing outwardly on the situation more than inwardly on ourselves. It is attending to what matters to us, in light of our values, but without anxious self-preoccupation: "it is when you are really in the present—working, thinking, lost, absorbed in something you care about very much, that you are living spiritually."[2] At such times the self is expressed without becoming the center of attention. Self-expression presupposes we care about our endeavors, relationships, and other things. We invest ourselves in them. We also find value in them, and give value to them. Self-expression involves expressing our personal values. Although it typically is accompanied by a tacit self-awareness, the self is not the focus of attention. Put paradoxically, self-expression has a *self-less* quality, in that there is no anxious self-consciousness, pretentiousness, or narcissistic desire to dominate.[3] We are absorbed in activities we care about and which bring enjoyment. We pay attention to what matters to us in skillfully pursuing particular activities, and we focus outward more than on inwardly on ourselves. This combination of features is found in psychologists' concept of "flow," discussed in later chapters.[4] Here I mention several of Ueland's favorite illustrations: writing, musical performance, and walking.

Self-less self-expression occurs in writing the first draft of a story, in the manner Ueland recommends. We write in a free, relaxed, bold, and personal way, leaving troublesome details for later revisions. The absorption in writing also occurs in revising, as we polish and perfect until the words leap off the page. In both instances a primary outward orientation on the writing becomes a way to express our values and identity: "to have things alive and interesting it [writing] must be personal, it must come from the 'I': what *I* know and feel."[5]

There are two ways to play a musical instrument. We can *play at it*, "grindingly" (with unpleasant effort), grudgingly (without desire), and without feeling (mechanically following imposed rules). Or we can *play in it*, identifying with the music, entering into it with feeling, and expressing ourselves as we play. At such times "the music—Mozart or Bach or whatever it is—suddenly is yourself, *your* voice and your eloquence."[6] We become immersed in the music by exercising our talent while caring for the activity. In this sense, to live in the present is to be fully present to the music. Even in playing music for an audience, enjoyment increases as we become less self-preoccupied, thereby lowering performance anxiety.

Walking is another favorite example. Ueland was athletic throughout her life, and she set an international swimming record for people eighty years and older. In her book on writing, however, she highlights her long daily walks. She reports that when she walked primarily for exercise or to reach a destination—she walked miles to work each day—she was doing something necessary, but there was no self-expression, no living in the present. Only when she relaxed, slowed down, and stopped thinking about the future did she have fresh thoughts and perceptions. She might have new ideas about a writing project, or she might see things usually overlooked: "Suddenly I was seeing how pretty the winter evening was, how black the trees in the phosphorescent moonlight, how the stars are different colors."[7]

Appreciation, the second aspect of living creatively, is akin to virtue-mindfulness. It consists in being attuned and responsive to sound values as they apply to our immediate situation, whether the values express excellence in writing, music, or perception of beauty. Commitments to sound values define our better, "true" self, which is a locus of activities rather than a fixed essence: "the true self is always in motion like music, a river of life, changing, moving, failing, suffering, learning, shining."[8] To live in the present can suggest that we "take time to love beauty."[9] Ueland understands beauty as eliciting but transcending subjective responses to it. Although she accents aesthetic experiences, as we might expect in a book about writing, she also highlights moral values that overlap with aesthetic values, in particular truthfulness and authenticity. Even more than beauty, truthfulness is essential in defining the true self, with its authentic responses to the world. She speaks of "microscopic truthfulness" in writing that is rich in accurate detail and clear understanding, and guided by honesty in expressing significant truth.[10] Achieving truthfulness, for example by avoiding clichés, requires effort, for we often deceive ourselves about what we think and feel.

Living in the present implies *not* dwelling on superficial aspects of the present that distract us from what is important. More positively, living in the present implies attunement to what is good in the present, rather than being preoccupied with past failures and future goals, and without being distracted by larger events in the future. Such preoccupation blinds us to the beauty, goodness, and opportunities directly in front of us. Ueland mocks the obsession with amassing wealth in order to enjoy a few end-of-life years at the expense of not enjoying life along the way. She does not, however, suggest that living in the moment requires obliviousness to the future and past. Far from it. For her, living in the moment implies living with optimism, with a horizon of faith and trust looking forward. Judging from her memoir published a year later, she possessed exceptional optimism: "I have not a touch of resignation about the future, or nostalgia, or poetic mournfulness for the days that are gone. I seem to be entirely cheerful and full of anticipation. I seem to be always holding my breath with suspense, as though something wonderful were going to happen the next day and the next."[11]

Ueland uses simple language to convey ideas I introduced using semi-technical terms: Living in the present implies attending to what matters in our situation in light of our values (personal-mindfulness) and in light of sound values (virtue-mindfulness). Next I illustrate how values also enter into understanding what the present is and how we attend to it.

WHAT IS THE PRESENT?

The *present* is vague, ambiguous, and elastic.[12] So is the *situation* and *context* in which we act. One ambiguity concerns whether time is specified objectively in terms of clocks and calendars, or subjectively in terms of human experience. Objectively, the present is understood in terms of the chronological time in which we act and respond. Even when we are asleep we live in the chronological present—until it recedes into the past and is replaced by the future. Yet the objective present can be measured in different ways that give it variable duration. It might be the instant dividing past from future, perhaps a moment having duration of a second, or perhaps having virtually no duration, akin to the mathematician's point in time. Or it might be an hour, day, month, season, year, or century. It might even be an entire lifespan, as when earthly existence is contrasted with the eternity of time. Religious, moral, and other values play a role in how we measure the present "objectively." Values also enter when the present is specified culturally or thematically. Broad cultural divisions include ancient, medieval, modern, and postmodern eras; shorter spans include the Renaissance, Enlightenment, and Romantic periods; still shorter divisions name cultural developments such as the eras of Jazz or the Internet.

In contrast, subjective time is specified in experiential terms. Here values play a much larger role, especially as embodied in emotions, attitudes, and commitments. On the one hand, the subjective present can be specified in terms of our current concerns—our ongoing endeavors, relationships, emotional states, bodily states, attention span, environment, observations, and thoughts. These things have a duration that can be measured objectively, but their identity is specified in terms of what we care about and value—what matters to us. Moreover, as John Dewey points out, this temporal arena of value-oriented activity is not only flexible but contains references to the past and future: "'Present' activity is not a sharp narrow knifeblade in time. The present is complex, containing within itself a multitude of habits and impulses. It is enduring, a course of action, a process including memory, observation and foresight, a pressure forward, a glance backward and a look outward."[13] Even in writing this paragraph I have a tacit sense of what went before and what follows—temporally, spatially, and conceptually.

On the other hand, the subjective present can be understand in terms of how we experience the passage of time—including its duration, pace, and how the present is framed in relation to the past and future.[14] We might live with joy and gratitude for being alive, as Ueland conveys. Or we might be depressed and anxious in ways that distort everything about the present, giving it a tedious or dreadful motion. We might feel serene about the smooth passage of time, panic that time is leaving us behind, disgust at wasting time, and excitement in looking ahead. Time flies when we are having fun, but during great stress an hour can feel like an eternity. Age, too, can influence how time is experienced. In *A Spool of Blue Thread*, Anne Tyler has her aging protagonist observe time, "How slow it is when you're little and how it speeds up faster and faster once you're grown. Well, now it's just a blur. I can't keep track of it anymore!"[15] Distortions of the pace of time also occur during illness, as Thomas Mann describes in *The Magic Mountain*. Chronologically, Hans Castorp's recovery from consumption (tuberculosis) expands from three weeks to several years. Experientially, his recovery becomes an enduring present that absorbs the past and future into itself—a "dimensionless present," "a continuous present, an identity, an everlastingness" of the same day, such that the usual units of time run together and disappear.[16] Mystics report similar experiences of time standing still, even though they know clocks continue to tick.

Again, we feel "pressed for time." Occasionally this feeling accents enjoyment of the present while pursuing an urgent commitment. But more likely the feeling generates a sense of being hurried, which lessens enjoyment and distorts usual priorities and commitments. In an ingenious (and slightly naughty) experiment, John Darley and Dan Batson arranged to have professors at Princeton's seminary program assign their students to write and deliver a sermon on the Good Samaritan story.[17] The topic primed them to be especially mindful of the importance of helping, reinforcing values of compassion and humanity in their planned careers. The experimenters then arranged to have each student walk across campus to deliver their Good Samaritan sermon at a particular time and using a particular route, through an alley where they passed the person who was (convincingly) pretending to be sick and in need of help. Students in one group were told they had ample time but might as well get underway. Most of them stopped to help. Students in a second group were told they were already late for their presentation and needed to hurry. Most of them, some 90 percent, did not stop to offer help. The crucial variable explaining the different conduct was feeling pressed for time.[18] All the students, in both groups, noticed the distressed person in the alley, as subsequent interviews revealed. But their judgment about what was most important in their immediate situation—stopping to help the person in need or instead meeting their responsibility to give the sermon as scheduled—was dramatically influenced by perceived time pressures. Incidentally, observers who insist that all *mindful* seminarians would have stopped to help are obviously asserting a value perspective that elevates altruism over educational duties.

As with the present, the past and future are malleable in how they are specified. Objectively, my past might include the time from my birth to the present moment, or specified as much narrower durations. Subjectively, it might refer to the most significant things I did and experienced prior to my current projects and relationships—significant in light of my present values.

And it might be experienced as a burden or instead as a proud heritage. Objectively, my full future might include everything from this moment until my death. Subjectively, it might refer to the major things I do and experience from now until I die. It might be experienced as exciting or bleak. And when the present is understood in terms of my ongoing concerns, parts of my past and anticipated future might be experienced as elements of my present.

BUFFERING AND BROADENING THE PRESENT

Whether the present is specified chronologically or experientially, *how* we attend to the present varies. In particular, we can shift attention from narrow to wider perspectives on the present, at times buffering the present from the past and future, and at times broadening the present by linking it to the past and future.

The Roman god Janus gazed on the past and future simultaneously and with equanimity. His dual vision did not render him oblivious to the present; far from it. As the god of transitions, he applied memory and foresight in understanding what matters in the moment, in order to evaluate and choose wisely. Similarly, one type of mindfulness is Janus-faced, broadening the moment by viewing it under wider horizons of time and value—horizons that themselves vary in scope. Another type of mindfulness, the one emphasized in psychologists' writings, narrows attention to the immediate present, buffering it from regrets and worries about things we cannot control. Both types of mindfulness involve living in the present by focusing on what matters in light of values. The difference lies in how the present is framed, either linking it to the future and past or isolating it from them. Both types of mindfulness have a role in good lives.

Living in the present has two facets (if not faces) that require continual integration. Buffering the present enables us to savor pleasures, appreciate good fortune, quiet anxieties about the past and future, and make the most of opportunities. It keeps us on track in completing essential tasks, perhaps creatively or perhaps like a blinkered horse. In contrast, broadening the present helps us understand the world by applying causal explanations, elucidating how what is came to be. More important, it helps us maintain relationships, long-term endeavors, and ties with communities. It helps us appreciate the present as pregnant with hope in light of enduring commitments. That is literally true for a rocket mathematician who was several months pregnant: "At home, she got the baby's room ready and started picturing her life as a housewife and mother. The small kicks within, growing stronger each day, made her mindful of the future."[19] Again, in making mindful decisions about spending and investing individuals might benefit from imaginatively bringing the future into the present, using "prospective hindsight": "imagine how they would feel if their action turned out positively versus how they would feel if the same act had negative consequences."[20] Either way—with a buffered or a broadened present—values are central in understanding mindfulness.

Although buffering and broadening are usually complementary, they can be in tension. Goethe explored the tension in his memoir *Italian Journey*. In 1786 he was thirty-seven years old, a famous novelist, a successful civil servant in the Weimar Republic, and on the verge of a mental breakdown. He abruptly took leave from his work and traveled to Italy, where he spent two years fulfilling his childhood dream of studying Roman art. During his travels, according to his biographer John Armstrong, "Goethe experienced a tension between the grandeur of the big view—'life, viewed as a whole'— and the needful thing for happiness: carelessness, seizing the moment."[21] I would recast Armstrong's contrast as two ways of finding happiness in the moment: experiencing the moment for the delights it yields, and experiencing it as part of a happy life overall. Goethe believed that a good life maximizes "reasonable and happy" values: "all really intelligent people recognize . . . that the moment is everything and that the sole privilege of a reasonable being is to behave in such a manner, in so far as the choice lies with him, that his life contains the greatest possible sum of reasonable and happy moments."[22] In his view, reasonable values include those of art, ideas, culture, love, morality, and physical expression, along with the pleasures attached to these values. Throughout his journey he tried to observe things as they are, looking with "clear, fresh eyes" and effacing "the grooves of old mental habits."[23] Almost immediately he found himself "mentally alert all the time" with "a new elasticity of mind."[24] He sustained this stance as he grounded his ideas in "real living contact with the things himself."[25]

Goethe undertook his journey partly to counter the dulling effects of bureaucratic work. He discovered, however, that even pleasure can become monotonous. Initially, he was attracted by the happy-go-lucky pleasure-seeking Neapolitans, with their ability to free themselves from cares that would otherwise erode enjoyment in the moment. Yet he came to regard their immersion in pleasure-seeking as subverting the pursuit of culture and knowledge.[26] His ideal of a good life combined self-expression with broad understanding and cultural appreciation. Although his novel, *The Sufferings of Young Werther*, helped usher in the Romantic Movement, with its celebration of joy and self-expression, he was critical of Romanticism because it made a fetish of the moment at the expense of cultural values. For him, enjoying the present includes understanding it, which requires connecting it with the past and envisioned future.[27]

Italian Journey was based on journals kept during his journey, but it was crafted by a much older man. He began writing it twenty-five years after the journey, and he completed the last part when he was almost eighty. That last part contains his depiction of the Roman Carnival as an extended metaphor for living well. The Carnival continues for days of tumultuous partying during which people release their inhibitions, with the sole official ban of fighting and killing. We might anticipate that Goethe would use the Carnival to celebrate the pleasures of giving oneself over to the moment with pleasure and joy, using masks to free us from inhibitions. In fact, he reasserts the tensions and perplexities inherent in being alive: "knowing that life, taken as a whole, is like the Roman Carnival, unpredictable, unsatisfactory and problematic," with "half uneasy sensations," and yet "how valuable is every moment of joy, however fleeting and trivial it may seem to be."[28]

Goethe and Ueland agree that the art of living consists in enjoying the moment in light of values. For both, living in the present requires integrating self-expression and appreciation in light of sound values, using both buffering and broadening of the present. Living in the present requires skill in narrowing and widening cognitive focus, sometimes in alternation as in using a zoom lens, and other times in using stereoscopic vision.[29] Inappropriate worries about the past and future can destroy the joy of the moment. But tunnel vision on the moment also carries risks. It can be short-sighted and irresponsible. It might amount to evading past wrongdoing for which we owe compensation, or at least deserve remorse and repentance. It might lead to ignoring injustices to which we should bear witness. It might make us ingrates for the love and kindness shown to us by others. It might also render us imprudent about the future, placing both us and people we love at risk. Whereas living in abstraction can blind us to goods and responsibilities immediately in front of us, focusing too much on the immediate situation can blind us to vital truths. As John E. Smith observes, "There is a price to be paid for making our thoughts speak to a limited experience and circumstance, the price of being so completely tied to the moment that we lose sight of the perennial or universal elements that bear on all moments."[30] Good judgment based on a sound value perspective helps us choose when and how to buffer the present from the past and future, and when and how to connect the present to wider horizons of meaning.

Focusing on the present does not guarantee good decisions. Countless factors can distort or undermine good judgment, and even luck plays a role in shaping what is most important in a situation, and thereby can affect what counts as good judgment, practical wisdom, virtue—and mindfulness.[31] I recall speeding and being casual about stop signs when I drove my wife to the hospital in the middle of the night to have our second baby. We made it with time to spare, but I would earn no kudos for mindfulness if I had caused a collision. On another occasion, while driving in the middle of the night across the Nevada desert, my wife and I saw a large truck on fire not far off the freeway. At a time before cell phones, I drove faster than I ever have to get to a nearby city where I could call for help. The emergency dispatcher said not to worry; the police knew about the truck and had decided to let it burn itself out. To this day I am unsure whether my speeding was mindful, reckless, or both (in different respects).

AESTHETIC MEDITATION

Most psychologists who discuss mindfulness emphasize a narrow focus on the moment, especially during meditation. They accent practices of engaging in brief episodes of contemplation during which usual activities are temporarily set aside, and with them our usual ways of connecting the present to the future and past in light of our values. In tune with this chapter's emphasis on aesthetic values, I discuss value-oriented mindfulness during aesthetic meditation. Christophe André's *Looking at Mindfulness: Twenty-Five Paintings to Change the Way You Live* is a charming book about appreciating beauty, as integral to good lives. André selects paintings that express specific themes about mindfulness. Self-awareness is involved but subsumed, and aesthetic themes are wedded to therapeutic themes of healing and being morally nonjudgmental.

According to André, "Mindfulness means intensifying our presence to the moment, stilling ourselves to absorb it, instead of escaping it or trying to alter it, through thought or action."[32] He emphasizes meditative states in which routine activities are temporarily suspended in order to focus closely on the immediate situation, buffered from worries about the past and future. Value judgments associated with those activities are also suspended, but otherwise aesthetic values are very much involved. They infuse perceiving, feeling, appreciating, and cherishing. André understands mindfulness as *giving importance* to things we usually neglect, suspending our practical values while acting on aesthetic values. For example, he has us imagine ourselves entering the wintry scene depicted by Claude Monet in *The Magpie*: "Just stay here, doing our best to perceive the countless riches of this moment: the clumps of snow that fall from the trees with a tiny, soft thud; the blue-white shadow of the hedge; the small movements of a magpie seeking a little warmth in the sun. Everything is perfect."[33] Everything is perfect in the painting *and* in our experience of it. To properly appreciate the painting induces a parallel experience in us, one that serves as a paradigm of mindfulness when we return to daily activities. Encountering art in the right spirit teaches us to pause, stand back, and cultivate discerning awareness of the world. Simultaneously, it makes us more attuned to the world and to our experiences of the world.

Similar themes are explored by Ueland and Goethe, but André adds a therapeutic twist. He is a psychiatrist, and his book reflects his therapeutic role. For one thing, his overall purpose is to alleviate suffering, or more exactly, to use meditation to help people free themselves from unnecessary suffering. Accordingly, he discusses works of art that have therapeutic as well as aesthetic aims. He intersperses them with recommendations for simple breathing exercises and body awareness aimed at relieving stress and increasing enjoyment. The daily practice of meditation, whether centered on works of art or our breathing, anchors us in the present in ways that promote calmer and healthier lives.

For another thing, André interweaves commentary on self-awareness throughout his discussions of art. In attending to a painting we become attuned to our sense impressions and emotions in response to the painting. More fully, our self-awareness occurs at three levels: (1) primary awareness, which consists of sense impressions and sensations; (2) awareness of ourselves, and of our perceptions and feelings as part of us; and (3) reflective or self-awareness in the form of explicitly observing our emotions, attitudes, and conduct.[34] Mindfulness is not a fourth level of awareness but rather a full integration of the three levels—where the term "integration" hints that values and purposes are involved. Its primary resource is attention, which is how the mind takes control of its direction and aims. Thus, a mindful response to a painting involves attending to the painting, but it equally involves attending to our interests and needs in experiencing the painting. So, too, mindfulness in everyday life implies attunement to what is important to our psychological well-being, including "our fundamental needs for slowness, calm and continuity" for our mind in a hectic world.[35] Mindful living, he says, generates "the greatest possible number of moments with our mind wide open. It means regularly stopping for a few seconds, minutes or more, to feel, intensely and wordlessly, whatever is happening inside and outside ourselves."[36]

Despite his outward orientation on art, ultimately André is preoccupied with mindfulness during meditation, rather than in pursuing everyday activities. He is preoccupied with episodic moments of immersion in feeling and perception, in which much routine thinking and everyday practical activities, and the values they are based on, are temporarily suspended. This preoccupation is fine, indeed illuminating. But the emphasis on mindfulness during meditative states should not lead to the neglect of mindfulness during daily activities.

TIME AND PSYCHOTHERAPY

Writers on mindfulness commonly decry how little time we spend living in the moment. In fact, most of us think about the present far more often than we think about the past and future. Roy Baumeister's experiments suggest that on average we think about the present twice as often as about the future, and six times more often than about the past. The bulk of our thoughts are about what we are doing: "the most common categories of thoughts about the present are all about doing," and reports from experimental subjects "clustered most heavily in the categories 'doing what I intend to do / doing what I am supposed to be doing' and 'paying attention / zeroed in on what I am doing.'"[37] At the same time, about 30 percent of these present-oriented thoughts were linked to a future horizon, whether near-term or longer-term. Moreover, among the responses of people who were thinking about the past, about half had implications for the future. We are pragmatic creatures whose evolution hardwired a primary attention on the present. Hence, calls to live in the present accentuate and increase a natural priority, and their primary import concerns the manner in which we attend to the present—with different thinkers advocating different modes of attention and awareness.

Different types of psychotherapy may selectively emphasize attending to the present, past, and future. Thus, therapies that employ mindfulness-based meditation for stress relief emphasize the immediate present. These therapies require immersion in the moment, radically buffering the present from the past and future, and suspending usual activities and the values that connect them to wider horizons of time and meaning. Patient/clients are instructed to suspend value judgments, activities, and wider time horizons. This value-suspending meditation has been shown to have therapeutic effectiveness for many individuals, but obviously it is not a model for value-based mindfulness in everyday activities.

In contrast, Freudian psychoanalysis emphasizes the past, delving into childhood traumas and the origins of unresolved conflicts. Although I say little about psychoanalysis, I appreciate its contribution to coming to grips with the past, and the difficulties in doing so. That theme involves accepting what cannot be changed in order to move on, putting mistakes and misfortunes in perspective within a life that has provided sufficient opportunities for us to create a life that is worth living, even fortunate. In most instances, a painful past is rarely literally forgotten. Instead we can learn not to dwell on it in ways that undermine hope and courage in looking to the future. Coming to grips with the past also requires forgiving ourselves, making amends for past wrongs where possible, and understanding in order to let go of mistakes. Regrets easily grow to excess in terms of their felt intensity, the time they absorb, or the importance we assign to them in evaluating our character and lives.[38]

Whereas therapeutic meditation accents the buffered present and psychoanalysis emphasizes retrospection, cognitive behavioral therapies emphasize connecting the present to the future. This connecting involves prospection—the ability and tendency to look forward. Martin E. P. Seligman observes that some variations of cognitive behavioral therapy are explicitly future-emphasizing: "Future-Directed Therapy," "Hope Therapy," "Solution-Focused Therapy," and "Goal-Setting Planning" interventions.[39] Seligman also calls for more research about the relative effectiveness of therapies like mindfulness-based meditation that isolate the present, and therapies that are more future-oriented.

> What are the merits of present-focused and future-focused therapies? The concept of mindfulness (an accepting awareness of present experience) has become more popular. . . . More research is needed to understand the benefits and risks of prospective [i.e., future-oriented] techniques versus present-centered techniques and to investigate the possibility that present-centered therapies actually work by correcting faulty prospection (e.g., by helping people to disengage from catastrophic thoughts about the future).[40]

In my terms, Seligman calls for additional research to assess the relative effectiveness of therapies that buffer the present or instead broaden the present by linking it to the future (and past). I believe that mindful living in the present centers more on *how* we connect the present to the past and future, and less on disregarding the past and future altogether. It centers on the meaning we give to the present in light of wider horizons of time and value, horizons that shape what we care about in general and in the moment. Occasionally focusing on the future or the past is necessary for getting through difficult times, if only enduring a root canal in a dentist's office. As Seligman reminds us, we need our hopes and faith in the future to keep moving forward in the present, and we need memories of happier times to remind us that time heals many a wound.

Although I applaud Seligman's call for further research into the relative effectiveness of therapies having different temporal orientations, I question his embrace of the dominant psychological paradigm of mindfulness as "an accepting awareness of present experience," which emphasizes being nonjudgmental in the sense of suspension of value judgments. The word "mindfulness" acquired that meaning in psychology from studies of meditation, but, to emphasize again, mindfulness is not limited to meditation. Mindfulness is an activity, skill, and virtue relevant to all aspects of good lives, and to all of us in pursuing good lives, not just to individuals who practice meditation. For the purpose of exploring mindfulness in good lives, the concepts of value-based mindfulness, personal-mindfulness, and virtue-mindfulness should be emphasized, far more than value-suspending mindfulness.

Is there a version of psychotherapy that explicitly integrates and balances perceptions of time in all its dimensions? There is. Philip G. Zimbardo and his colleagues developed a version of cognitive behavioral therapy called Time Perspective Therapy (TPT). TPT contrasts positive and negative orientations toward the past events, present, and future in our lives. Zimbardo distinguishes many categories, but he highlights the following subset. (1) Past-positive orientation consists in pronounced positive attitudes toward the past, often romanticizing it and experiencing frequent nostalgia for the good old days. (2) Past-negative orientation emphasizes past failures, regrets and guilt, and abuses from others, frequently shown in high levels of depression. (3) Present-hedonistic orientation is living and seeking pleasure in the present, which carries a risk of falling into addictions. (4) Present-fatalistic orientation centers on believing that the present is beyond our control, and as a result not taking control when we should. (5) Future-positive orientation is constantly thinking ahead in order to plan and meet deadlines, sometimes at the risk of becoming a workaholic. (6) Future-negative orientation emphasizes attitudes about the future that are despairing, defeatist, and fatalistic. (7) Transcendental-future orientation is believing that life after death is more important than life in this world, and constantly seeking to connect one's current activities to that future life.[41] Zimbardo develops a "Time Perspective Inventory" that enables individuals to classify themselves. He also develops criteria for assessing the likely outcomes of holding these attitudes.

Zimbardo is a distinguished scientist who insightfully connects psychotherapy with values. Each of his broad categories have many variations that range from "moderate" (tolerable, desirable) to "extreme" (problematic, undesirable). Furthermore, the attitudes involved in the orientations can be combined in various ways, some more desirable than others. He even contends there is one "optimal" perspective: "the ideal time-perspective profile is high in past-positive, moderately high in future, moderately high in present-hedonistic, low in past-negative, and low in present-fatalistic time perspectives."[42] Which value criteria underlie such judgments? They are familiar criteria in psychological discussions of mindfulness: mental health, happiness, and a personal sense of meaning.[43] Each of these categories contains value judgments, including those embodied in the concept of mental health. Certainly the practical application of his categories involves value judgments. For example, Zimbardo applies TPT in depicting Donald Trump as manifesting extreme, unbalanced, unbridled present-hedonism orientation which, combined with his narcissism and bullying behavior, renders him "mentally unfit to be President of the United States."[44] Without disagreeing with that assessment, I regard it as a moral judgment that goes beyond value-neutral science. In general, moral evaluations are often in the background when psychologists and psychiatrists discuss mental health, especially when they apply their research to case studies. This observation is by no means mine alone. It is shared by many critics,[45] although it has not been as widely discussed in connection with mindfulness as it deserves to be.

To conclude, living in the present is not something we always and automatically do, even though we do far more of it than the mindfulness literature generally suggests. Instead it is a choice and a strategy we can adopt or resist, both as a habit and in particular situations.[46] Depending on the context, the strategy can be straightforward or difficult to implement, and beneficial or disastrous in its results. As a skill associated with value-based mindfulness, it is as much about values as about time. What we attend to in the present is shaped by values that indicate what matters. In addition, values influence the duration of the present that interests us. They enter into our choices about what to downplay or disregard in the present, and also about when to buffer or broaden how the present relates to the future and past. Values also influence which modes of attention we choose to adopt in particular situations, as discussed in the next chapter.

NOTES

1. Ram Dass [born Richard Alpert] popularized this phrase in what is possibly the strangest book in the mindfulness literature: *Be Here Now* (San Cristobal, NM: Lama Foundation, 1971).
2. Brenda Ueland, *If You Want to Write*, 2nd ed. (Saint Paul, MN: Graywolf Press, 1987[1938]), 59.
3. Herbert Fingarette elucidates such paradoxical phrasings in connection with "mystic selflessness" in *The Self in Transformation: Psychoanalysis, Philosophy, and the Life of the Spirit* (New York: Basic Books, 1963), 294–341.
4. Mihaly Csikszentmihalyi provides a helpful sketch of his concept of flow in *Creativity: Flow and the Psychology of Discovery and Invention* (New York: HarperCollins, 1996), 111–113.
5. Ueland, *If You Want to Write*, 71.
6. Ueland, *If You Want to Write*, 57.
7. Ueland, *If You Want to Write*, 45.
8. Ueland, *If You Want to Write*, 112.
9. Ueland, *If You Want to Write*, 56.
10. Ueland, *If You Want to Write*, 102–115.
11. Brenda Ueland, *Me: A Memoir* (Duluth, MN: Holy Cow! Press, 2016 [1939]), 364.
12. For complications, see Alan Burdick, *Why Time Flies: A Mostly Scientific Investigation* (New York: Simon and Schuster, 2017).
13. John Dewey, *Human Nature and Conduct: An Introduction to Social Psychology* (New York: Modern Library, 1957[1922]), 259.
14. See William James, "The Perception of Time," *The Principles of Psychology*, vol. 1 (New York: Dover Publications, 1918[1890]), 605–642.
15. Anne Tyler, *A Spool of Blue Thread* (New York: Alfred A. Knopf, 2015), 161.
16. Thomas Mann, *The Magic Mountain*, trans. H. T. Lowe-Porter (New York: Vintage Books, 1969), 184, 183.
17. John M. Darley and C. Dan Batson, "From Jerusalem to Jericho: A Study of Situational and Dispositional Variables in Helping Behavior," *Journal of Personality and Social Psychology*, 27 (1973): 29–40.
18. Robert Levine studied how the experienced pace of life in a society or location dramatically influences how much we are willing to help others. See *A Geography of Time: The Temporal Misadventures of a Social Psychologist, or How Every Culture Keeps Time Just a Little Bit Differently* (New York: Basic Books, 1997).
19. Nathalia Holt, *Rise of the Rocket Girls: The Women Who Propelled Us, from Missiles to the Moon to Mars* (New York: Little, Brown and Company, 2016), 49–50.
20. Paul Sullivan, "Why the Wealthy Should Keep a Budget," *New York Times* (January 12, 2019), B-6.
21. John Armstrong, *Love, Life, Goethe: Lessons of the Imagination from the Great German Poet* (New York: Farrar, Straus and Giroux, 2006), 191.
22. J. W. Goethe, *Italian Journey*, trans. W. H. Auden and Elizabeth Mayer (New York: Penguin, 1970), 405.
23. Goethe, *Italian Journey*, 38.
24. Goethe, *Italian Journey*, 38.

25. Goethe, *Italian Journey*, 347.
26. Goethe, *Italian Journey*, 199, 221.
27. Goethe, *Italian Journey*, 165.
28. Goethe, *Italian Journey*, 470.
29. See Robert Nozick, *The Examined Life: Philosophical Meditations* (New York: Simon and Schuster, 1989), 122.
30. John E. Smith, *The Spirit of American Philosophy* (New York: Oxford University Press, 1966), xii.
31. Some classic readings on the role of moral relevance of luck are collected in Daniel Statman, ed., *Moral Luck* (Albany: State University of New York Press, 1993).
32. Christophe André, *Looking at Mindfulness: Twenty-Five Paintings to Change the Way You Live*, trans. Trista Selous (New York: Blue Rider Press, 2014), 8.
33. André, *Looking at Mindfulness*, 12.
34. André, *Looking at Mindfulness*, 80–81.
35. André, *Looking at Mindfulness*, 132.
36. André, *Looking at Mindfulness*, 243.
37. Roy Baumeister, "Pragmatic Prospection," in Martin E. P. Seligman, Peter Railton, Roy F. Baumeister, and Chandra Sripada, eds., *Homo Prospectus* (New York: Oxford University Press, 2016), 157–189, at 165.
38. See Janet Landman, *Regret: The Persistence of the Possible* (New York: Oxford University Press, 1993), 11.
39. Martin E. P. Seligman with Ann Marie Roepke, "Prospection Gone Awry: Depression," in Seligman, Railton, Baumeister, and Sripada, *Homo Prospectus*, 281–304, at 209–291. See also Martin E. P. Seligman and John Tierney, "We Aren't Built to Live in the Moment," *New York Times* (May 21, 2017), 1, 6. Seligman and Tierney's title (and thesis) would be closer to the truth by inserting "only" after "Live."
40. Seligman and Roepke, "Prospection Gone Awry: Depression," 295.
41. Philip Zimbardo and John Boyd, *The Time Paradox: The New Psychology of Time That Will Change Your Life* (New York: Free Press, 2009), 52, 334–336. Zimbardo's highlighted list varies; for example (5) and (6) are usually combined into one category ("future oriented") having two variations. See also Philip G. Zimbardo and Rosemary K. M. Sword, *Living and Loving Better with Time Perspective Therapy: Healing from the Past, Embracing the Present, Creating an Ideal Future* (Jefferson, NC: Exposit, 2017), 15–16, 183–184.
42. Zimbardo and Boyd, *The Time Paradox*, 322.
43. Zimbardo and Boyd, *The Time Paradox*, 246–247; and Zimbardo and Sword, *Living and Loving Better with Time Perspective Therapy*, 158–159.
44. Philip Zimbardo and Rosemary Sword, "Unbridled and Extreme Present Hedonism: How the Leader of the Free World Has Proven Time and Again He Is Unfit for Duty," in Bandy X. Lee, ed., *The Dangerous Case of Donald Trump: 27 Psychiatrists and Mental Health Experts Assess a President* (New York: St. Martin's Press, 2017), 25–50, at 45.
45. See, for example, James Davison Hunter and Paul Nedelisky, *Science and the Good: The Tragic Quest for the Foundations of Morality* (New Haven: Yale University Press, 2018).
46. See Jean Améry, "Existence and the Passage of Time," in *On Aging: Revolt and Resignation*, trans. John B. Barlow (Bloomington: Indiana University Press, 1994), 1–26.

Chapter Four

Ways of Attending

To *attend* is to direct the mind to something. It might be to look or listen, to be present (at a class, for example), take heed (of a teacher's instructions, for example), tend (to a chore, for example), or take care of (a sick person, for example).[1] To be *mindful* is to direct the mind to things that matter in a situation. It often suggests being aware of, taking heed, bearing in mind, appreciating, and being attuned to what matters in the situation. The two terms overlap in meaning, especially where values are involved in guiding attention. But mindfulness accents the role of values. Usually it implies a degree of success in implementing relevant values—for example success in noticing, appreciating, and taking into account what we attend to. Whether things matter in their own right and ought to be cared about, or whether they matter simply because we care about them, the attending involved in mindfulness is value based.

The attending involved in mindfulness has various modes, including perceptual (seeing, listening, tasting, smelling, touching, kinesthesia), intellectual (quantitative, narrative, imagination, reasoning), and emotional (affection, fear, anger). In this chapter I sort out a few modes of attending that recur in the mindfulness literature: modalities of scope (open awareness versus focused attention), engagement (participants versus spectators), direction (inward versus outward), time and pace (slow versus swift), and value-oriented skills (e.g., honest versus self-deceptive attending).[2] These modes are often complementary or overlapping, but at times they are in tension and require choices about *how* we attend, in addition to choices about *what* we attend to.

VALUES AND ATTENTION

In their Invisible Gorilla Experiment, psychologists Christopher Chabris and Daniel Simons made a short video of a basketball game between a team wearing white shirts and a team wearing black shirts. The researchers then ask experimental subjects to count the passes made by the white-shirt team. The task is demanding because the passes are frequent and quick, and because the experimental subjects must repeatedly distinguish between passes made by the two teams while counting only the passes of the white-shirt players. Midway through the video a person dressed up as a gorilla appears and walks slowly across the basketball court, pausing midway to thump its chest. Remarkably, half the experimental subjects fail to notice the gorilla impersonator (henceforth "gorilla"). When another researcher repeated the experiment using an eye tracker, he discovered that all experimental subjects look directly at the gorilla for about a second, even though only half of them report seeing it.[3]

Chabris and Simons conclude that the experiment documents "the illusion of attention": the mistaken belief that we discern more of what we look at than we actually do discern. The experiment demonstrates that "When people devote their attention to a particular area or aspect of their visual world, they tend not to notice unexpected objects, even when those unexpected objects are salient, potentially important, and appear right where they are looking."[4] No doubt most of us know of this limitation in the abstract, but in practice we tend to exaggerate our personal skills in paying attention to things. Thus, the experimental subjects who fail to notice the gorilla tend to be surprised or shocked when they notice it while re-watching the video. They may even briefly protest: Surely, they say, I would have noticed that; perhaps the experimenters were conning me with technology, substituting a new video rather than replaying the original one. Ultimately, however, they become reminded of how easy it is to *look* in the direction of something and yet fail to *see* (notice, discern) it because they are concentrating on something else. In general, most of us are overly confident about how much control we have over our attention. We overestimate our capacities, skills, and sheer energy in focusing and remaining focused. All this helps explain why eyewitnesses frequently provide unreliable testimony at the scene of an accident or crime. It also helps explain why so many people continue to use cell phones and other digital devices while driving, confident they are in control and driving safely, even after learning about the power of the devices to distract.

The Invisible Gorilla Experiment provokes questions about mindfulness. In particular, does failing to notice the gorilla indicate an absence of mindfulness? The answer depends on how mindfulness is defined. If mindfulness were awareness of everything in our situation, then failing to notice the gorilla indicates a lack of mindfulness, or full mindfulness. But if mindfulness is paying attention to what matters in light of values, then we must inquire further. What actually matters in the situation, as a participant in the experiment? And what matters most? One plausible answer is that the gorilla is what matters, given its bizarre appearance during a basketball exercise. A contrasting but equally plausible answer is that the passes of the white-shirt team, and an accurate tally of them, are what matter. After all, that is what the experimental subjects were told to focus on, what they agreed to attend to, and what they reasonably believed to be their proper task during the experiment. Suppose that experimental subjects slowed or stopped their counting of passes once they noticed the gorilla, and as a result counted less accurately. Would these subjects be more mindful by focusing on the gorilla at the expense of counting accurately? Or would they be less mindful because they failed to count as accurately as possible, which was their assignment in the experiment? Or should we simply say they were mindful about one thing and mindless about another, and leave it at that?

I will not attempt to answer these questions. Perhaps Wittgenstein's remark applies here: "Say what you choose, so long as it does not prevent you from seeing the facts. (And when you see them there is a good deal that you will not say.)"[5] The key point is that questions about who is being mindful depend on what we consider important in a situation, and what we should consider important. At least if we use the concept of value-based mindfulness, determining what matters in the situation turns on relevant values and priorities.

Furthermore, if we conclude that the gorilla-blind group of experimental subjects were *mindless*, at least regarding the gorilla, then we should remind ourselves of the pejorative connotations of that term. Mindlessness frequently suggests failing to attend to something that should be attended to. It suggests being inattentive, careless, absentminded, rash, or stupid. It may imply irresponsibility, as when we speak of mindless violence. "Mindless," like "mindful," is typically used when something matters, either in terms of our purposes and values (personal-mindfulness) or in terms of sound values (virtue-mindfulness). Accordingly, disagreements about who is being mindful or mindless often turn on differing value judgments about what it is important and should be carefully attended to.

Paying *careful* attention is more than being conscious (versus comatose), awake (versus sleeping), or alert (versus groggy). It is being conscious of, taking heed of, and attending to what matters in light of relevant values. At some level, all attention can be an evaluative activity, but especially the careful attention involved in mindfulness. Indeed, Robert Nozick suggests that "the fundamental evaluative activity is selectivity of focus, focusing here rather than there."[6] To believe that all things are equally valuable and worthy of attention might sound open-minded, generous, and nonelitist. In fact, it makes nonsense of both attention and values: "Whether or not it is good economics, laissez-faire does not constitute an acceptable attitude toward life in general."[7] A call to be mindful of everything, at all times and in all places, would be a recipe for incoherence and chaos. It would also undermine responsibility, insofar as responsible conduct requires attending to what is morally important.

William James made a similar point in terms of stimuli and interests. He was struck by how we are constantly bombarded by stimuli but attend to relatively few of them. Our consciousness "picks out" particular sense impressions "as worthy of its notice and suppresses all the rest. We notice only those sensations which are signs to us of things which happen practically or aesthetically to interest us."[8] James intended "interest" to include what we value, either because of its perceived inherent value or because we give it value by caring about it. Values also enter into modes of attention—for example, general ways of perceiving, thinking, and feeling. In the rest of this chapter I sort out a few of the modes of attention highlighted in the mindfulness literature.

SCOPE: GENERAL VERSUS FOCUSED

Wandering-mind is consciousness that flits from one thing to another, with little focus and with varying degrees of alertness. It is the brain's default mode of attention and awareness. In the mindfulness literature, the wandering-mind is usually contrasted with mindful attention. Typically, concepts of mindfulness specify modes of attention that involve more heightened and sustained focus than typically occurs during wandering-mind, which is a domain of constant distraction. Thus, Rick Hanson says "Being mindful means staying present in this moment as it is, moment after moment, rather than daydreaming, ruminating, or being distracted."[9]

Mindfulness heightens the awareness of the wandering-mind by altering the scope, selectivity, and strength of attention, or perhaps increasing the care with which we bear something in mind. For example, during meditation we usually remain aware of the passing thoughts and feelings of the wandering-mind, but we are said to be mindful of what we choose to focus on—perhaps our breathing, or perhaps other objects of attention.[10] Applying my trio of concepts, value-based mindfulness is focusing on what matters in light of our values (personal-mindfulness) or in light of sound values (virtue-mindfulness), while restricting the distractions of the wandering-mind.

Scope of attention refers to how much is encompassed in present awareness (where the "present" is flexibly defined). It concerns the breadth and range, and quantity and variety of things attended to in the present. For example, mindful individuals might bring together a wide range of considerations in solving problems, or instead focus on a few things and filter out more fluff than is typical of the wandering mind. Sometimes we go too far and inadvertently exclude significant matters, perhaps missing the gorilla right in front of us. Thales was so absorbed in meditating on the stars that he became mindless about where he was walking, and fell into a ditch.[11] Absentminded Adam Smith fared worse: "Once, walking along in earnest disquisition with a friend, he fell into a tanning pit, and it was said he had brewed himself a beverage of bread and butter and pronounced it the worst cup of tea he had ever tasted."[12] Again, there is a video from a shopping-mall camera showing a woman who, preoccupied with a call on her cell phone held in one hand while carrying a shopping bag in the other hand, trips into the mall's fountain, spontaneously performs a somersault into the water, then quickly recovers and climbs out of the fountain to continue walking, all within fifteen seconds.[13] Given the contemporary emphasis on mindfulness as awareness of our immediate situation, we are likely to say that Thales, Smith, and the shopper were momentarily mindless. Indeed they are paradigm instances of mindlessness. Yet we could instead say that they were mindful about one thing (the stars; an intellectual issue; an important phone call) and mindless about another thing (where they were walking; making tea). Or they were mindful in one way but not in another way. Once again, citing Wittgenstein's dictum, we can say what we like as long as we are clear about the facts.

The mindfulness literature standardly distinguishes between open awareness and selective attention, both of which are specified as more heightened and focused than the wandering-mind. *Open awareness* (or *general attention*) is wide-scoped alertness to the situation, perhaps along with self-awareness of our experience of the situation.[14] In contrast, *selective attention* is focus on individual items in our environment or stream of consciousness that hold our interest, usually because we regard them as important or interesting in some way. Open awareness and selective attention are undergirded by different brain functions.[15] Each requires mental effort and energy, whether minimal or demanding, depending on the situation and our state. The same is true of acts of *redirecting attention*: voluntarily shifting attention from one item to another.

All these types of attention can interfere with each other. Excitement or anxiety occurring during open awareness, for example, might result in lapses in the selective focus on important aspects of our job, perhaps leading to workplace injuries, significant miscalculations, or incoherent sentences while writing. Again, selective attention might require paying undivided attention, intentionally restricting open awareness so as to shut out things deemed less important. Thus, Chabris and Simons directed their experimental subjects to focus on the passes of the white-shirt team, predisposing them to miss the (black-colored) gorilla. Likewise, teachers might wish for such attention from their students throughout the day, but occasionally they explicitly call for it: "May I have your undivided attention, please." Open awareness and selective attention need not conflict, however, and frequently they complement each other. We integrate them, for example, when we focus on a conversation while remaining peripherally aware of our surroundings. Again, during meditation we might easily manage shifts from general awareness of our ideas and feelings to the concerted effort to focus on one thing, such as our breathing or an object in the room. Most everyday mindfulness combines wide-ranging awareness with concentration on selected objects. In this way we can be alert to a wide variety of sights, sounds, and ideas, while dwelling on one or two of them in a given moment. This ability is surely one of the gifts of evolution, an ability that helped humans survive in a world of danger and opportunity.

Strength of attention refers to the intensity of focus. Intensity is not a feeling, although it might be accompanied by various feelings, perhaps effort and energy, or perhaps calmness and serenity. Intensity and strength mean heightened alertness. This alertness is manifested and measured, for example, in how many details we discern concerning an object, or in how richly we can relate the object to other things in our field of perception or reasoning. Strength can also refer to intensity in the form of extended duration—attending to something longer than is usual. And strength concerns the scope of attention: *concentrating* mainly or exclusively on one thing, for example watching our young child play on monkey bars where they are tempted to climb higher than is safe for them.

Intensity often involves *selective monitoring*, whereby we maintain open awareness in order to pick out and then concentrate on what matters for a given purpose. Thus, we might monitor the weather by checking it periodically, perhaps at regular intervals. Or a stock broker might monitor the stock market throughout the day or week, in order to buy or sell at appropriate times. *Bearing in mind* is related to selective monitoring. To bear in mind is to remember something important, perhaps something tempting or easy to forget, and to take it into account in our reasoning and choices. For example: "mindful of the pressures and compromises that can come with bigger budgets and preexisting brands, some filmmakers find themselves choosing smaller, more personal films."[16] Bearing in mind usually does not require continuous awareness of what is borne in mind. Thus, if I am mindful of the errand I promised a friend after work, I might think of the errand (focus on it) occasionally during the day, perhaps reminding myself using silent self-talk: "Remember to. . . ."[17] Or I might write a Post-It note to myself, place it on my steering wheel, and not think about that errand again until I leave work. Again, safe driving requires both open awareness and focused attention. We have open awareness of many factors—other cars, pedestrians, etc. We then increase attention to stop signs once we spot them, and focus on red traffic signals in order to accelerate when they turn to green. Our driving speed needs to be monitored with periodic attention focused on the speedometer, although less so when we are in slow traffic or when we put the car on cruise control (or into self-driving mode, using new technologies).

TASK ATTENTION: PARTICIPANTS AND SPECTATORS

Mindfulness is sometimes stereotyped as a serene state of attention during meditation, in which usual activities and value judgments are suspended. But mindfulness is also involved in practical activities, in coping effectively in response to a situation, perhaps to a problem or special challenge, regardless of whether serenity is present. As such, it requires valuing and responding based on values. This is especially true in *task attention* (or *task focus*): paying attention to what we are doing in order to do it well, avoid mistakes, and minimize undesirable side effects.

With regard to simple activities, task attention might involve concentrating on one thing, such as counting the passes of the white-shirt team. With regard to more complex tasks it is exercising appropriate care in performing multiple specific activities that together constitute the task.[18] Think how many small tasks are involved in driving safely, beyond simply staying on the road: identifying and coming to full stops at stop signs, watching for and not hitting pedestrians, identifying correct turns and properly signaling, and so forth. We can also pursue several tasks simultaneously (in the same day, hour, or even moment), for example writing an essay, planning a trip, and listening to music. Yet mindfulness frequently implies concentrating on what is most important in the present (understanding the present as flexibly defined), perhaps because it is most demanding or urgent, or perhaps because we have chosen to make it a priority for some other reason.

The *participant-spectator* distinction is familiar in the mindfulness literature. Agents can be participants in an activity or spectators of it, allowing of course that observing is itself an activity. The participant-spectator distinction is rough, and it needs to be applied relative to the context. We might play both roles in a situation, in different ways. For example, actors are the participants in performing a play, and members of the audience at a play are observers. But even as observers, audience members are agents who participate with emotional engagement and applause at appropriate times. Again, we are observers when we watch the basketball video in the Invisible Gorilla Experiment, but we participate in the experiment when we interact with the video by counting passes. And meditation is often depicted as suspending everyday activities in order to observe our breathing or experiences, but we are participants in the activity of meditating.

The participant/agent and spectator/observer distinctions figured prominently in twentieth-century philosophy of mind. Gilbert Ryle dissolved the myth that acting attentively (mindfully) involves an accompanying self-observation of what we are doing.[19] To this end, he emphasized that acting intentionally and attentively, and knowing what we are doing, does not consist in watching ourselves. Wittgenstein also emphasized that attention in performing activities is not a mysterious inner process. Doing things attentively is doing them competently by exercising skills we have learned. For example, to read a story attentively typically involves noticing what occurs in the story, especially noteworthy things: "What result am I aiming at when I tell someone: 'Read attentively'? That, e.g., this and that should strike him, and he be able to give an account of it."[20] Of course, reading skills come at various levels. A child who reads attentively might demonstrate her skill by being able to recall the main plot line, but an advanced reader can identify nuanced symbolism and character development. Wittgenstein also sought to dispel the illusion of singular mental processes by using the example of attending to colors and shapes, which can involve different activities.[21] One case is that someone asks you to bring a blue book to them, and you do so. Bringing a yellow book shows you are not paying attention, or perhaps do not understand English. Another case is that someone tells you to purchase some blue paint and you enter a store and find there is none available. In another case you are painting and reflect on how close the tint is to the sky. And so forth.

DIRECTION: INWARD VERSUS OUTWARD

Discussions of mindfulness typically emphasize a distinction between two directions (and objects) of attention (and awareness): inwardly on oneself (self-awareness) or outwardly on the world (situational awareness). The distinction has already been noted above, and it cuts across the distinctions between open awareness and focused attention, and between participant and spectator awareness. But a few additional comments should be added by way of linking it to some of the thinkers I discuss.

The inward-outward distinction enters explicitly into most discussions of mindfulness, but in different ways and with alternative emphases. For example, recall how Christophe André's concept of mindfulness integrates self-awareness with outward-directed attention to art. Likewise, David M. Levy, a computer and information scientist, discusses mindful self-awareness as a way to improve outward-oriented attention is using digital technologies (chapter 10). Most striking, an emphasis on one direction or the other characterizes the two most influential concepts of mindfulness: Jon Kabat-Zinn's inward emphasis during meditation (chapter 6) and Ellen J. Langer's outward emphasis during problem solving (chapter 7).

Inward and outward focus often combine and complement each other. Thus, we might briefly observe and reflect on ourselves in order to improve our performance, identifying weaknesses and strengths as a critic might. Yet self-observing can also interfere with effective agency. For example, while teaching self-consciousness tends to make me anxious. Typically I do best by focusing away from myself, remaining centered on students and on the relevant subject matter, all the while maintaining open awareness of the time, room temperature, and a host of additional ambient matters. Again, mindful drivers are agents driving attentively, paying heed to pedestrians, cyclists, slowing traffic, drunk drivers, and so on. They might briefly become self-spectators in order to monitor how well they are driving. But extended self-observation and introspection can be a dangerous distraction while driving in busy traffic.

Latin etymology for "attention" accents outwardness: *attendere* means to reach or stretch toward to the world.[22] During the Invisible Gorilla Experiment, the attention of experimental subjects is deliberately directed outwardly, in order to efficiently and accurately count the passes of the white-shirted team. The subjects are self-aware in the sense of knowing what we are doing, but their effectiveness in counting the passes would be undermined by simultaneously explicitly attending to themselves. Likewise, many activities in everyday life are best or most enjoyably performed by focusing outward, with less than usual self-preoccupation, as in Brenda Ueland's selfless self-expression, and as in "flow" when self-consciousness diminishes as we become enjoyably engaged in activities that elicit our interest and skills.[23] The self is not entirely forgotten, and if asked what we are doing we can usually readily reply, in that moment becoming explicitly self-reflective.[24] But during most flow experiences, the self remains in the background of consciousness.

In contrast, many discussions of mindfulness during meditation emphasize turning inward, explicitly focusing on ourselves—whether our moment-to-moment thoughts and feelings, or broader aspects of ourselves such as habits, attitudes, and character traits. During self-reflection the outward world is usually not eclipsed, but it becomes secondary and part of the background of consciousness. Explicit self-awareness is integral to most serious discussions of mindfulness. Indeed, a standard objection to the mindfulness movement is that, overall, mindfulness turns us inward far too much, multiplying self-preoccupation to the point of narcissism (see chapter 12).

One object of self-awareness plays a special role in the mindfulness literature: our attention itself. *Meta-attention* is attention to our attention; attention to how and what we attend to, or perhaps briefly to our inattentiveness itself.[25] It is a sub category of both selective attention and open awareness. Meta-attention occurs during meditation when we notice our mind wandering and shift it back to our breathing or other object of concentration. But it is integral to everyday activities as well, in which we are primarily focused outward but use moments of meta-attention to direct or redirect our activities. For example, we catch our minds wandering and deliberately refocus them on the task at hand. Eric Harrison elevates self-awareness as the hallmark of task attention, of becoming mindful of our activities in order to improve them or to avoid mistakes: "To be mindful of something means to consciously perceive and evaluate it. We can train ourselves to be mindful of our actions by asking two simple questions: 'What am I doing?' and 'How well am I doing it?' These few seconds of perception and evaluation have the potential to improve an action or ameliorate any bad outcomes on the spot."[26] (Notice Harrison's emphasis on values, which I share and comment further on in chapter 12).

To repeat, although meta-attention is often useful, sometimes it is undesirable. For example, athletes undermine themselves during a competition by thinking too much about the techniques they are employing.[27] Again, concentrating on the keys we are striking interferes with the speed of typing and thinking about what we are writing. And it slows us down when counting passes during the Invisible Gorilla Experiment. This differential speed brings us to the next distinction.

SPEED: FAST AND SLOW THINKING

Psychologists contrast two processes and systems of thinking, in terms of speed. One system is reflexive—automatic, quick, and requires little experience of effort. The other is reflective—slower, and involves a sense of effort and control. For example, the fast process identifies the answer to "$1 + 1 = ?$" and the slow process works out the answer to "$949 \times 761 = ?$" Daniel Kahneman describes the two systems this way:

> *System 1* operates automatically and quickly, with little or no effort and no sense of voluntary control.
> *System 2* allocates attention to the effortful mental activities that demand it, including complex computations. The operations of System 2 are often associated with the subjective experience of agency, choice, and concentration.[28]

The distinction applies to attention and mindfulness. Thus, a mindful driver swerves to avoid an accident, using the quick and largely automatic action (System 1). Or a mindful driver, confused about directions to a particular destination, might pull safely to the side of country road to look at a map, whether the map is in paper or digital form (System 2). Kahneman sometimes associates attention with System 2, thereby equating attention with effortful concentration. But I understand System 1 as also involving attention in the form of automatic attentiveness and quick attention.

Writers on mindfulness might associate mindfulness with one or both systems, or instead combine elements from both systems. The meditation literature emphasizes slowing down (System 2)—perhaps standing back, observing and reflecting at greater length and in more detail, or perhaps engaging in a task more slowly and deliberately. Effort might be required to achieve concentration. Yet the eventual aim might be to enter a state of mindfulness in which effort dissipates and we respond automatically to objects with care (System 1). In contrast, Ellen J. Langer associates mindfulness with active and inventive reflection (System 2). She depicts much automatic thinking (System 1) as mindless: "Habit, or the tendency to keep on with behavior that has been repeated over time, naturally implies mindlessness."[29] In contrast to Langer, I regard both habits and automatic actions as potentially involving mindfulness in the sense of attending to what matters. Mindfulness can include careful attention using either System-1 or System-2 thinking.

SKILL AND VIRTUE

All the preceding forms of attention can be engaged in with competence or incompetence, intelligence or stupidity, creativity or conventionality, and honesty or dishonesty. These terms refer to normative modes of attention—modes defined in terms of skills and values. There are also competent and incompetent choices about which type of attention to employ in a given situation. For example, it takes skill to know when to attend and act quickly, and when to pause to reflect. Skillful attending enters centrally into value-based mindfulness, in that values guide how and when we attend, as well as what we attend to. Some values and skills are nonmoral, such as skill in accurately counting basketball passes in the Invisible Gorilla Experiment. Other values and skills are moral, such as attending honestly and conscientiously, and being attentive to our work responsibilities rather than being negligent. Of course, paying attention can be skillful in some ways but not others. We might attend with focus, concentration, and reflection, and yet fail to notice something important. Perhaps we fail to notice something in part because we are concentrating on something else, as demonstrated in the Invisible Gorilla Experiment.

Everyday mindfulness typically implies success in noticing what is important, where *noticing* means gaining knowledge by attending.[30] It may also imply some degree of success in appreciating what matters, and in generating responses that are appropriate, responsible, or otherwise desirable. Specifically, virtue-mindfulness suggests *caring* and giving *due consideration* to what matters in a situation in light of sound values, not simply identifying it. It also suggests exercising *good judgment* in understanding our situation and responding to it appropriately. Mindlessness, in contrast, suggests inattentiveness in ways involving carelessness, obliviousness, or negligence. If, as detached observers, we attend closely to the scene of an accident without doing what we can to help (at least calling for help) we are not being mindful, at least not in the sense of virtue-mindfulness.

Attending with honesty and integrity is central to moral mindfulness—mindfulness concerning moral matters. In particular, it is central to being truthful and avoiding objectionable forms of self-deception. Objectionable self-deception can involve highly skillful attending in identifying areas of concern combined with irresponsible acts of refusing to attend more fully, choosing instead to turn away. Writing in the eighteenth century, Joseph Butler understands self-deception as willful ignorance due to intentional inattention to what matters. He observes how easily we discern flaws in the character of other people while remaining blissfully blind to our own flaws, despite having "at least an implicit suspicion" where our faults lie:

> it is much the same as if we should suppose a man to have had a general view of some scene, enough to satisfy him that it was very disagreeable, and then to shut his eyes, that he might not have a particular or distinct view of its several deformities. It is as easy to close the eyes of the mind, as those of the body: and the former is more frequently done with willfulness, and yet not attended to, than the latter; the actions of the mind being more quick and transient, than those of the senses.[31]

R. G. Collingwood developed a related idea of "corrupt consciousness":

> we direct our attention towards a certain feeling, or become conscious of it. Then we take fright at what we have recognized: not because the feeling, as an impression, is an alarming impression, but because the idea into which we are converting it proves an alarming idea. We cannot see our way to dominate it, and shrink from persevering in the attempt. We therefore give it up and turn our attention to something less intimidating.[32]

Avoiding harmful instances of self-deception is an important part of honesty and integrity, but it is only a part. There is the much larger field of conscientiousness in being a moral agent, including within specialized roles. Thus, if there were a book on mindfulness in medicine we might expect it to be rooted in a virtue-oriented perspective on what it means to be a caring, skilled, and responsible physician. In fact, there is such a book. In *Attending: Medicine, Mindfulness, and Humanity*, Ronald Epstein says mindfulness is "remembering who you are and what is important, every moment of everyday," which is an idealized version of what I call virtue-mindfulness.[33] Specifically, he understands physicians' mindful attention as value-based in terms of ethics and excellence in medicine: "Applying focused attention is a *moral* choice, not just a skill. We pay attention to that which we consider important, and by virtue of paying attention to something, we make it important. All physicians take a vow to do their best to relieve suffering and not do harm."[34]

Crucial to being a good doctor, or to exercising professional expertise in any field, is "the ability to alternate—effortlessly—between automatic and effortful cognitive processing," and "only if the [professional] practice is mindful will people learn to switch from automatic to effortful, to slow down when they should."[35] Epstein uses the example of a nurse taking blood pressure as a routine part of her work, while chatting with a patient. Suddenly she slowed down, rechecked the gauge, and retook the pressure. Noticing high numbers transformed the automatic into the effortful. She knew when to do so because she was being mindful. Epstein says that mindfulness requires a kind of *executive attention*, which enables us to move freely among modes of fast and slow attention: "Executive attention is our 'inner manager,' which helps us to prioritize one source of information over another."[36] Epstein sometimes speaks as if "executive attention" is a special form of attention, involving a combination of meta-attention (attention to how we are attending) and choices about how best to attend in a given situation. I would say instead that mindfulness involves exercising the entire mind in making choices about how to attend in particular situations, rather than itself another form of attention. Related kinds of executive attention enable us to shift between buffered and broadened understandings of the present, between task-attention and spectator-attention, and between open awareness and focused attention.

To conclude, I have emphasized the role of values in connection with various modes of attending that recur in discussions of mindfulness. I have not attempted an exhaustive categorization of ways to attend, whatever that would be like. In the next chapter I remain focused on values, illustrating how the values that guide mindfulness can be elaborated on within general perspectives on good lives.

NOTES

1. Gay Watson, *Attention: Beyond Mindfulness* (London: Reaktion Books, 2017), 16–17.

2. Many of the distinctions drawn in this chapter are discussed by Daniel Goleman in *Focus: The Hidden Driver of Excellence* (New York: HarperCollins, 2013), 39–40. See also Anna C. Nobre and Sabine Kastner, eds. *The Oxford Handbook of Attention* (New York: Oxford University Press, 2014); and Wayne Wu, *Attention* (New York: Routledge, 2014).

3. Christopher Chabris and Daniel Simons, *The Invisible Gorilla* (New York: Crown Publishers, 2010), 13. The eye-tracker researcher was Daniel Memmert of Heidelberg University, in "The Effects of Eye Movements, Age, and Expertise on Inattentional Blindness," *Consciousness and Cognition*, 15 (2006): 620–627.

4. Chabris and Simons, *The Invisible Gorilla*, 6–7.

5. Ludwig Wittgenstein, *Philosophical Investigations*, 3rd ed., trans. G. E. M. Anscombe (New York: Macmillan Company, 1958), 37, Remark 79.

6. Robert Nozick, *The Examined Life: Philosophical Meditations* (New York: Simon and Schuster, 1989), 120.

7. Nozick, *The Examined Life*, 120. In this passage Nozick playfully alludes to his former libertarian outlook, which he disavows on 286–302.

8. William James, *Psychology: Briefer Course* (New York: Collier Books, 1962), 184, italics removed.

9. Rick Hanson, with Forrest Hanson, *Resilient: How to Grow an Unshakable Core of Calm, Strength, and Happiness* (New York: Harmony Books, 2018), 23.

10. An exception occurs when the wandering-mind becomes part of the open awareness that enters into creative problem solving.

11. Some accounts have Thales falling into a well rather than a ditch. See Frederick Copleston, *A History of Philosophy*, new revised edition (Garden City, NY: Image Books, 1962) vol. I, part I, 38.

12. Robert L. Heilbroner, *The Worldly Philosophers*, revised 7th ed. (New York: Simon and Schuster, 1999), 42.

13. David M. Levy cites the event to open his book *Mindful Tech: How to Bring Balance to Our Digital Lives* (New Haven, CT: Yale University Press, 2016), 1. I discuss Levy's book in chapter 10.

14. The terms "open monitoring" and "focused attention" are preferred by Yanli Lin, Megan E. Fisher, Sean M. M. Roberts, and Jason S. Moser, "Deconstructing the Emotion Regulatory Properties of Mindfulness: An Electrophysiological Investigation," *Frontiers in Human Neuroscience*, 10 (2016). (https://doi.org/10.3389/fnhum.2016.00451.)

15. See Daniel J. Levitin, *The Organized Mind: Thinking Straight in the Age of Information Overload* (New York: Plume, 2015), 39, 68.

16. Josh Rottenberg and Daniel Miller, "Hollywood's Director Shuffle," *Los Angeles Times* (September 13, 2017), A1 and A10.

17. Charles Fernyhough studies the general importance of silent self-talk in *The Voices Within: The History and Science of How We Talk to Ourselves* (New York: Basic Books, 2016).

18. See A. R. White, *Attention* (Oxford: Basil Blackwell, 1964), 8–16.

19. Gilbert Ryle, *The Concept of Mind* (New York: Barnes and Noble, 1949), 137–143.

20. Ludwig Wittgenstein, *Zettel*, trans. G. E. M. Anscombe, ed. G. E. M. Anscombe and G. H. von Wright (Berkeley: University of California Press, 1967), 17, Remark 91.

21. Wittgenstein, *Philosophical Investigations*, 16, Remark 33.

22. Goleman, *Focus*, 4.

23. Mihaly Csikszentmihalyi, *Flow: The Psychology of Optimal Experience* (New York: HarperCollins, 1990), 71.

24. In Jean-Paul Sartre's jargon, we are "pre-reflectively" engaged in the world, which is accompanied by a tacit, "non-positional awareness" of the self. At any time we can shift to "reflective awareness" in which we become explicitly aware of ourselves, "positing" aspects of ourselves as the explicit objects of consciousness. Jean-Paul Sartre, *Being and Nothingness*, trans. Hazel E. Barnes (New York: Washington Square Press, 1966).

25. In the same spirit, law professor Peter H. Huang says that "meta-mindfulness" is being mindful about whether we are being mindful; for example, we can mindfully catch ourselves not being attentive and focused. With a jarring oxymoron, however, he speaks of "mindless mindfulness," which he says is being "mindful in a mindless fashion." He seems to mean we can be mindful of some things but not others, which of course we can. Peter H, Huang, "Meta-Mindfulness: A New Hope," *Richmond Journal of Law and the Public Interest*, vol. xix: iv (2016): 303–324, at 316.

26. Eric Harrison, *The Foundations of Mindfulness: How to Cultivate Attention, Good Judgment, and Tranquility* (New York: The Experiment, 2017), 110.

27. Goleman, *Focus*, 29.

28. Daniel Kahneman, *Thinking, Fast and Slow* (New York: Farrar, Straus and Giroux, 2011), 20–21.

29. Ellen J. Langer, *Mindfulness*, 25th anniversary ed. (Boston, MA: Da Capo Press, 2014), 17–18.
30. See White, *Attention*, 23.
31. Joseph Butler, *Fifteen Sermons Preached at the Rolls Chapel*, ed. W. R. Matthews (London: G. Bell and Sons, 1964), 159. See also Herbert Fingarette, *Self-Deception* (Berkeley: University of California Press, 2000[1969]); Mike W. Martin, *Self-Deception and Morality* (Lawrence: University of Kansas, 1986); Alfred R. Mele, *Self-Deception Unmasked* (Princeton, NJ: Princeton University Press, 2001).
32. R. G. Collingwood, *The Principles of Art* (New York: Oxford University Press, 1958).
33. Ronald Epstein, *Attending: Medicine, Mindfulness, and Humanity* (New York: Scribner, 2017), 244, n15.
34. Epstein, *Attending*, 34.
35. Epstein, *Attending*, 180–189.
36. Epstein, *Attention*, 29.

Chapter Five

Thoreau's Wakefulness

Value perspectives on mindfulness draw together the primary values in light of which we pay attention to what matters—whether it matters in light of our current values (personal-mindfulness) or it matters in light of sound values (virtue-mindfulness). In addition, value perspectives might indicate rough priorities among values, clarify what it means to live in the present, and recommend practices for cultivating mindfulness. The perspectives reflect, or just are, conceptions of good lives—lives that are meaningful, morally decent, healthy, authentic, happy, and fulfilling. Henry David Thoreau's value perspective on mindfulness provides a good illustration. It is relatively familiar and connects with a variety of contemporary interests, including individualism, ethical pluralism, democracy, capitalism, and environmentalism. It reminds us that value perspectives can be set forth in many different ways, including in philosophical argument, fiction, literary nonfiction, religious writing, blogs, and social media. It illustrates how any proffered value perspectives on mindfulness is open to dispute. And it reminds us that mindfulness can be discussed without using the word.

MINDFULNESS AS WAKEFULNESS

Wakefulness is Thoreau's term for virtue-mindfulness: to be mindful is to be morally and spiritually awake. We know this from the full context of *Walden*, with its nuanced themes and tropes. We know this as well because so many thinkers invoke and celebrate Thoreau as providing a paradigm conception of mindfulness. For example, Jon Kabat-Zinn writes that "Henry David Thoreau's two years at Walden Pond were above all a personal experiment in mindfulness. He chose to put his life on the line in order to revel in the wonder and simplicity of present moments."[1] Again, Rick Fields praises

Thoreau for being the first American to sympathetically explore Asian concepts of *sati*.[2] Although *Walden* was published in 1854, three decades before T. W. Rhys Davids translated *sati* as "mindfulness," Thoreau's wakefulness resonates with Buddhist and Hindu themes of attentiveness, enlightenment, simplicity, self-discipline, attunement to the moment, and spiritual awakening—even though he develops these themes in more individualistic terms than Asian religions do. In addition, countless environmentalists celebrate Thoreau's environmental mindfulness a century before alarms were raised about the environmental crisis.[3]

Thoreau centers his value perspective on virtues—on ideals of character rather than rules and duties (although at times he calls ideals of character "principles"). He invokes over a hundred moral virtues,[4] all of which connect with values of health, morality, and enlightened cherishing. Because *Walden* is a literary work rather than a systematic treatise in philosophy, Thoreau depicts ideals of character using metaphor rather than formal definition, and imagery rather than analysis. When he occasionally defines a key term, he is likely to offer a persuasive definition aimed at changing attitudes. For example, he defines philosophers as everyone who loves wisdom and seeks to live with simplicity, independence, and nobility (14).[5] As with many of Thoreau's key concepts, wakefulness blends the literal and metaphorical, the natural and normative, and the physical and spiritual. Physically, wakefulness is being conscious and alert rather than slumbering. Spiritually, it is being attuned to what matters in light of sound values.

As virtue-mindfulness, wakefulness is a dependent virtue—its full substance depends on additional values and virtues it helps implement. In addition, wakefulness combines many value-laden elements, including attention, appreciation, deliberateness, truthfulness, and authenticity. *Attention*, to begin with, is value-guided focusing that results in value-infused awareness. It is experiencing the world with intelligence and discernment, in ways that enable us to appreciate what matters. In general terms, what matters includes everything that contributes to a good life, including physical well-being, mental exertion, meaningful relationships, and aesthetic responsiveness. It can be manifested in every aspect of daily life, not just during meditation. Serious reading and writing, for example, require mindful attentiveness as much as alertness to nature's sounds and scenes.

Appreciation combines esteem and gratitude. On the one hand, it is esteeming or valuing genuine goods contained in our immediate situation. "To be awake is to be alive" to the good in front of us (90). That implies discerning and responding to beauty, spiritual realities, and moral possibilities. On the other hand, it is gratitude for our good fortune in being alive. Life is a gift, not a burden, regardless of how difficult it becomes on occasion (78). These two meanings of appreciation coalesce, so that gratitude for being alive is manifested in responding to the richness of our situation (333). Thoreau's value perspective is a naturalistic version of American transcendentalism. He understands the authentic self, the natural environment, and the very fabric of the universe in terms of natural elements infused with spiritual values.[6] When he occasionally refers to God, he intends something closer to Spinoza's pantheism than a conventional deity. Values are reflected in a wholesome and beneficent universe, a spiritual reality embedded in the natural world and in the higher nature of each of us.

Deliberateness is living in earnest, with a commitment to pursuing a rich and fulfilling life. Deliberateness implies intelligence and self-control, and personal and moral autonomy. It is acting with purpose, with aims that are reasonably chosen and pursued with steadfastness, as well as nuance and appropriate flexibility (97). Although deliberation can enjoin urgent action, deliberateness opposes the "desperate haste to succeed, and in such desperate enterprises," which Thoreau found ubiquitous in mid-nineteenth-century society (326). He discusses deliberateness in connection with everything from reading books to building his cabin at Walden Pond (45, 101). His decision to live at Walden Pond illustrates careful planning and moral purpose: "I went to the woods because I wished to live deliberately, to front only the essential facts of life, and see if I could not learn what it had to teach" (90). And his decision to leave Walden Pond after two years was a choice guided by a sense that he had "several more lives to live"—the most important of which turned out to be writing *Walden* (323).

Truthfulness is caring about truth in understanding ourselves and the world, as well as in communication and relationships. Thoreau is confident there are important truths to discover and live by, and he prioritizes truth as a value: "Rather than love, than money, than fame, give me truth" (330). At its root, truthfulness is trying always, or at least in important matters, to make contact with reality, which lies beneath "the mud and slush of opinion, and prejudice, and tradition, and delusion, and appearance" (97). It is heeding standards of reason in acquiring, communicating, and acting on truth, standards that include creativity and authenticity. Thoreau would be repelled by the casual and calculated dishonesty of today's politics, and even more by the radical subjectivity of contemporary postmodernism.

Authenticity combines honesty, self-respect, and autonomy. It begins with truthfulness and trust in our independent judgment—listening to our own drummer. It requires moving beyond convention to discover our interests, talents, and what manner of life suits us. It also requires accepting aspects of our nature that we can do nothing to change.[7] Authenticity puts mindfulness into action: "Let everyone mind his own business, and endeavor to be what he was made," stepping "to the music which he hears" (326). Our own music invariably has conventional elements, but it also requires going beyond convention. Each of us must struggle to find our way—a good life for us—not oblivious to values but implementing them intelligently, honestly, and with self-respect. He suggests that if we live sincerely and communicate honestly, an account of our lives will read like a report from "a distant land" (4).

Thoreau is an ethical pluralist who celebrates the immense variety of authentic lives: "I desire that there may be as many different persons in the world as possible," so long as each is authentic rather than unthinkingly imitative (71). This emphasis on authenticity blends with all his major themes. As a result it can be unclear when he is making value judgments intended to apply generally, and when instead he expresses elements of a good life for him. For example, he suggests we spend too much time in the company of other people. Is this suggestion intended as a universal moral pronouncement, or an expression of his personal preference for solitude, or simply an invitation to reflect on how best to allocate our precious time? Usually his intent is clear enough, however, at least with the aid of biographical resources. For example, he was a lifelong bachelor, but that does not mean he hated marriage and sought the solitude of bachelorhood. On the contrary, he courted Ellen Sewall, but found his love unrequited, or at least she was prevented by her father from marrying him. Despite such uncertainties, *Walden* succeeds in weaving together enduring themes about authenticity with more controversial value judgments about particular issues.

THOREAU'S LIVING PRESENT

To live in the present is to be fully *present* to it. It is to be awake to the large and small goods in our situation that we usually take for granted, to bring fresh attunement even to the morning sun (17). The present situation is ambiguous and elastic. It can be specified objectively with clocks and calendars, for example the two years, two months, and two days Thoreau lived at Walden Pond. Alternatively, it can be specified in terms of our current stage of life, such as childhood, early adulthood, or old age. In some contexts it can refer to an entire lifetime, for example when earthly life is contrasted with eternity. As he lay dying, and a minister asked him about the next life, Thoreau quipped "One world at a time."[8] Most important for Thoreau, the present can be specified subjectively in terms of emotions in response to the passage of time, or experientially in terms of the time needed to complete current activities and commitments. *Living* in the present refers to the experiential present, especially as pursued with passion. Regardless of what clocks indicate, "morning is when I am awake and there is dawn in me" (90). Stated more prosaically in my terms, whatever the objective duration of the present, living in the present is understood in light of sound values to which we are attuned.

The "now and here" is sacred (97). Thoreau is always eager to "improve the nick of time"—"the meeting of two eternities, the past and the future, which is precisely the present moment" (17). Living in the present is an ideal of mindfulness: "We should be blessed if we lived in the present always" (314). To waste the present is to waste life, "As if you could kill time without injuring eternity" (8).

Wakefulness requires refusing to allow regrets and worries to undermine the possibilities contained in the moment.[9] It does not, however, imply disregarding the future and past. Always it implies viewing the present in light of the future. It involves appreciating opportunities in the present that reach into the future, and living with hope, anticipation, and trust in the future—with "an infinite expectation of the dawn" (90). Living well in the present also involves learning from the past, and respecting ourselves for what we have accomplished, or at least appreciated. With that Janus-faced perspective, it involves slowing down, without our usual "hurry and waste of life," in order to savor the moment (93).

Wakefulness is continual reawakening and self-renewal. "Moral reform is the effort to throw off sleep" so as to improve each day, making our lives worthy of contemplation in their details as well as overall patterns (90). Doing so involves living in the moment but also cultivating general habits that express sound values.

CULTIVATING MINDFULNESS

Although habits can be mindless, they can also be engaged in mindfully, with attention and deliberation. In turn, they can also be used to cultivate mindfulness. Some habits are standardized and communal, but many are tailored to individual temperaments and needs. Thoreau is particularly interested in habits of contemplating nature with an eye to fusing its physical and moral meanings. In doing so he combines appreciation of beauty as well as practical reflection aimed at self-improvement (222). The opening lines of "Solitude" contain a famous example: "This is a delicious evening, when the whole body is one sense, and imbibes delight through every pore" (129). The passage continues with details about his daily walks along the shore of Walden Pond, during which he listens to gentle waves, bullfrogs, and whippoorwills, and sees night hunters such as foxes and skunks. These walks became a spiritually restorative ritual.

In contemplating nature, Thoreau interweaves the perspectives of a naturalist, scientist, philosopher, artist, spectator, and participant. His mindful responses to nature are nuanced and varied. He identifies with wildlife. He condemns killing of animals for sheer sport, as distinct from hunting for food. With empathy for the victim, he notes that even a rabbit cries out in pain like a child does (212). At the same time, he finds inspiration in "the tonic of wildness" and the "inexhaustible vigor" of nature (317–318). Aware of what wildness entails, he can "cheer" the wild spectacle of animals eating animals, on a vast scale that "rained flesh and blood" (318). Although he can cherish a tender plant, he concludes that "compassion is a very untenable ground" as a general response to nature, at least the truthful response of an observer (318).

Another enlivening ritual is swimming in Walden Pond. A bracing morning swim becomes a "religious exercise" (88). The cool and sometimes *cold* water serves to awaken him, physically and spiritually. He compares the pond to the bathtub of kings, and envisions his swim as the stimulus for heroic striving. No doubt there were enjoyable variations in the ritual, perhaps at times a calming immersion and at times a challenging exercise, perhaps usually initiated with enthusiasm but sometimes reluctantly.

Rituals associated with raising food were important for sustenance and symbolism alike. In particular, tending to his bean field, to raise more beans than he could possibly eat, demanded daily effort that "attached me to the earth" (155). Like swimming, caring for the plants became a spiritual practice that was demanding without being onerous and tedious, at least for the most part. To cultivate the plants is simultaneously to cultivate patience and care. It is also to gain knowledge. As a naturalist and amateur botanist, he also studied bean plants. He learned about everything from the effect of the sun on their sprouting to the pests that attacked them. He kept careful financial records of the costs in raising them and the income from selling them, thereby linking the economic side of farming to themes of frugality that permeate *Walden*.

Reading is an essential activity that requires and cultivates mindfulness. So is writing, even though he says little about it in *Walden*. He kept a daily journal at Walden Pond that provided the basis for the two books he would publish during his lifetime. The first book, *A Week on the Concord and Merrimack Rivers*, was published within two years of leaving the pond. But he spent five years writing *Walden*, putting it through at least seven major drafts.[10] In doing so, he condensed two years of experienced time into one year of narrative time, while doubling the original length. For him writing is a physical, mental, and moral practice. It combines periods of contemplation and disciplined problem solving.

Each of us discovers and cultivates our preferred mindfulness-enriching practices that awaken and sustain us in our pursuit of a good life for us. We also need to become mindful of when rituals have grown constrictive, perhaps numbingly routine, and need to be modified, abandoned, or temporarily suspended. Thoreau's daily walks around Walden Pond provided endless variety of possible experiences. After two years, however, they began to feel limiting, like the "ruts of tradition," and were relinquished when he moved from Walden Pond (323).

HEALTH, HAPPINESS, AND SOCIETY

Thoreau's perspective on mindfulness in good lives intertwines with his critique of the society he lived in—"this restless, nervous, bustling, trivial Nineteenth Century" (329). Although he sustains a positive tone, there is no mistaking the underlying themes of human suffering and compassion: "The mass of men lead lives of quiet desperation" and "unconscious despair" (8). He is convinced that most of our suffering is self-inflicted. It is generated by mistaken beliefs, harmful attitudes, and misguided desires.

One source of self-inflicted suffering is exaggerated self-hatred in the form of what Freud would call neurotic guilt. With playful hyperbole he depicts his fellow citizens as "doing penance in a thousand remarkable ways," no less extreme than Hindu holy men who contort their bodies to the point of causing permanent injuries, or who chain themselves to a tree for life (4). In addition, many unwarranted guilt feelings are based on exaggerated duties of charity owed to others. He also chides people who "*somewhat hastily*" conclude that the aim of life is to glorify God, conceived as a supernatural Creator (91).

A second source of self-inflicted suffering, this time oriented to the future, is the obsession with getting ahead. Embracing conventional beliefs, we enslave ourselves to the endless pursuit of material wealth. Even those individuals who have the "misfortune" to inherit much material wealth are burdened with pushing that wealth for the rest of their lives in a metaphorical cart loaded with rocks, a task as onerous as twelve labors of Hercules (4–5). The resulting "incessant anxiety and strain" is not healthy; it is a "disease" (11). Thoreau's response is to argue that most of the things we desire are not necessities ("necessaries"). We waste our lives, frittering them away with endless pursuits of trivial goods. Instead, we should concentrate on the essentials for a good life: "Simplicity, simplicity, simplicity!" (91). To simplify our lives, in Thoreau's sense, is to center our lives on what is essential—on what matters most in light of sound values.

A third source of unnecessary suffering is the most damaging of all: lack of self-respect. *Self-respect* means properly valuing ourselves—knowing our inherent worth, caring about our well-being, and appreciating our strengths as well as our flaws.[11] It implies taking care of our bodies (221), developing our minds, and paying due regard to our health and happiness. Self-respect is a moral virtue that includes but is not reducible to *self-esteem*, understood as the psychological state of feeling good about ourselves. Thoreau is not merely offering the contemporary cliché that our suffering derives from low self-esteem. Self-renewal implies moral self-scrutiny, which is positive oriented but also sober-minded. Thoreau reports regularly experiencing "a certain doubleness" in which he simultaneously acts and observes himself acting (135). He also reports that he never knew a person more flawed than himself—although undoubtedly he wrote with irony, since he also claims the only person he knows well is himself (78).

How we think of ourselves indicates our fate (7). And we should seek to live in a manner that warrants self-affirmation during our most elevated and critical hours (90). Human nature intertwines spiritual and animal tendencies that are worthy of reverence but require reasonable integration (210). In this way, the lack of self-respect underlies the other sources of suffering: We degrade ourselves by uncritically accepting conventional duties and conventional obsessions with money. The cure is to increase simplicity and foster self-respect (222).

Happiness is rooted in self-respect, as well as health and simplicity. Although the word "happiness" appears only once or twice in *Walden* (e.g., 193), all pages pulse with themes of happiness in its various hues—enjoyment, cheerfulness, contentment, serenity, and exuberance. Thoreau sets out to write a hymn to joy rather than an ode to dejection (84). He urges readers to "Love your life, poor as it is" (328). In social terms, he is convinced that each of us can and should achieve a happy life, not by maximizing financial wealth and other external goods, but by development of our talents and character.

CRITIQUES OF THOREAU'S VALUE PERSPECTIVE

Thoreau's social critique strikes many readers as extreme, even peculiar. So does his value perspective on mindfulness in good lives. Whatever our response to his perspective, he illustrates an important general point. Perspectives on mindfulness in good lives are invariably subject to criticism and disagreement. In concluding I mention a few of the recurring criticisms of his views.

First, the austerity he recommends would make many of us miserable. Even if we agree with him that materialism easily becomes excessive. Most people report that they are mostly happy.[12] They do not regard themselves as living in quiet desperation, and I suspect that was true in Thoreau's day. We can agree that Thoreau provides valuable reminders of how materialism easily becomes excessive. We might even agree that a degree of frugality is a virtue for the rich and poor alike. But when Thoreau proclaims that "Money is not required to buy one necessary of the soul" (329), he forgets that books and education carry a price tag, especially Ivy-League educations like the one he received at Harvard.

Second, many readers are appalled by his views on philanthropy. Thoreau lambastes philanthropy as overrated and usually rooted in tainted motives. He calls philanthropy "greatly overrated," and claims it serves to expiate guilt more than bring joy and change lives (76). If philanthropy is voluntary giving for public purposes,[13] whether in the form of money or volunteered time, then his criticisms are at most one-sided and underappreciate virtues of generosity and compassion in giving. At worst, they are rationalizations of his own relative poverty that limited his ability to help others. They also smack of ingratitude and hypocrisy, for he benefited greatly from the largesse of his friend Ralph Waldo Emerson who permitted him to live on land he owned at Walden Pond, a gift he does not acknowledge in *Walden*. Thoreau wrote a classic and enduring essay celebrating peaceful, civil disobedience. Yet he naively admired and supported John Brown, the murderer who orchestrated the horrifying butcher of innocent people in the name of fighting slavery.[14] In addition, Thoreau made blunders he was painfully aware of (78), such as inadvertently (and mindlessly) starting a campfire that destroyed three hundred acres, an event that mortified him for years. And needless to say, he never attempts to offer anything like a social agenda that could guide contemporary responses to environmental crises like climate change.

Third, in the eyes of some critics, Thoreau's value perspective is excessively individualistic. It neglects, or underappreciates, the convivial values of friendship and community. Leon Edel even charges Thoreau with narcissism: he was "a meditative narcissist with more feeling for trees and plants than for humans."[15] Again, "Thoreau's life is a tragic life, that of a man of enormous feelings that have shriveled up within him."[16] Edel goes too far, in my view. Granted, Thoreau's individualism, illustrated in his views of philanthropy, require greater balance with the claims of community. Granted, too, his personality was more introverted than, say, Emerson's expansive disposition. But although his thinking contains usual elements of egoism, his thought overall is anything but narcissistic. It is oriented to moral, spiritual, and social themes, and his voice on these themes remains relevant. Charges of narcissism and excessive inward turning are sometimes raised against the contemporary mindfulness movement (chapter 12). But Thoreau at least attempts to combine honest self-assessment with an outward orientation to large issues in good lives.

Finally, Thoreau's version of mid-nineteenth-century American transcendentalism—with its strong individualism, material austerity, nascent environmentalism, and spiritual richness—was suitable for him, and it appeals to many readers in at least some respects, and contains ideas still worthy of consideration. Yet it clashes with many other value perspectives that reasonable persons might hold. At the level of general philosophical theories, it clashes with various forms of rights ethics, duty ethics, and utilitarianism, and even alternative varieties of virtue ethics. It clashes with a host of religious perspectives. And it clashes with many everyday value perspectives that apply ordinary values like love, forgiveness, generosity, without weaving them into anything like a systematic theory.[17] These differences among value perspectives are reflected in different understandings of virtue-mindfulness.

All value perspectives on mindfulness are controversial. It should be clear why. Mindfulness is not a stand-alone value. It is always linked to a host of additional virtues and values that give it substance, values that are more or less unified within conceptions of good lives. Personal-mindfulness—attending to what matters in light of our present values—leaves open the possibility that our values might be immoral, irrational, unhealthy, or otherwise indefensible. Accordingly, patterns of personal-mindfulness are open to criticism using concepts of virtue-mindfulness: attending to what matters in light of sound values—values that are worthy of being acted on. Value perspectives articulate what sound values are, but those perspectives are themselves open to controversy as being flawed, even if we adopt a pluralistic framework that acknowledges a host of different value perspectives as reasonable though conflicting. Accordingly, virtue-mindfulness is not a philosophers' stone that transmutes base value perspectives into the gold of philosophical wisdom. Instead it must always be understood in conjunction with particular value perspectives judged reasonable on independent grounds, beyond a simple appeal to mindfulness itself.

To conclude, Thoreau sets forth a value perspective on mindfulness as part of a wider perspective on good lives. In doing so, he illustrates the centrality of values in understanding mindfulness. He exemplifies in rich detail how perspectives on mindfulness lead directly to broader questions about sound values in good lives, including values of health, happiness, and appreciating nature. In all these ways, Thoreau's perspective prepares us to explore psychologists' approaches to mindfulness. Do psychologists distinguish conceptual, empirical, and moral matters in discussing mindfulness? Or do they blend and blur them, in a manner akin to Thoreau—but with less explicit appreciation of the role of values in understanding mindfulness? We expect seamless integration of mindfulness and other values in a literary masterpiece like *Walden*. In turning to psychological accounts of mindfulness that aspire to scientific objectivity, however, we should remain alert to background assumptions about values that need to be made transparent.

NOTES

1. Jon Kabat-Zinn, *Wherever You Go There You Are*, Tenth Anniversary Edition (New York: Hachette Books, 2014), 24.

2. Rick Fields, *How the Swans Come to the Lake: A Narrative History of Buddhism in America*, 3rd ed. (Boulder, CO: Shambhala, 1992), 62.

3. See *American Earth: Environmental Writing since Thoreau*, ed. Bill McKibben (New York: Penguin Putnam, 2008).

4. See Philip Cafaro, *Thoreau's Living Ethics: Walden and Pursuit of Virtue* (Athens: University of Georgia Press, 2004).

5. Parenthetical page references in this chapter are to Henry D. Thoreau, *Walden* (Princeton, NJ: Princeton University Press, 2004).

6. See, for example, Kevin Dann, *Expect Great Things: The Life and Search of Henry David Thoreau* (New York: Penguin Random House, 2017).

7. On the distinction between individual and general human nature see Joel Feinberg, "Absurd Self-Fulfillment," in Joel Feinberg, *Freedom and Fulfillment* (Princeton, NJ: Princeton University Press, 1992), 297–330.

8. Susan Cheever, *American Bloomsbury* (New York: Simon and Schuster, 2006), 168.

9. See Scott Slovic, "*Walden* and Awakening: Thoreau in a Sophomore American Literature Survey Course," in Richard J. Schneider, ed., *Approaches to Teaching Thoreau's Walden and Other Works* (New York: The Modern Language Association of America, 1996), 105–112.

10. On Thoreau's process in writing *Walden*, as well as insightful commentary, see Robert E. Spiller, Willard Thorp, Thomas H. Johnson, Henry Seidel Canby, and Richard M. Ludwig, *Literary History of the United States*, 3rd ed. rev. (New York: Macmillan Company, 1963), 388–415; Robert Sattelmeyer, "The Remaking of *Walden*," in James Barbour and Tom Quirk, ed., *Writing the American Classics* (Chapel Hill: University of North Carolina Press, 1990), 53–78; Denis Donoghue, *The American Classics: A Personal Essay* (New Haven, CT: Yale University Press, 2005), 137–76; and Jay Parini, *Promised Land: Thirteen Books That Changed America* (New York: Doubleday, 2008), 106–30.

11. See Robin S. Dillon, ed. *Dignity, Character and Self-Respect* (New York: Routledge, 1995).

12. Most Americans score their happiness level between 7 and 8 on a scale of 10. See Sonja Lyubomirsky, *The How of Happiness: A Scientific Approach to Getting the Life You Want* (New York: Penguin, 2007), 42.

13. See Mike W. Martin, *Virtuous Giving: Philanthropy, Voluntary Service, and Caring* (Bloomington: Indiana University Press, 1994).

14. See Robert Penn Warren, *John Brown: The Making of a Martyr* (Nashville, TN: J. S. Sanders, 1993); and Cheever, *American Bloomsbury*, 162.

15. Quoted by Jeanne McCulloch in an interview with Leon Edel in George Plimpton, ed., *Writers at Work: The Paris Interviews*. Eighth Series (New York: Penguin, 1988), 25–72, at 53.

16. Jeanne McCulloch in an interview with Leon Edel, in *Writers at Work*, 59. See also Leon Edel, *Henry D. Thoreau* (Minneapolis: University Of Minnesota Press, 1970).

17. Perhaps overstating his claims, but offering an important reminder, Michael Ignatieff argues that the everyday ethics of most people bear little resemblance to systematic ethical theories taught in university seminar rooms. *The Ordinary Virtues: Moral Order in a Divided World* (Cambridge, MA: Harvard University Press, 2017).

Part Two

Concepts of Mindfulness

Chapter Six

Meditation and Morality

During a Buddhist meditation retreat in 1979, Jon Kabat-Zinn experienced a vision, lasting no more than ten seconds, which revealed his right livelihood and karmic assignment. He would recontextualize meditation within mainstream health care, setting aside its detailed ties to Buddhist doctrines while retaining its general aim to "relieve suffering and catalyse greater compassion and wisdom in our lives and culture."[1] He was well prepared to undertake this task. Not only had he practiced meditation for fourteen years, beginning when he earned his doctorate in molecular biology at MIT, but he was currently teaching in the medical school at the University of Massachusetts where health-care innovation was encouraged. A few months following his vision he established a science-oriented clinic to treat stress by using what he later called mindfulness-based stress reduction (MBSR). The success of his clinic inspired hundreds of similar programs around the world.[2] It also promulgated a concept I call *value-suspending mindfulness*: nonjudgmental attention to and awareness of our immediate experience, where nonjudgmental implies suspending value judgments.

To suspend value judgments is not to abandon them. It is to set them aside during meditation, rather than acting on them or even guiding attention in light of them. On the surface, then, value-suspending mindfulness is the opposite of value-based mindfulness: paying attention to what matters in light of our values (personal-mindfulness) or sound values (virtue-mindfulness). At another level, however, value-suspending and value-based mindfulness are compatible and connected. As Kabat-Zinn emphasizes, background values provide the motivation and rationale for temporarily suspending value judgments during therapy-oriented meditation. These background values may center on mental health, happiness, and general well-being. They may also include the moral and spiritual values of compassion, love, and peace that initially attracted him to Buddhism.

KABAT-ZINN ON VALUES

Initially Kabat-Zinn defined mindfulness in terms of *attention*: "paying attention in a particular way: on purpose, in the present moment, and nonjudgmentally."[3] But midway through his career he defined mindfulness in terms of *awareness* achieved through attention: "the awareness that emerges through paying attention on purpose, in the present moment, and nonjudgmentally to the unfolding of experience."[4] At times he gave equal emphasis to them: "placing one's attention and awareness in the present moment with an attitude of non-judgemental acceptance."[5] These shifts are noteworthy. Whereas attention is a mental activity of directing consciousness in particular directions, awareness is a state of apprehension and appreciation. Attending and paying attention are activity concepts: they refer to activities we engage in. In contrast, awareness and becoming aware are reception-concepts and often success-concepts: they refer to noticing, knowing, and receiving information.[6] Awareness often suggests attending to what matters, and thereby becomes value-based mindfulness.[7]

Exactly what does Kabat-Zinn mean by nonjudgmental, and nonjudgmental acceptance? The terms have several meanings in his writings.

> Sense 1: *not judgmental*, by avoiding unreasonably negative evaluations, and unduly blame-oriented attitudes.
> Sense 2: *not negative*, meaning avoiding all negative judgments.
> Sense 3: *accepting* and *affirming*, in the sense of acknowledging something and judging it to be benign or even good in some way.
> Sense 4: *not judging* (nonjudging, non-evaluative), by avoiding or suspending all evaluations, both positive and negative evaluations, and both explicit value judgments and reactions based on them, such as emotions, attitudes, commitments, and actions.

Not judgmental (Sense 1), which is the primary everyday meaning of nonjudgmental, suspends negative value judgments that are unjustifiably negative. Not negative (Sense 2) goes further by suspending all negative value judgments, including those which are justified or unjustified. Accepting or affirming (Sense 3) implies making positive value judgments, tacitly evaluating them as benign or even good in some way. Not judging (Sense 4) means that all value judgments are suspended, both negative and positive ones, along with actions and emotions based on them.

Although Kabat-Zinn slides among these senses, the primary meaning he uses in defining mindfulness is not judging (Sense 4): Mindfulness "involves suspending judgment and just watching whatever comes up, including your own judging thoughts, without pursuing them or acting on them in any way."[8] At least, it involves *trying* to suspend value judgments and reactions based on them. Suspending evaluation can be difficult, even during brief sessions of meditation. This is because everyday attention and awareness are infused with value judgments that intrude during meditation. For example, everyday experiences and awareness of emotions of envy, anger, and self-hate express value judgments about perceived bads; and everyday awareness of our success, pleasure, and self-worth are based on positive value judgments about perceived goods. During therapy-oriented meditation we are told to simply notice value-charged emotions and thoughts when they arise, and then set them aside.

Meditation based on value-suspending mindfulness has many variations, but the most familiar and elemental version is to focus on our breathing. While sitting or lying down, and with eyes closed, we slow, deepen, and steady our breathing. We maintain open awareness to ideas, feelings, sensations, and explicit value judgments as they drift through consciousness. But we simply note them without reacting to them, and return focused attention to our breathing. During therapeutic meditation we become observers or spectators on our experience and situation, including our breathing and wandering thoughts, buffering our immediate experience from our past and future. We do not react to our immediate experience in our role as valuers and agents, as we do in everyday life. As an aid in defusing and distancing ourselves from troublesome thoughts, meditation might involve explicitly identifying random feelings and saying things to ourselves sotto voce—for example, "I am having the thought that I am failing at work"—before letting the thought drift away. At other times the "I" and the sense of self disappear altogether, as we observe "There is worry about work."

When practiced regularly, value-suspending meditation can reduce stress and distress, both episodically during meditation and systemically throughout life, at least for many people.[9] It can relax the body, calm the mind, increase a sense of control, and improve concentration. It can defuse anxiety-producing value judgments, so that we stop beating ourselves up with self-blame and self-hate. It has been widely adapted to treat a host of ailments, including addictions, compulsions, phobias, and depression. Beyond healing ailments, it has also been used to enhance a sense of well-being and to improve performance in sports, education, and work.[10] By temporarily removing us from everyday value-charged awareness, meditation paves the way for fresh alternatives in how we view the world and ourselves. It prepares us to challenge our usual obsession with ranking ourselves and other people. It might lessen our tendency to shut out people through intolerance and indifference, and to nurture greater tolerance and acceptance. Many practitioners testify that value-suspending mindfulness during regular meditation increases self-knowledge by helping identify recurring patterns of thought, feeling, and conduct.[11]

Even though values are suspended during meditation, values do play a role in practices of meditation. We engage in value-suspending mindfulness during meditation *because* we value its benefits: relaxation, a sense of control, an improved sense of well-being, and perhaps increased self-knowledge. We act on such values in committing to practicing meditating. Moreover, even during meditation, in its elemental version, we tacitly *give value* to the otherwise commonplace activity of controlling the pace of our breathing, as a means to relieve stress. We also give value to being attuned to our immediate experience, rather than taking our breathing and our passing thoughts for granted (as we usually do). Awareness and control of our breathing, along with open awareness of the contents of our wandering mind, take on importance; they matter to us in the moment. In this way, paradoxically, values justify value-suspending during meditation. Defusing the paradox, *some* of our values motivate and provide the rationale for temporarily suspending *other* values we hold.

Kabat-Zinn emphasizes that in order for meditation to be effective, it needs to be motivated and justified by background values that comprise a *personal vision*, rooted in a conception of a good life for us: "Your vision should be what you believe is most fundamental to your ability to be your best self, to be at peace with yourself, to be fully integrated as a person, to be whole."[12] He reports he once believed that value-suspending meditation "was so powerful in itself and so healing" that it eventually brings about personal growth, but he soon learned that a personal vision is essential: "to achieve peace of mind, people have to kindle a vision of what they really want for themselves and keep that vision alive in the face of inner and outer hardships, obstacles, and setbacks."[13] Indeed, practicing meditation can help keep that vision alive, in addition to being motivated by it.

Exactly which values enter into our personal vision is just that—personal. The values are a matter of individual commitment, and they vary widely among patient/clients. For some individuals the vision is simply to have a healthier, less-stressful way of living. For others, as with Kabat-Zinn, the vision includes moral and spiritual values—especially peace, compassion, kindness, and love. But while visions are personal, some attitudes and qualities "support all meditation practice."[14] They include patience, generosity, trust, compassion, self-respect, and tolerance. These are *moral* virtues, of course, even though he usually does not label them as such. They contribute to successful meditation by calming the mind, reducing its "endemic restlessness and impatience" and reducing the anger that underlies its usual turmoil.[15] Their moral and health benefits, in turn, can spread throughout a life when meditation is practiced regularly.

Researchers and therapists are bound by professional standards that forbid imposing values on clients: do not cause harm, help patients by meeting standards of due care, and respect patients' privacy and autonomy.[16] Usually this requires therapists to maintain therapeutic neutrality, encouraging clients to develop and maintain their personal value perspective without imposing values on them. At most, therapists might collaborate with clients by offering suggestions about a personal vision for their consideration, but ultimately professional ethics requires them to respect their clients' autonomy in forming and acting on their value perspective. Even so, as Kabat-Zinn emphasizes, it is entirely appropriate for therapists to be motivated by their personal value perspective in working with client/patients. In addition to a need to earn a living, it is desirable for health professionals to be sustained in their work by their moral and religious ideals. In particular, Kabat-Zinn was inspired to create his clinic and conduct workshops because of his experiences in practicing Buddhist meditation, with the Buddhist-inspired aim of increasing compassion and wisdom in the world.[17] And as a therapist, Kabat-Zinn adopts a stance of unconditional acceptance and affirmation toward patients. He says to clients and readers, with a mind-bending reassurance, "you are already perfect just as you are, in the sense of already being perfectly who you are, including all the imperfections."[18]

In addition to being a clinician and scientist, however, Kabat-Zinn writes popular-audience books in which he explores mindfulness in good lives. In his books he encourages each of us to develop a personal vision for meditating. Yet he also conveys his value perspective on good lives, at times tacitly inviting readers to share it. That perspective, again, centers on humanitarian love—on compassion, kindness, and peace. Technically, he contrasts two aims using mindfulness-based meditation: (1) the therapeutic aim of treating stress disorders, depression, and other illness, and (2) the moral/spiritual aim of developing awareness "systematically in the service of self-understanding and wisdom," where wisdom is a guide to virtues such as authenticity, self-respect, love, compassion, kindness, gratitude, and peace.[19] In his role as a therapist, he encourages client/patients to suspend all value judgments during meditation *and* to develop and apply a personal value perspective that provides a rationale and motive for meditating—including for suspending evaluation during meditation. In his role as a writer on spiritual matters, he expresses his personal vision, and encourages others to share or otherwise respond to it. Yet, in his popular-audience books, he does not maintain a sharp line between understanding mindfulness as value-suspending and discussing it as value-based. Moreover, in those books he retains the same definition of value-suspending mindfulness introduced in his clinical work.

Using his concept of value-suspending mindfulness, how can mindfulness foster "a commitment to ethical behavior," and promote wisdom and ethical conduct?[20] As I interpret his claim, value-suspending mindfulness does not by itself generate wisdom and decency. Instead, it does so when guided by an appropriate personal vision, which provides the framework for both therapeutic meditation and the moral contribution of mindfulness in daily life. Admittedly, in some passages he seems to claim that just any personal vision combined with disciplined meditation will produce wisdom: The "nonjudging orientation," he says, will make us "more balanced, more effective, and more ethical in our activities."[21] But that claim is utterly implausible. For the claim ignores the possibility of value-suspending attention being used for immoral purposes—calming and steadying the mind in pursuing sheer evil. Mindfulness-based meditation does not contribute to good lives by itself, but only in conjunction with *sound* values that enter into a personal vision. That is, Kabat-Zinn implies that the power of meditation to improve lives requires, from the outset, grounding it in sound values for practicing meditation. Value-suspending mindfulness during meditation can express and reinforce sound values, but does not magically create them wholesale. In order for ethical and spiritual benefits to accrue, meditators must sincerely practice meditation "in the service of wisdom, self-understanding, and recognizing our intrinsic interconnectedness with others and with the world, and thus in the service of kindness and compassion."[22]

In offering the above interpretation of Kabat-Zinn's popular writings I am not suggesting that he is entirely clear or consistent in how he states his views. Confusion is produced when he conflates various uses of the term *nonjudgmental*. Here are three examples.

First, he often conflates *not judgmental*, using the pejorative sense of "judgmental" as unduly negative in making value judgments (Sense 1) with *not judging* in the sense of not evaluating (Sense 4). He consistently maintains that we avoid being judgmental in the pejorative sense in all areas of our lives, not only during meditation. And usually he emphasizes that during meditation we temporarily suspend *all* value judgments. Yet in some passages he introduces a technical meaning of "judging" as unjustified evaluation, and contrasts it with "discernment" as justified evaluation. Thus, he associates *judging* with "black-and-white, either/or seeing and thinking [that] leads rapidly to fixed and limiting judgments, often arrived at reflexively, automatically, without reflection. . . . *Discernment*, on the other hand, as differentiated from *judging*, leads us to see, hear, feel, perceive infinite shades of nuance, shades of gray between all-white and all-black, all-good and all-bad."[23] This distinction is disconcerting. For in ordinary language discernment involves judging in the sense of making value judgments. Discernment is evaluating in reasonable, sensitive, and nuanced ways. The crucial point is that he never uses the term "discernment" when he defines mindfulness. He never says the mindfulness involved in mindfulness-based meditation consists in discerning-attention-and-awareness in the moment. If he had, he would have been talking about value-based mindfulness all along—indeed about virtue-mindfulness. He would also have undermined his scientific studies, by requiring that patients make discerning evaluations during meditation, rather than suspending evaluations while meditating.

Second, he invokes Thoreau frequently and extensively to illustrate what mindfulness means. As we saw in chapter 5, Thoreau's concept of wakefulness is value-based, not value-suspending. It expresses Thoreau's views about virtue-mindfulness in good lives. Yet Kabat-Zinn writes as if he and Thoreau use the same concept of mindfulness. He regards Thoreau's wakefulness as a paradigm of mindful living, and he extensively quotes from *Walden* in developing his own themes.[24] Granted, occasionally he alerts his readers about discussing mindfulness in the new context of daily life, rather than the clinic where patients are treated for special health problems.[25] Nevertheless, he never acknowledges that he is using two different concepts of mindfulness in the two different contexts.

Third, compounding confusion, in places he introduces selected value judgments into some forms of mindfulness-based meditation for therapeutic purposes, thereby contradicting his official definition of mindfulness as value-suspending. In particular, during "loving-kindness meditation" "we consciously invite feelings of love and kindness toward ourselves to arise," perhaps using phrases like "May I be free from inner and outer harm; may I be happy; may I be healthy; may I live with ease."[26] These hopes and wishes are then extended to other individuals, explicitly cultivating feelings of kindness, compassion, and forgiveness toward them. In these contexts he recommends that client/patients "try"—experiment with—loving-kindness meditation, rather than officially advocating it (as a therapist). He also retains value-suspending with regard to negative and distressful matters, so that loving kindness meditation is actually a mixture of value-suspending and value-based mindfulness. Nonetheless, he tacitly goes against his official definition of mindfulness as requiring the suspension of all value judgments and value-based reactions.

Putting things together, Kabat-Zinn might have stated his views more clearly and consistently by distinguishing from the outset several categories of value judgments: negative judgments about things as bad or undesirable; unduly negative and nondiscriminating judgments rooted in attitudes of blame, guilt, shame, failure, and undesirable ways of ranking people; accepting judgments in the form of acknowledging the presence of something as benign; and positive and discriminating judgments rooted in loving, kindness, gratitude, generous forgiving, hope, open-hearted embrace of diversity, and mental health. He could then specify that all mindfulness-based meditation involves suspending negative value judgments, especially unduly negative value judgments, and most types of meditation involve temporarily suspending all moral value judgments, both negative and positive ones. Only *most*, because some forms of meditation incorporate positive values. In particular, loving-kindness meditation involves making positive and discriminating value judgments about love, self-respect, compassion, and peace. Furthermore, although most values are suspended during meditation in the clinical setting, in meditating we do act on the values contained in our personal vision. Outside the clinical setting, in most areas of our lives, mindfulness and meditation may remain fully value-based: they are attached to and help implement our vision of a good life (personal-mindfulness) and ideally a sound and discriminating vision (virtue-mindfulness).

NONJUDGMENTAL AWARENESS

Kabat-Zinn was the catalyst for the scientific study mindfulness-based meditation. He inspired thousands of research papers on mindfulness and myriad practical applications in clinical settings. Under his influence, the concept of value-suspending mindfulness spread rapidly through popular culture. It is now reflected in the entry for "mindfulness" in *Merriam-Webster's Collegiate Dictionary*: "the practice of maintaining a nonjudgmental state of heightened or complete awareness of one's thoughts, emotions, or experiences on a moment-to-moment basis."[27] Notice the emphasis on "awareness" rather than "attention" in this definition. Notice especially the operative term "nonjudgmental," with all its ambiguity. That term permeates psychologists' writings on mindfulness (as well as therapy in general).

In 2004, after surveying the psychological literature on mindfulness, Scott Bishop and his colleagues formulated this influential summary definition: "nonelaborative, nonjudgmental, present-centered awareness in which each thought, feeling, or sensation that arises in the attentional field is acknowledged and accepted as it is."[28] *Nonelaborative* awareness means we perceive, observe, or otherwise take note of objects without trying to explain or otherwise reason about them. But what does Bishop mean by *nonjudgmental* awareness? Does he mean *not judgmental*, using the pejorative sense of "judgmental" as making unduly negative, excessively blame-oriented, and unjustifiably punitive valuations (Sense 1); *not negative*, that is, avoiding all negative judgments (Sense 2); *accepting* and *affirming*, which implies acknowledging the existence of a thing but also judging it benign or even good in some way (Sense 3); or *not judging* by avoiding or suspending all evaluations of what we are experiencing (Sense 4)?

As usually interpreted, Bishop intends Sense 4. That is, he intends what I call value-suspending mindfulness: paying attention to something in ways that involve suspending all value judgments about it, both positive and negative evaluations, and both explicit evaluations and reactions based on them such as emotions, attitudes, thoughts, commitments, and actions. Nevertheless, as it stands, Bishop's definition is vague and ambiguous. Hence it behooves researchers who adopt his definition to specify how they interpret the slippery term "nonjudgmental." Otherwise they risk confusion about what is being studied in their experiments. Are they studying the therapeutic efficacy of suspending *all* value judgments during meditation, suspending *negative* value judgments, suspending *unduly negative* and blame-oriented judgments, or perhaps allowing and encouraging *positive* value judgments? Failing to specify exactly what they are studying can result in unsound experiments and misinterpretations of the results of experiments.

For clarity, researchers probably do best to avoid the term "nonjudgmental" altogether.[29] If they do use the term, however, they should immediately stipulate its meaning. To his credit, Michael A. West does exactly that. According to him, mindfulness combines four elements.

1. Awareness—of all possible experiences such as sensations in the body, thought, emotions, sights, and sounds. . . .
2. Sustained attention—this involves gently but firmly bringing attention back to the current moment; reducing rumination; reducing anxious thoughts about the future; and bringing attention back to the here and now.
3. Focus on the present moment—rather than becoming immersed or lost in thoughts about the past, the future, plans, and preoccupations.
4. Nonjudgmental acceptance—this involves not making judgments about experience; not labeling or reacting to experience in the current moment as good or bad, desirable or undesirable, but instead allowing experiences to arise without blocking, controlling, changing, or avoiding them.[30]

The last element is stated with admirable explicitness. West stipulates that nonjudgmental acceptance means awareness, attention, or acknowledgment while suspending *all* value judgments, both positive and negative ones, explicit and tacit ones, and also reactions such as emotions and attitudes based on evaluations. His definition provides clarity about what is being studied. It also provides operational guidelines for experimental subjects who are instructed to suspend or set aside all value judgments while meditating—including explicit value judgments, tacit value judgments, and responses and actions based on value judgments.

If removing the ambiguities surrounding "nonjudgmental" is important in conducting experiments, it is equally important in communicating with the public, for example in self-help books and in popular-audience books conveying scientific studies. Consider Ronald D. Siegel's book, *The Mindfulness Solution: Everyday Practices for Everyday Problems*. Siegel presents himself as a scientist, one who has taught for decades in Harvard's Medical School. Yet he also writes as a practical ethicist who sees moral benefits from practicing mindfulness. As the title of his book suggests, he contends that mindfulness helps us grapple with the panoply of daily problems. He defines mindfulness as "awareness of present experience with acceptance."[31] He then proceeds to shift among different meanings of "acceptance," as suits his aims in discussing specific topics.

For example, when he highlights the calming effects of sustained attention to our breathing, nonjudgmental acceptance means suspending all evaluation.[32] When he highlights the harm caused by negativity and blaming, acceptance means not judgmental—that is, not "judgmental" in the pejorative sense.[33] When he highlights engagement with our immediate situation and experiences, acceptance means honest acknowledgment, in contrast with untruthful evasion.[34] And when he highlights being compassionate and savoring the moment, acceptance means affirmation, appreciation, and positive evaluation.[35] In some passages he obviously intends (what I call) virtue-mindfulness. For example, he asks whether mindfulness could be used to serve undesirable purposes, such as helping calm a sniper who kills innocent victims. He answers that it could not. Malevolent snipers do not manifest the appropriate "attitude of mind": "What is missing for the sniper is acceptance, or nonjudgment. This adds warmth, friendliness, and compassion."[36] Again, in a chapter on "mindful ethics" he contends that all unethical behavior involves a lack of mindfulness by "not really noticing its consequences in our own mind."[37] This "noticing" is guided by moral evaluation, not value-suspending mindfulness.

Value-suspending mindfulness and value-based mindfulness are compatible and complementary when used in their appropriate contexts. One appropriate context for value-suspending mindfulness is the clinical setting, where value judgments are temporarily set aside with therapeutic goals in mind, perhaps in addition part of scientific studies of meditation. Other contexts include temporarily suspending routine value judgments with aims of relaxation or in gaining self-knowledge. In contrast, the appropriate context for value-based mindfulness includes almost everywhere else in daily life. It would be morally subversive to replace value-based mindfulness with value-suspending mindfulness in all areas of life. It would also be incoherent, insofar as the therapeutic aims of health have moral dimensions. Mental health is important because people are morally important.

Morality and mental health overlap and interweave at many junctures. There are moral, as well as health reasons for not being judgmental in the pejorative sense—that is, unduly negative in making judgments about oneself and other people. There is also a moral basis for rejecting unrealistically high moral ideals that cause excessive shame and guilt.[38] Furthermore, value-suspending mindfulness in its proper place can contribute to morality as well as to therapy. Thus, we might feel anger, envy, and hatred toward a boss, in ways that damages important work relationships. The temporary suspension of these negative judgments during meditation can enter into identifying and rethinking harmful value preconceptions, opening a door to greater compassion and respect for others. It can increase self-knowledge and self-control—not by itself, but when tethered to moral convictions and commitments.

At multiple points, then, value-suspending mindfulness during meditation connects to value-based mindfulness. Value-based mindfulness can make us more attuned to how unduly negative judgments (about ourselves and others) can cause great harm. Value-based mindfulness can also play a role in mindful valuing (chapter 8) and in forming what Kabat-Zinn calls a personal vision that motivates and justifies the practice of value-suspending meditation. In fact, in some ways, value-suspending mindfulness can be subsumed to value-based mindfulness. We might envision value-suspending mindfulness during meditation as *giving importance to* otherwise commonplace things—such as our breathing or thoughts—with the wider purpose of promoting background values of health and moral values. Nevertheless, it is important to be clear about the striking differences between value-suspending and most value-based mindfulness. To accent that contrast I conclude by discussing Buddhist concepts of value-based mindfulness and meditation.

BUDDHIST RIGHT MINDFULNESS

Kabat-Zinn's influence in promulgating mindfulness-based meditation sometimes resulted in equating mindfulness and meditation in popular culture. Yet they are distinct. He implies as much in speaking of mindfulness-*based* meditation—that is, meditation based on value-suspending mindfulness. In everyday usage, *meditation* is contemplating something, using more or less extended reflection—what Daniel Kahneman calls slow thinking rather than fast thinking. Meditation might consist in studying an event in order to understand it, reasoning about a problem in order to find a solution, dwelling on a scene to appreciate its beauty, reading scripture for spiritual enlightenment. Thus, after a novelist gets an idea for a story there comes "a period of more or less conscious meditation, then the first draft, and finally the revision."[39] And when the peripatetic Thales fell into a well while gazing at the stars, he was very much meditating—just not about where he was walking. In these instances, meditation does not imply suspending values. On the contrary, if we say that mindfulness is involved, we probably have in mind paying careful attention to what matters in our present experience or situation in light of values. Only during Kabat-Zinn style meditation is value-suspending mindfulness required.

Although meditation and mindfulness are distinct concepts, many of the distinctions concerning mindfulness, drawn in chapter 2, carry over to meditation. Thus, the *objects* during meditation—the things we attend to—might be features of ourselves, for example our breathing, or the ideas and feelings that stream through our wandering consciousness. Instead they might be things external to us, such as music or flowers. Either way, they might also involve our values, such as beauty, love, and compassion. The *modes of attention* can be general awareness (or open monitoring), focused attention (concentration), or normative modes such as honest self-scrutiny. The generic *purpose* of therapeutic meditation is to improve or maintain health. Its specific purpose might be to reduce anxiety, depression, compulsions, phobias, or physical pain. Beyond healing ailments, therapeutic meditation might serve to enhance concentration during sports or study, or to augment a sense of well-being and happiness. In contrast, the purpose of other types of meditation might be to pursue moral and spiritual aims, as in Buddhism. Of course, the goals of therapeutic and spiritual meditation can overlap, and perhaps usually do. Health values include selected moral values, for example self-respect and respect for others, and spiritual values can include care of our body and mental well-being. Nevertheless, spiritual-oriented meditation makes moral values central, in contrast with therapy-oriented meditation that tends to leave moral values in the background. In this way, spiritual meditation connects straightforwardly with value-based mindfulness, and specifically with virtue-mindfulness.

Meditation practices were commonplace in world religions long before psychology even emerged as a science.[40] The practices include prayer, study of scripture, communal singing, revering religious icons, and attunement to nature as sacred. I choose Buddhism to illustrate the explicit value orientation of religious mindfulness and meditation, for two reasons. First, as we have seen, Buddhism played a key role in inspiring Kabat-Zinn's development of his influential mindfulness-based meditation. Although he set aside esoteric Buddhist doctrines, he never abandoned his personal vision of good lives as centered on Buddhist values such as love, kindness, peace, and compassion, values he readily shares in his popular books.[41] Second, mindfulness is often associated with Buddhism in popular culture.

Mindfulness is understood in many ways during Buddhism's 2,600-year history, but the general concept of *right mindfulness* is directly traceable to the Buddha. He introduced it as a key virtue in his Noble Eight-Fold Path to spiritual enlightenment and nirvana. He does not equate it with periods of meditation that are set aside and buffered from the rest of daily life. In particular, sitting forms of meditation are only one of many applications of right mindfulness in good lives. Right mindfulness, and even meditative attitudes and practices, are advocated in all areas of daily life.

Early Buddhist scripture does not explicitly define mindfulness. It does, however, bathe mindfulness in themes about remembering what matters spiritually. *Sati* is illustrated using terms such as "remembrance," "recollection," "recall," "keeping in mind," "absence of floating" (mental drifting), and "absence of forgetfulness."[42] The same emphasis on remembering occurs in definitions of mindfulness in later exegetical texts of the Theravada tradition: "*Sati* is that by means of which [the qualities that constitute the mind] remember, or it itself is what remembers, or it is simply remembering."[43] It requires guarding against intrusive, especially objectionable thoughts. In order to keep the mind concentrated, it requires deliberately disrupting the mind's natural tendency to drift. Stated more positively, it implies remembering and concentrating on what we *ought* to be doing at the time. One important thing, of course, is to remember to practice meditation each day. Another important thing is to concentrate on the specific rituals in various forms of meditation, for example focusing on our breathing or posture. In addition, guarding implies remembering important values that should guide everyday life when we are not meditating. Above all, we need to remember to cultivate compassion, and to act with compassion toward ourselves and others. Guarding involves being cautious and wary so as to identify hostile attitudes (such as anger, hatred, envy) and greedy behavior (for example obsessions with money, drugs, sex), and then to discipline or root out excesses. In this way, *sati* is explicitly value-based mindfulness. It is the attitude and virtue of bearing in mind sound values, "standing guard" on behalf of sound values, and on behalf of one's commitment to those values, remembering to implement them in our lives at appropriate moments and in appropriate ways. When manifested during meditation, *sati* calms, centers, and concentrates the mind around sound values.

The Buddha widened the meaning of *sati* that was current in his time, connecting it to the new spiritual doctrines and practices he introduced. He used *sati* to mean general memory but also the specific readiness to bear in mind and implement the values and principles he advocated. *Sati* became an immediate, in-the-moment awareness of what matters. In translating *sati* as mindfulness, T. W. Rhys Davids underscored the Buddha's expansion of *sati*, and the specification of the spiritual heeding he taught his followers:

> Etymologically Sati is Memory. But as happened at the rise of Buddhism to so many other expressions in common use, a new connotation was then attached to the word, a connotation that gave a new meaning to it, and renders "memory" a most inadequate and misleading translation. It became the memory, recollection, calling-to-mind, being-aware-of, certain specified facts. Of these the most important was the impermanence (the coming to be as the result of a cause, and the passing away again) of all phenomena, bodily and mental. And it included the repeated application of this awareness, to each experience of life, from the ethical point of view.[44]

Because right mindfulness is explicitly attached to other Buddhist values, it sharply contrasts with the value-suspending attention emphasized in psychologists' therapeutic meditation. During meditation, as well as throughout daily life, right mindfulness involves removing false ideas and unjustified evaluations involved in "attachment" to worldly things, and replacing them with true ideas and justified evaluations. Its overall role is to advance spiritual understanding and ultimately full enlightenment. It can perform this role when it involves proper conceptualization and justified evaluation. As Bhikkhu Bodhi explains:

> The practitioner of mindfulness must at times evaluate mental qualities and intended deeds, make judgments about them, and engage in purposeful action. In connection with right view, mindfulness enables the practitioner to distinguish wholesome qualities from unwholesome ones, good deeds from bad deeds, beneficial states of mind from harmful states. In conjunction with right effort, it promotes the removal of unwholesome mental qualities and the acquisition of wholesome qualities.[45]

In my terms, right mindfulness is a version of virtue-mindfulness: paying attention to what matters in light of Buddhist values. These values include compassion, peace, and love. What matters also includes negative things—things that are important because they constitute threats to sound values and doctrines and as such need to be guarded against and combatted, such as temptations of greed, anger, and callous indifference to suffering.

The connections between Buddhist virtue-mindfulness and Buddhist values and doctrines are complex, and they vary among different Buddhist traditions. And perhaps needless to add, even central values such as compassion are sometimes perverted, as in the recent oppression of the Muslim minority in Myanmar. But one core teaching is found in all traditions: The Four Noble Truths. These Truths are that life involves suffering; desire is the source of that suffering; removing desires ends suffering; and the Eightfold Path is the way to remove those desires and alleviate suffering. Suffering (*dukkha*) includes physical pain, some of which is inevitable and irremovable, but most importantly it includes unnecessary experiences of anxiety, fear, envy, and hatred, all of which arise because of our desires (interacting with influences from the world). The Eightfold Path is: "right view, right thought, right speech, right action, right livelihood, right effort, right mindfulness, right concentration."[46] Right mindfulness plays a key role within this progression. It combines lucid awareness of each item in our present experience with clear comprehension of it—comprehension of its nature and meaning in light of basic truths and values. The truths include the centrality of suffering, its origins, and how it can be overcome. They also include impermanence, as a basic feature of everything that exists, and the doctrine of the no-self: persons are processes, not substances. The values include compassion in response to suffering (one's own and that of others), and attitudes of love and kindness.

Practicing meditation cultivates the ability to concentrate, compose, and calm the mind. But far more than that, meditating cultivates mindfulness as a virtue centered on compassion in response to suffering and to insight into the impermanence of all things. Martine Batchelor emphasizes that concentration (*samatha*) must be complemented with experiential inquiry (*vipassana*) centered on the "four great efforts" (reflected on during meditation and applied during everyday life): to prevent negative states (undesirable attitudes, emotions, desires); to release negative states when they arise; to cultivate positive states (desirable attitudes, emotions, desires); and to sustain positive states that arise.[47] She illustrates these experiential inquiries with sayings of the Buddha that resonate with contemporary cognitive therapy. Many of them reflect moral common sense, for example explore concrete ways to replace greed with simple acts of kindness and generosity, think through the harmful consequences of harmful desires, empathetically place yourself in the situation of the suffering person, and slow down the frantic pace of action in order to enjoy the present more fully. The important point is that mindfulness as attention and concentration is not enough in Buddhism. Virtue-mindfulness is required: attention to what is genuinely important, in light of sound values implemented with caring and good judgment. This virtue implies cultivating and exercising habits of compassion and caring in response to the suffering of others and oneself.

Right mindfulness sharply contrasts with the value-suspending mindfulness used in contemporary therapy. In recontextualizing mindful meditation in a therapeutic setting, Kabat-Zinn promulgated a palimpsest of the Buddhist version of virtue-mindfulness (even though he restores much of his Buddhist background in his popular-audience books). Interestingly, the transition was paved earlier by the German-born monk Nyanaponika Thera, who coined and popularized the term "bare attention" in the 1960s. For him the term meant observing things as stripped of their usual meaning and connotations. To *bear* in mind Buddhist values is a contrary of *bare* attention, or what I call value-suspending mindfulness. But there is a bridge between them. Nyanaponika Thera introduced bare-attention for the explicit purpose of cultivating morally desirable forms of detachment from the world.

> Bare attention is the clear and single-minded awareness of what actually happens to us and in us, at the successive moments of perception. It is called "bare" because it attends just to the bare facts of a perception as presented either through the five physical senses or through the mind. . . . [A]ttention or mindfulness is kept to a bare registering of the facts observed, without reacting to them by deed, speech, or by mental comment, which may be one of self-reference (like, dislike, etc.), judgement or reflection.[48]

Robert H. Sharf points out that the idea of bare attention (though not the word) was introduced earlier in the twentieth century by Burmese monks, and occasionally it surfaced earlier in Buddhist traditions, including eighth-century Zen Buddhism in China.[49] Sharf also points out that bare attention meditation was intended for laypersons who do not have an understanding of Buddhism. At least until the twentieth century, it was also regarded as a heretical practice. It would be patently false to claim that value-suspending mindfulness is the core idea of mindfulness in Buddhism's long history. If anything, it is closer to the activity that induces what Zen Buddhists call *emptiness*—a sickness the Buddha associated more with mindlessness than mindfulness.[50] Nevertheless, it was one of the bridges between Buddhism and Western culture, including Kabat-Zinn's bridge between Buddhist and therapeutic meditation.

To conclude, in this chapter I compared and contrasted three concepts of mindfulness: value-suspending mindfulness, value-based mindfulness, and right mindfulness. Right mindfulness refers to Buddhist versions of virtue-mindfulness—versions, because Buddhist value perspectives can vary. Each concept is useful, although for different purposes, within their natural habitats: respectively, therapeutic meditation, everyday activities, and Buddhist spirituality. In my terms, Kabat-Zinn's advocacy of value-suspending mindfulness during meditation is rooted in his hope and faith that it will contribute to virtue-mindfulness in everyday life. Value-suspending mindfulness is not, however, a general paradigm of mindfulness as it contributes to good lives. It may not even contribute to good lives unless it is accompanied by a personal vision involving sound values. Owing to Kabat-Zinn's influence, value-suspending mindfulness became the predominant concept of mindfulness in psychology. As we will see, however, some psychologists have developed strikingly different concepts of mindfulness in exploring topics other than meditation.

NOTES

1. Jon Kabat-Zinn, "Some Reflections on the Origins of MBSR, Skillful Means, and the Trouble with Maps," in J. M. G. Williams, and J. Kabat-Zinn, eds., *Mindfulness: Diverse Perspectives on Its Meaning, Origins and Applications* (New York: Routledge, 2013), 281–306, at 285.

2. A recent sample of Kabat-Zinn's influence is found in the collection of essays edited by Michael A. West, *The Psychology of Meditation: Research and Practice* (New York: Oxford University Press, 2016).

3. Jon Kabat-Zinn, *Wherever You Go, There You Are: Mindfulness Meditation in Everyday Life*, Tenth Anniversary Edition (New York: Hachette Books, 2014), 4.

4. Jon Kabat-Zinn "Mindfulness-Based Interventions in Context: Past, Present, and Future," *Clinical Psychology: Science and Practice, 10*, no. 2 (2003): 144–56, at 145.

5. J. Kabat-Zinn, L. Lipworth, and R. Burney, "The Clinical Use of Mindfulness Meditation for the Self-Regulation of Chronic Pain," *Journal of Behavioral Medicine, 8* (1985): 163–90.

6. See Alan R. White, *Attention* (Oxford: Basil Blackwell, 1964), 4, 22, 39.

7. See Eric Harrison, *The Foundations of Mindfulness: How to Cultivate Attention, Good Judgment, and Tranquility* (New York: The Experiment, 2017), 301.

8. Jon Kabat-Zinn, *Full Catastrophe Living: Using the Wisdom of Your Body and Mind to Face Stress, Pain, and Illness*, revised edition (New York: Bantam Books, 2013), 23, italics removed.

9. One meta-analysis reaches a modest conclusion: "meditation programs can result in small to moderate reductions in multiple negative dimensions of psychological stress." Madhav Goyal et al., "Meditation Programs for Psychological Stress and Well-Being: A Systematic Review and Meta-Analysis," *JAMA Internal Medicine, 174*, no. 3 (March 2014): 357–68.

10. The work might be writing. See Alice Walker, "Metta to Muriel and Other Marvels: A Poet's Experience of Meditation," in John Darnton, ed., *Writers on Writing* (New York: Henry Holt and Company, 2001), 246–50.

11. I say "testify," because whether value-suspending meditation succeeds in advancing self-knowledge depends greatly on the knowledge persons bring to meditation. See, for example, the hyperbolic celebration of meditation by the highly educated world historian Yuval Noah Harari in *21 Lessons for the 21st Century* (New York: Spiegel and Grau, 2018), 314–23.

12. Kabat-Zinn, *Full Catastrophe Living*, 38.

13. Kabat-Zinn, *Full Catastrophe Living*, 37.

14. Kabat-Zinn, *Wherever You Go, There You Are*, 47. See also Kabat-Zinn, *Full Catastrophe Living*, 21.

15. Kabat-Zinn, *Wherever You Go, There You Are*, 48.

16. Kabat-Zinn, "Some Reflections on the Origins of MBSR, Skillful Means, and the Trouble with Maps," in Williams and Kabat-Zinn, eds., *Mindfulness*, 218–306, at 294. Ethics in mindfulness-based therapies are explored more fully in Lynette M. Monteiro, Jane F. Compson, Frank Musten, eds., *Practitioner's Guide to Ethics and Mindfulness-Based Interventions* (Cham, Switzerland: Springer International Publishing, 2017).

17. Kabat-Zinn, "Some Reflections on the Origins of MBSR, Skillful Means, and the Trouble with Maps," 285.

18. Kabat-Zinn, *Full Catastrophe Living*, 38.

19. Kabat-Zinn, *Wherever You Go, There You Are*, xvii. See also xix, 5.

20. Kabat-Zinn, *Wherever You Go, There You Are*, 47.

21. Kabat-Zinn, *Wherever You Go, There You Are*, 57.

22. Jon Kabat-Zinn, *Meditation Is Not What You Think: Mindfulness and Why It Is So Important*, Book One (New York: Hachette Books, 2018), xxxiv.

23. Jon Kabat-Zinn, *Coming to Our Senses: Healing Ourselves and the World through Mindfulness* (New York: Hyperion, 2005), 46. See also Jon Kabat-Zinn, *Mindfulness for Beginners: Reclaiming the Present Moment—and Your Life* (Boulder, CO: Sounds True, 2016), 85.

24. See Kabat-Zinn, *Wherever You Go, There You Are*.

25. Kabat-Zinn, *Wherever You Go*, xix.

26. Kabat-Zinn, *Full Catastrophe Living*, 214.

27. *Merriam-Webster's Collegiate Dictionary*, 11th ed. (Springfield, MA: Merriam-Webster, 2014).

28. S. Bishop, M. Lau, S. Shapiro, L. Carlson, N. Anderson, J. Carmody, Z. Segal, S. Abbey, M. Speca, D. Velting, and G. Devins, "Mindfulness: A Proposed Definition," *Clinical Psychology: Science and Practice, 11* (2004): 230–241, at 232.

29. Cf. Harrison, *The Foundations of Mindfulness* (New York: The Experiment, 2017), 313.

30. Michael A. West, "The Practice of Meditation," in West, ed., *The Psychology of Meditation: Research and Practice*, 3–25, at 16.

31. Ronald D. Siegel, *The Mindfulness Solution: Everyday Practices for Everyday Problems* (New York: Guilford Press, 2010), 27, italics removed.

32. Siegel, *The Mindfulness Solution*, 84.

33. Siegel, *The Mindfulness Solution*, 83.

34. Siegel, *The Mindfulness Solution*, 33, 38.

35. Siegel, *The Mindfulness Solution*, 31.

36. Siegel, *The Mindfulness Solution*, 32.

37. Siegel, *The Mindfulness Solution*, 256.

38. Sigmund Freud's most trenchant attack on traditional morality is in *Civilization and Its Discontent*, trans. James Strachey (New York: W.W. Norton, 1989[1930]). An early and powerful critic of Freud is Philip Rieff, *The Triumph of the Therapeutic* (Chicago: University of Chicago, 1987[1966]). On the general issue of the therapeutic influence on ethics see Mike W. Martin, *From Morality to Mental Health: Virtue and Vice in a Therapeutic Culture* (New York: Oxford University Press, 2006).

39. Malcolm Cowley, "How Writers Write," *The Paris Review Interviews*, First Series, ed. Malcolm Cowley (New York: Penguin Books, 1960), 3–21, at 7.

40. For samples and sources, see Michael A. West, "The Practice of Meditation," in West, ed., *The Psychology of Meditation*, 3–25.

41. Kabat-Zinn says as much in "Some Reflections on the Origins of MBSR, Skillful Means, and the Trouble with Maps," in Williams and Kabat-Zinn, eds. *Mindfulness*, 288.

42. Rupert Gethin, "On Some Definitions of Mindfulness," in Williams and Kabat-Zinn, eds., *Mindfulness*, 270.

43. Quoted by Rupert Gethin from the Theravada exegetical texts, in "On Some Definitions of Mindfulness," in Williams and Kabat-Zinn, eds., *Mindfulness*, 272.

44. T. W. Rhys Davids, quoted by Bhikkhu Bodhi in "What Does Mindfulness Really Mean? A Canonical Perspective," in Williams and Kabat-Zinn, eds., *Mindfulness*, 19–39, at 23.

45. Bhikkhu Bodhi, "What Does Mindfulness Really Mean? A Canonical Perspective," in Williams and Kabat-Zinn, eds., *Mindfulness*, 26. See also Bhikkhu Bodhi, *The Noble Eightfold Path: Way to the End of Suffering* (Onalaska, WA: BPS Pariyatti Editions, 1994).

46. See *Buddhism: The Illustrated Guide*, ed. Kevin Trainor (New York: Oxford University Press, 2001), 70.

47. Martine Batchelor, "Meditation and Mindfulness," in Williams and Kabat-Zinn, eds., *Mindfulness*, 159–160. See also, Martine Batchelor, "Meditation: Practice and Experience," in West, ed., *The Psychology of Meditation: Research and Practice*, 27–47.

48. Nyanaponika Thera, *The Heart of Buddhist Meditation* (San Francisco: Weiser, 1962), 30. Quoted by Bodhi, "What Does Mindfulness Really Mean? A Canonical Perspective," 29.

49. See Robert H. Sharf, "Is Mindfulness Buddhist? (and Why It Matters)," in Robert Meikyo Rosenbaum and Barry Magid, eds., *What's Wrong with Mindfulness (and What Isn't): Zen Perspectives* (Somerville, MA: Wisdom Publications, 2016), 139–151.

50. See Harrison, *The Foundations of Mindfulness*, 12–17, 162–164.

Chapter Seven

Mindful Decision Making

"Mindlessness is pervasive. In fact I believe virtually all of our problems—personal, interpersonal, professional, and societal—either directly or indirectly stem from mindlessness."[1] This is an astounding generalization, especially coming from a distinguished experimental psychologist like Ellen J. Langer. It overlooks vastly many problems that stem from causes beyond our control, including natural disasters, economic calamities, and genetic diseases. Setting aside the many types of bad luck, however, I agree that mindlessness causes many problems, and mindfulness helps prevent and solve even more problems—*if* by mindfulness we mean a robust version of virtue-mindfulness: paying attention to what matters in light of sound values, those which are not immoral, irrational, or unhealthy. But that is not what Langer means. Her concept of *flexibility-mindfulness*, as I call it, builds in the values of flexibility, inventiveness, and openness to new information and viewpoints. To that extent it is a version of virtue-mindfulness, but it is an anemic version. It omits any requirement of sound values—of moral decency, rationality, truthfulness, or even mental health. Tyrants, terrorists, and thieves might employ flexibility-mindfulness in causing problems for their victims.

Langer began studying mindful decision making and problem solving during the 1970s, shortly before Jon Kabat-Zinn opened his clinic to study mindfulness-based meditation.[2] Unlike him, she has little interest in meditation. Like him, at key junctures she assumes moral values in the background, values that she never officially connects to mindfulness.[3] Making those values transparent invites a rethinking of flexibility-mindfulness, so as to transform it into a robust version of virtue-mindfulness. John Dewey's discussion of intelligent problem solving provides a resource for that rethinking.

FLEXIBILITY-MINDFULNESS

In *Mindfulness*, her most acclaimed book, Langer lists three "key qualities of a mindful state of being: (1) creation of new categories; (2) openness to new information; and (3) awareness of more than one perspective."[4] *Creation of new categories* means being inventive by reframing situations using fresh ideas and distinctions, rather than responding from habit and automatic mind-sets. *Openness to new information* means a willingness to acquire and consider additional information. *Awareness of more than one perspective* means sympathetically considering new points of view that contrast with what we currently believe. In each instance, what is new is identified relative to the self; it is new with regard to an individual's current categories, information, and perspectives.

Elsewhere Langer augments the three qualities, although more by way of elaboration than revision. Thus, she specifies that mindful decisions include *acting* on new concepts and perspectives, rather than merely thinking them: mindfulness is "the process of actively noticing new things, relinquishing preconceived mindsets, and then acting on the new observations."[5] She also underscores sensitivity to the immediate situation and context: "When we are mindful, we implicitly or explicitly (1) view a situation from several perspectives, (2) see information presented in the situation as novel, (3) attend to the context in which we are perceiving the information, and eventually (4) create new categories through which this information may be understood."[6] The word *understood* may seem to imply a *rational* or *intelligent* interpretation of available information, based on sound values such as rationality, moral decency, and mental health. But Langer immediately blocks that implication: "From a mindful perspective, one's response to a particular situation is not an attempt to make the best choice from among available options but to create options."[7] As a result, her concept of flexibility-mindfulness remains seriously deficient as an account of mindful decision making and problem solving.

Mindfulness in everyday decision making centers on using information and viewpoints to solve problems in *desirable* ways—or at least not patently irrational, unhealthy, and immoral ways. Such decision making is guided by good reasons, sound reasoning, and ideals of rationality. More fully, the locus of practical reasoning is the question "why?"—the "why" of justification. This "why" of *justification* concerns reasons, in contrast with the "why" of *explanation* that concerns causes. As Arthur Murphy reminds us, intelligent decision making turns on answering this "why" of justification in terms of sound values, intelligently applied: "Given alternatives for action, why *should* we act in one way rather than another? What's the good of it, and how will this action serve to bring about that good?"[8] In particular, moral decision making connects with "*reasons*, as considerations of moral relevance to a judgment of the over-all merits of the situation in which a choice between alternatives is made."⁹ A plausible conception of mindfulness in decision making and problem solving will connect directly with moral and other kinds of practical reasoning. Langer's flexibility-mindfulness omits this crucial connection with reasons and reasoning.

Flexibility-mindfulness also omits ideals of *truthfulness*, including intellectual and moral honesty, and also *good judgment*, especially in connection with moral reasoning. Truthfulness involves openness to evidence and new perspectives, but the converse does not hold: openness to evidence and new viewpoints is sometimes used in a spirit of cynical dishonesty. Above all, truthfulness implies respect and caring for truth. It implies caring that new evidence is true, that new viewpoints help us get at the truth, and that reasoning is justified and sound. It implies a serious attempt to get at the truth about important matters by *reasonably* weighing evidence and alternative perspectives. Moral mindfulness does not entail complete success in exercising good judgment, but it does imply a conscientious attempt to exercise good judgment. Moral mindfulness also includes respect for other persons who struggle to arrive at honest and intelligent views. Langer's flexibility-mindfulness omits any commitment to acting *responsibly* on *sound* values, using good judgment. It makes no mention of morally good judgment in reasoning and conduct, so as to implement justice, self-respect, decency, and compassion. An individual could be open-minded about new evidence and views but still exercise poor and perverse judgment in how they weigh and act on the evidence and views. In fact, flexibility-mindfulness could be used by a sociopath like Ted Bundy in inventively plotting rape and murder; by Bernard Madoff in cleverly bilking billions of dollars from investors; by Osama Bin Laden in using innovative ways to demolish New York City's Twin Towers; and by Nazi officials in conducting the Holocaust with horrifying novelty. In each case I suspect it was.

In discussing openness, flexibility, and newness, Langer also uses flexibility-mindfulness to highlight several important aspects of creativity, as "a process of actively making novel distinctions about objects in one's awareness."¹⁰ Here, too, her account of creativity strikes me as inadequate. Langer understands creativity as a *process* of mindfulness rather than achieving desirable *outcomes*.¹¹ She emphasizes the use of intuition rather than reasoning, inventiveness rather than isolated mind-sets, openness to the new rather than being shaped by habits, and authenticity in expressing one's genuine feelings.¹² She also understands the new and inventive as entirely relative to oneself—as distinct from new relative to the world, for example within a domain such as science or art, or to a group or society. In all these ways, she omits any mention of results that are valuable, rather than merely new. She eclipses the sense in which creativity involves achieving and inventing *valuably* new results.¹³ In debunking standards, reasons, and values in connection with mindful creativity, she implausibly claims that "Everybody has an equal talent for everything."[14]

By itself, flexibility-mindfulness is at most an anemic version of virtue-mindfulness that highlights the values of flexibility and openness. It is a narrow and instrumental rationality that might be used to serve either moral or immoral aims, healthy or unhealthy desires, reasonable or unreasonable choices, and creative achievements or crass self-indulgence. Nevertheless, *in practice* Langer tacitly employs a more robust version of virtue-mindfulness than she acknowledges. In applying flexibility-mindfulness to case studies Langer presupposes additional values centered on moral decency, mental health, and reasonableness. Here are five illustrations, each involving moral values.

   a. An airline pilot conducts a routine pre-flight check but fails to notice icy conditions outside the airplane.[15] The pilot, she says, acts mindlessly by blindly following habit in a situation where new information should have been acquired and taken into account. Agreed! But *why* should the pilot have noticed the icy conditions and taken them into account by refusing to fly until it was safe to do so? What makes that information about the icy conditions relevant, important, and even decisive in mindfully making the decision not to fly? The answer, of course, is that the pilot is responsible for the safety of the passengers, not to mention the airline's property and the pilot's own safety. In any ordinary sense, the pilot's mindlessness is not merely failing to notice the ice and to consider it in making a decision about whether to take off. It is failing to assess relevant information in light of sound values, and exercising good judgment in applying sound professional and moral values. Suppose the pilot notices the icy weather conditions, envisions alternative possibilities and perspectives on whether to fly, and then deliberately takes off. The pilot might be morally callous, for example. Or perhaps the pilot is a terrorist who intends to commit suicide and mass murder by causing an airline disaster. Perhaps the pilot suffers from a delusion and envisions a bizarre—but new—possibility most of us would never consider, such as aliens are about to attack the airplane if it stays on the ground. (This possibility is not entirely fanciful: Paranoid schizophrenia can involve episodes of "uncanny wakefulness" mixed with crazy delusions.[16]) In any case, such a morally reckless pilot could manifest flexibility-mindfulness—openness to new information, alternative perspectives, and fresh ideas. The reckless pilot does not manifest virtue-mindfulness in any robust sense connected with sound values. Langer assumes sound values in the background, but never explicitly connects mindfulness to them.

b. In her most famous experiment, Langer discovered that residents in nursing homes live longer and are happier when they have greater freedom and responsibility, if only in small matters such as taking care of a potted plant.[17] Invoking her experiment in discussing flexibility-mindfulness, Langer takes for granted that longevity is desirable, that health and happiness are important values, and that reasonable and mindful individuals would recognize as much. She also studies people who are basically sane, decent, and willing to assume responsibility for simple things. She does not encounter, or even envision, violent individuals who throw their potted plant at a window or nurse, perhaps as an inventive expression of their frustration. In depicting her experimental subjects as mindful, she takes for granted they are individuals who connect new information and perspectives to desirable choices in light of sound values of morality and mental health, not to mere openness to new information and possibilities.

c. Langer recommends flexibility-mindfulness as a tool for overcoming bigotry. To overcome prejudice (discrimination in the pejorative sense) individuals need to become more discerning (discriminating in the honorific sense). According to her, discernment comes from drawing more and fresh distinctions. People need to be educated to make more extensive and careful distinctions about themselves and other people, rather than relying on simplistic stereotypes: "A mindful outlook recognizes that we are all deviant from the majority with respect to some of our attributes."[18] Langer makes an important point. Yet she obviously assumes that bigotry is bad, that racist beliefs and sexist attitudes are indefensible, and that mindfulness involves truthfulness and good faith, rather than cynical self-promotion. She assumes that the relevant "new" distinctions are rooted in accurate assessment of new information, and moral attitudes of humaneness and fairness. She proceeds in the faith that experimental subjects are at some level committed to decency, so that their hatred diminishes once they are given morally relevant evidence and new ideas. These value assumptions reach well beyond mere flexibility, inventiveness, and awareness of new ideas and views.

d. Langer recounts and reinterprets Stanley Milgram's classic study of obedience to authority. The subjects in Milgram's experiments were told they were participating in a learning experiment. They were instructed to inflict a series of increasingly severe electrical shocks on learners, when the learners failed to answer as they were supposed to.[19] There were no actual shocks inflicted, and the learners only pretended to feel pain, but the subjects were deceived into believing they were inflicting pain. Milgram documents the alarming degree to which people are willing to obey authorities perceived as legitimate, even when doing so harms innocent persons. In interpreting the experiment, Langer says the experimental subjects were mindless, in that they acted from their habitual attitudes, rather than from imaginative awareness of alternatives. She also emphasizes the incremental nature of the directives and actions, which seduced experimental subjects into lessened awareness about what they are doing. This is an astute observation. In making it, however, she presupposes that moral values specify what counts as harm in the situation, and she assumes the moral mandate not to harm innocent people. These background values establish a foothold for invoking talk of mindlessness and mindfulness in understanding the experiment. If Milgram had included self-aware sadists as his experimental subjects, Langer would have little basis for interpreting them as mindless in her sense. Sadists lack compassion, but they do not necessarily lack imaginative vision and even empathic understanding, in the sense of knowing what their victims are feeling.

e. Playfully, Langer has us imagine we are awakened in the middle of the night by an eccentric and seemingly financially well-off person conducting a scavenger hunt. The person offers us $10,000 for any piece of wood three-by-seven feet.[20] Most of us, she speculates, would react mindlessly by failing to envision the obvious solution: unhinge our front door, which fits the eccentric's specifications, and exchange it for the money. But is this *the* obvious solution, which a mindful individual would identify, and if so why? Suppose we live in a dangerous neighborhood where well-off gangsters occasionally drive through. Good judgment then indicates we should do precisely the routine thing: keep our door closed to intrusive strangers in the middle of the night. Langer tends to assume that mindfulness always involves selecting novel solutions, so that acting on habit is mindless (as discussed more fully below). In fact, many novel perspectives should be discarded as unreasonable from the outset. For example, an imaginative solution would be to grab a buzz saw and cut a suitably sized hole in our roof, causing damage that is costly, inconvenient, and dangerous. In assuming the problem has only one mindful solution, Langer presupposes values such as simplicity, efficiency, safety, and personal profit. She also presupposes these values will be balanced in optimal or at least reasonable ways.

In all these examples Langer gestures toward a more substantive concept of virtue-mindfulness, one explicitly grounded in spectrum of sound values. She comes close to acknowledging as much when she writes, "A mindful attitude involves identifying the positives in a situation, regardless of whether the situation itself initially seems positive or negative."[21] The term *positives* is vague, but it hints that substantive values beyond openness and inventiveness are at play. It conceals what the values are, let alone how they should be applied. Are the values merely those an individual holds, with no restriction about their soundness, as in personal-mindfulness? Or are they defensible values connected with what is genuinely desirable (worthy of desire), or at least not irrational, immoral, and unhealthy? If the latter are intended, then she has shifted from anemic flexibility-mindfulness to a robust concept of virtue-mindfulness. She has also moved beyond the role of a research scientist, who describes and explains the world, to the role of an advisor on mindfulness in good lives.

MORALITY AND HABITS

Why does Langer officially omit the values of rationality, morality, and even mental health in defining mindfulness, even though she presupposes those values when she applies her concept of flexibility-mindfulness? At least part of the answer lies in her beliefs about morality, evaluation, and habits. To begin with, she reduces morality to individual and group preferences, with no possibility of objective standards. Indeed, she says all values (moral, aesthetic, religious, etc.) are subjective preferences and declares herself a "moral relativist" in judging choices and conduct.[22] She also stereotypes morality as a simplistic, black-and-white, blame-and-punishment system.[23] She says we should minimize moral evaluations, or at least that is "the direction in which we might want to move."[24]

To elaborate, she says that in criticizing a thief or rapist we are merely expressing our preferences; the thief and rapist have different preferences.[25] Moreover, she charges us with being mindless when we evaluate other people and their actions as cruel or unjust. These evaluations reveal a failure on our part to grasp and appreciate their perspectives: "behavior makes sense from the actor's perspective, or else she or he wouldn't have carried it out. When we find ourselves being judgmental, we are being mindless."[26] In this and other passages Langer conflates several meanings of "judgmental": (1) making *unduly* negative moral judgments about them—that is, being "judgmental" in the pejorative sense, (2) making any negative moral judgments about others, and (3) making moral judgments of any sort, negative or positive. She implies that our negative moral assessments of the thief or rapist are judgmental in the pejorative sense. She also indulges in uncritical therapeutic optimism by implying that everyone is well-intentioned. Likewise, in an interview where she reiterates that "Virtually all the world's ills boil down to mindlessness," she says that a mindful understanding of other people precludes anger toward them: "If you can understand someone else's perspective, then there's no reason to be angry at them, envy them, steal from them."[27] But on the contrary, we might have every reason to be angry at the thief or rapist, and the thief or rapist might well understand the perspectives of their victims they inflict suffering on.

In places Langer assigns a pejorative meaning to the word "evaluation," and advocates not using it. Echoing a passage from Kabat-Zinn, she recommends replacing "evaluation" with "discrimination"—in its positive sense of discernment.[28] This wordplay facilitates smuggling in assumptions about truth and rationality under the rubric of discrimination, assumptions that should be made explicit. It is also misleading, for in ordinary language the positive sense of "discrimination" implies making evaluations—discerning and reasonable evaluations. In other passages, she grants that moral evaluation can have a point, but the point is merely to make us happy: "We are rarely immediately conscious of the purpose of our evaluations. Evaluation is something we use to make ourselves happy."[29] Here, as always, she reduces evaluation and values to subjective matters. Most self-evaluation fails in this regard by lowering self-esteem, as we contrast ourselves unfavorably with other people. We should stop judging ourselves and stop suffering from regret, guilt, and shame. When we make mistakes we should remind ourselves that we thought we were doing right at the time and on that basis stop criticizing ourselves.[30]

It is true, of course, that guilt, shame, self-hatred, and even regret cause enormous harm when they grow beyond any reasonable boundaries. It is also true that many moral judgments are close-minded, lacking in nuance and contextual sensitivity, or otherwise inhumane. Moral evaluation easily drifts into outlooks that are judgmental in the pejorative sense: unduly negative and blame oriented, self-righteous and narrow-minded, and employing simplistic dichotomies between totally good versus totally bad. It does not follow, however, that all moral judgments are mindlessly judgmental in these ways. Surely we can understand why rapists, murderers, thieves, terrorists, and tyrants do what they do, and we can explain how their actions proceed from their beliefs, and yet still be justified in criticizing them and their conduct as immoral. Whether positive or negative, moral judgments can be humane, nuanced and sensitive to context, and virtue-mindful—attentive to what matters in light of sound values.

It is also true that in *some* contexts negative moral judgments should be suspended, in limited ways, for a limited time, or for special purposes. One such context is working as a professional therapist who may have a responsibility to bolster clients' self-esteem. Other contexts include friendship, love, and therapeutic meditation. But extending value-neutrality from these special contexts to all contexts is a recipe for amorality. Ultimately, Langer's flexibility-mindfulness is largely that—amoral. It celebrates newness, openness, and inventiveness without anchoring them in sound moral values; indeed, without anchoring them in any substantive values beyond happiness. Her moral relativism and negative stereotype of morality, combined with her therapeutic optimism, help explain why she does not take morality seriously in understanding mindfulness.

Habits, too, get short shrift in Langer's discussion of flexibility-mindfulness. She stipulates that acting on habit is always mindless: "Habit, or the tendency to keep on with behavior that has been repeated over time, naturally implies mindlessness."[31] *Naturally*? Only if mindfulness means flexibility-mindfulness, which specifies newness and inventiveness. If instead mindfulness is understood as virtue-mindfulness, many habits can be engaged in mindfully.[32] For example, most routine and habit-guided work, driving, cooking, cleaning, and other daily activities can be mindful in that they are performed attentively in light of relevant values. Virtue-mindfulness plays a role in ensuring that good habits are carried out properly, rather than being undermined by distractions. Conversely, breaking good habits by acting on new information and outlooks is sometimes undesirable. Thus, envisioning and pursuing adultery might demonstrate openness to new information and possibilities, and thereby demonstrate flexibility-mindfulness. But adultery is often morally mindless, at least where marriages and other committed relationships are involved.[33]

Obviously *some* habitual behavior is mindless, in the sense of oblivious to what matters in light of relevant values. Richard H. Thayer and Cass R. Sunstein observe, "In many situations, people put themselves into an 'automatic pilot' mode, in which they are not actively paying attention to the task at hand."[34] We are absentminded and distracted while driving. We forget appointments. We eat while concentrating on other things: "Many of us simply eat whatever is put in front of us," a tendency that compounds problems of obesity.[35] In a humorous experiment conducted by Brian Wansink, people were given a large bowl of soup and advised to eat as much as they wanted: "Unbeknownst to them, the soup bowls were designed to refill themselves (with empty bottoms connected to machinery beneath the table). No matter how much soup is eaten, the bowl never empties. Many people just kept eating, not paying attention to the fact that they were really eating a great deal of soup."[36] Langer's concept of flexibility-mindfulness potentially illuminates such examples but only when conjoined with a robust version of virtue-mindfulness linked to healthy eating.

To be fair, in one passage Langer qualifies her sweeping denigration of habitual behavior as mindless. She points out that we cannot always be mindful in her sense. Constant novelty is impossible and inefficient, and habits are necessary (even though mindless, in her view). If she had developed this suggestion she might have broadened her account to allow that we can be mindful in acting on habits, depending on the situation and the values relevant to it—for example, in practicing meditation (recalling Kabat-Zinn) or walking (recalling Brenda Ueland and Thoreau). But instead of allowing that habits can be mindfully acted on, she simply extends her concept of flexibility-mindfulness to a new level. She says that mindfulness includes a second-order dimension: mindfulness about when to be mindful. That is, flexibility-mindfulness includes being flexible, open-minded, and multi-perspectival about which topics to exercise flexibility-mindfulness at a given time.[37] Like the CEO of a large corporation who delegates work to others, mindful individuals discern when to act automatically and when to rethink their habits; when to seek new information and when they have sufficient data; and when to seek and adopt fresh perspectives. Langer's idea of second-order mindfulness is useful, but it would be more useful if connected to virtue-mindfulness. That is, we should be attentive to what matters most by reasonably setting aside, disregarding, delegating, postponing, or leaving less important matters to habit.

In sum, flexibility-mindfulness highlights openness to new information but is silent about using that information with good judgment in seeking reasonable beliefs. It highlights openness to new outlooks but is silent on seeking desirable perspectives. It emphasizes inventiveness but omits creativity as finding *valuably* new solutions that serve worthwhile goals. It defines away the possibility of mindfully acting on good habits and conscientiously maintaining moral and healthy habits. Although it occasionally hints at "understanding" new information, it fails to specify that the relevant understanding is sensible, rational, and humane. Langer's concept of flexibility-mindfulness needs to be rethought, and her experiments on mindfulness reinterpreted, in light of a more robust conception of virtue-mindfulness in decision making, problem solving, and learning. One such conception was set forth by John Dewey.

DEWEY ON INTELLIGENCE

John Dewey (1859–1952) is a psychologist, as well as a philosopher, social critic, educational theorist, and advocate of democracy. He develops his conception of mindfulness under the heading of *intelligence*. As much as Langer, Dewey celebrates flexibility, openness to new ideas and information, inventiveness, and active problem solving. Like her, he renounces the preoccupation with blame and guilt that infects much everyday morality. Unlike her, he calls for intelligent decision making centered on truthfulness, moral responsibility, mental health, and good judgment. In doing so, he is an ethical pluralist who celebrates the diversity of moral outlooks and perspectives, while rejecting crass ethical relativism that reduces morality to social customs. He also rejects ethical subjectivism that reduces it to individual feelings and preferences. In this way he restores much of what is omitted in Langer's flexibility-mindfulness, while bridging ethics and psychology in understanding mindful decision making.[38]

Dewey discusses intelligent decision making throughout his voluminous writings. I draw mainly on *Human Nature and Conduct: An Introduction to Social Psychology*, with additional references to his books on education. Intelligence is not limited to general analytical abilities as measured by IQ tests, nor does it primarily consist in possessing abstract knowledge. Instead it is *practical* intelligence, as manifested in rational engagement with problems and concerns. In addition to analytical skills, it includes creative problem-solving skills.[39] Most important, it emphasizes *reasonable* perceptions and assessments of evidence, *healthy* perspectives and habits, and *moral responsibility* in deliberations, choices, and attitudes. It clarifies and "liberates" impulses and desires, reshaping them into rational plans that are effectively put into action.[40] In addition to creative problem solving, it includes common sense in developing and acting on habits. It also includes what is today called emotional intelligence (social aptitude) in developing and sustaining relationships. Dewey explores general features of intelligent problem solving in all areas of life, what he sometimes calls "the method of intelligent action."[41] At the same time, he highlights how most of us show intelligence in some areas of our lives but not others. He would welcome contemporary research showing that intelligence and creativity are not global abilities that automatically carry over from one type of activity to all others.[42]

Practical intelligence combines *knowing-that* relevant information is true (or has "warranted assertibility"), *knowing-how* to tackle problems, and *knowing-why* we act and should act in light of defensible values. Values connect the present to the past and future. He uses the illustration of intelligently building a house. The design for the house takes into account its envisioned use, past experience in building and using houses, and relevant knowledge about construction materials.[43] Intelligent design is the opposite of unthinking and uncritical action on irrational desires. In general, intelligence clarifies and liberates desires, modifying and integrating them. It selectively puts desires into action: "Intelligence converts desire into plans, systematic plans based on assembling facts, reporting events as they happen, keeping tab on them and analyzing them."[44]

In sharp contrast with Langer's stipulation that habit-based actions are mindless, Dewey celebrates intelligent habits. Taken together and as interpenetrating, habits largely constitute a unified character.[45] To act attentively on reasonable habits in appropriate situations counts as mindful activity. In my terms, virtue-mindfulness can be manifested in how we pursue habits, perhaps slowing down in order to pay due attention to what is important. It can also be manifested in good habits that enable us to quickly identify and remain attuned to what matters in a situation. Habits include all acquired forms of activity involving systematic patterns of response and motivations and having a dynamic quality reaching into the future.[46] As such, they include patterns of overt behavior, both good patterns like going to the gym and bad patterns such as excessive gambling. They also include habits of attending and thinking, of emotion and attitude, of valuing and evaluating, and of virtues and vices. All intelligent (good) habits are "conditions of intellectual efficiency," and intelligent habits in attending are crucial to focusing on important activities in the present moment.[47]

Intelligent habits are not the entirety of intelligent conduct, of course. Habits can grow old, cause boredom, and lead to the blinkered mind-sets that Langer warns against. Moreover, we often face novel situations in which habits by themselves cannot guide us, perhaps because they conflict with other habits, or perhaps where habits are irrelevant. When we face such "problematic situations," which call for fresh thinking, we need to decide what matters in the situation, perhaps including which habits are desirable in it. In moral dilemmas, for example, conflicting values (commitments, habits) point in different directions. Adjustments need to be made, values and habits rethought, reintegrated, and perhaps some abandoned. Deliberation (reflection) and intelligence are exercised in order "to resolve entanglements in existing activity, restore continuity, recover harmony, utilize loose impulse and redirect habit."[48]

Deliberation in solving problems is a kind of mental experimentation. We imaginatively think through alternative responses: If I do A, B will follow; if I do C, D, and E will occur. Consequences, including their impact on our ideals, need to be considered until an optimal or satisfactory solution is found. Equally sound values might come into conflict. Intelligent, mindful deliberation is needed to integrate them in desirable ways. The integration is always contextualized for Dewey, and he refuses to rank values in an absolute hierarchy. Deliberation involves setting priorities in the present situation. Choice is not so much the creation of a preference as "the emergence of a unified preference out of competing preferences," based on creative reasoning.[49]

The tendency to engage in rational deliberation on appropriate occasions is itself a habit. It is an overarching and second-order habit (recasting Langer's idea) that guides the revision of first-order habits. Dewey discusses a host of additional habits, skills, attitudes, and desires integral to intelligence and rationality. "Reflective thought" is not abstract, passionless reasoning. In addition to general and practice-specific skills, it is powered by truth-centered desires and attitudes, all three of which he highlights: open-mindedness, wholeheartedness, and responsibility. *Open-mindfulness* is "freedom from prejudice, partisanship, and such other habits as close the mind and make it unwilling to consider new problems and entertain new ideas;" more positively, "it includes an active desire to listen to more sides than one; to give heed to facts from whatever source they come; to give full attention to alternative possibilities; to recognize the possibility of error even in the beliefs that are dearest to us."⁵⁰ Dewey's open-mindedness is essentially Langer's flexibility-mindfulness with a key addition: it is aimed at knowledge and reasonable beliefs. *Wholeheartedness* is throwing oneself "heartily" into learning and additional practical activities, paying attention and holding one's mind on a subject matter. And *responsibility* centers on concern for intellectual integrity and truthfulness, combined with the skills of good practical judgment. Responsibility involves the exercise of good judgment in weighing the relative claims of values: "a person of sound judgment is one who, in the idiomatic phrase, has 'horse sense;' he is a good judge of relative values; he can estimate, appraise, evaluate, with tact and discernment."⁵¹ Sound practical judgment consists in discerning the *meaning* of facts, both identifying their implications for additional truths and appreciating how they connect with defensible values and goals.

Dewey is a pragmatist, usually considered the greatest of the classical American pragmatists, although he prefers to call his value perspective "experimentalism" and "instrumentalism," thereby highlighting his commitments to science and technology.⁵² Admittedly, in celebrating science and technology he sometimes presupposes the values of a social progressive, and in doing so opens himself to the criticism that he idealizes science and technology.⁵³ Although pragmatism takes many forms, one shared emphasis is on the plurality of values and the variety of good lives.⁵⁴ Dewey is an ethical pluralist who celebrates the diversity of value perspectives and the variety of good lives. His worldview is secular, and he understands personal identity without invoking a soul that endures after death. The character of a person is not a mental substance, but instead the interwoven complex of habits exercised throughout a lifetime. It is formed and changes throughout a lifetime, largely because the self must interact with a constantly changing society. His pragmatism is more community-oriented than Thoreau's extreme individualism, and more socially optimistic than traditional Buddhism. In connection with spirituality, he even embraces "a common faith," so long as it is understood in humanistic terms—that is, as nondogmatic, secular, democratic, and centered on intelligence and intelligent ideals.⁵⁵ Dewey never lapses into wholesale relativism and subjectivism.

Practices designed to cultivate mindfulness appear in Dewey's writings under the heading of *education*, understand expansively. Education includes all methods of increasing intelligent activity. Formal methods of schooling within institutions should emphasize assigning problems for students to solve, and raising questions that engage students and develop habits of reflection. Formal education is preparation for work, as well as for later education, but it is also intelligent activity that consists in "making the most of immediately present life."⁵⁶ Education combines concentrated attention designed to master information with mind-wandering consciousness in which the imagination ranges freely, perhaps playfully in new directions.⁵⁷ Like all deliberation, education takes place in the present, but a present that is connected to the past and future. Education accommodates the future to the past and utilizes the past as a resource in developing the future.[58]

Education can occur anywhere, at any time. It is a lifelong process, and methods of learning also include all practices in which we engage the world intelligently. Education "is that reconstruction or reorganization of experience which adds to the meaning of experience, and which increases ability to direct the course of subsequent experience."[59] As such, it includes all types of growth and self-development, development of talents and valuable potentialities, and thinking that increases meaning by making connections with wider horizons of meaning. Although education encompasses all kinds of learning and associated values, moral values invariably enter, especially honesty, self-realization, open-mindedness centered on truthfulness, breadth and reasonable balance in outlook, and accepting responsibility. The centrality of all such values needs to be kept salient, in contrast with Langer's one-sided emphasis on newness.

In sum, Dewey's conception of mindful, intelligent decision making and problem solving shares Langer's themes of flexibility, open-mindedness, and inventiveness. But it ties each of those elements to a spectrum of sound values. It foregrounds, rather than conceals, the values that enter into good lives, values that are embedded in useful habits in good lives, and values that specify what matters in particular situations. These values are many and varied, and they require integration and balance by exercising good (intelligent) judgment. In this way, Dewey offers a conception of mindfulness in decision making that makes salient the role of values, while welcoming the ongoing empirical studies conducted by psychologists and social scientists.

NOTES

1. Ellen J. Langer, *Mindfulness*, 25th Anniversary Edition (Boston: Da Capo Press, 2014), xiii. See also 80.

2. Langer's early, 1970s, discussions of mindfulness include E. Langer, A. Blank, and B. Chanowitz, "The Mindlessness of Ostensibly Thoughtful Action: The Role of Placebic Information in Interpersonal Interaction," *Journal of Personality and Social Psychology*, 36 (1978): 635–642.

3. Daniel J. Siegel suggests and (in my view) exaggerates additional similarities between Langer and Kabat-Zinn in *The Mindful Brain: Reflection Atonement in the Cultivation of Well-Being* (New York: W. W. Norton and Company, 2007), 231–256.

4. Langer, *Mindfulness*, 64.

5. Langer uses this wording in her teaching, according to Cara Feinberg, "The Mindfulness Chronicles: On 'the Psychology of Possibility,' *Harvard Magazine*" (September–October 2010). http://harvardmagazine.com/2010/09/the-mindfulness-chronicles.

6. Ellen J. Langer, *The Power of Mindful Learning*, 2nd ed. (Boston: Da Capo Press, 2016), 107. See also Amanda Ie, Christelle T. Ngnoumen, and Ellen J. Langer, eds., *The Wiley Blackwell Handbook of Mindfulness*, Volume 1 (Chichester, England: John Wiley and Sons, 2014).

7. Langer, *The Power of Mindful Learning*, 111. Italics removed.

8. Arthur Edward Murphy, *The Theory of Practical Reason*, ed. A. I. Melden (La Salle, IL: Open Court Publishing, 1964), 5.

9. Murphy, *The Theory of Practical Reason*, 415.

10. E. Langer, M. Cohen, and M. Djikic, "Mindfulness as a Psychological Attractor: The Effect on Children," *Journal of Applied Social Psychology*, 42(5), (2012): 1114–1122, at 1114. See also Ellen J. Langer, *On Becoming an Artist: Reinventing Yourself through Mindful Creativity* (New York: Random House, 2006), 16.

11. Brewster Ghiselin, one of my teachers, was fascinated with the processes of achievement-creativity, but he emphasized that those processes must be understood in light of values used to guide and assess outcomes and skills. See Brewster Ghiselin, ed., *The Creative Process: A Symposium* (New York: Mentor Books, 1952), 11–31.

12. Langer, *Mindfulness*, 113–129; and *On Becoming an Artist*, especially 3–21 and 41–73.

13. On creativity as achieving valuably new outcomes, see Vincent Tomas, "Creativity in Art," in Vincent Tomas, ed., *Creativity in the Arts* (Englewood Cliffs, NJ: Prentice-Hall, 1964), 97–109 at 100; Mihaly Csikszentmihalyi, *Creativity: Flow and the Psychology of Discovery and Invention* (New York: HarperCollins, 1996); Margaret Boden, *The Creative Mind: Myths and Mechanism* (New York: Parker, 2004); and Mike W. Martin, *Creativity: Ethics and Excellence in Science* (Lanham, MD: Lexington Books, 2007). For an opposing view, see Robert W. Weisberg, *Creativity: Understanding Innovation in Problem Solving, Science, Invention, and the Arts* (Hoboken, NJ: John Wiley and Sons, 2006), 60–70.

14. Langer, *On Becoming an Artist*, 171 (italics removed).

15. Langer, *Mindfulness*, 6.

16. Sylvia Nasar, *A Beautiful Mind: The Life of Mathematical Genius and Nobel Laureate John Nash* (New York: Simon and Schuster, 2001), 324.

17. Langer, *Mindfulness*, 3.

18. Langer, *Mindfulness*, 165.

19. Langer, *Mindfulness*, 50.

20. Langer, *Mindfulness*, 11.

21. Christelle T. Ngnoumen and Ellen J. Langer, "The Essence of Well-Being and Happiness," in Itai Ivtzan and Tim Lomas, eds., *Mindfulness in Positive Psychology: The Science of Meditation and Well-Being* (New York: Routledge, 2016), 97–107, at 99.

22. Langer, *On Becoming an Artist*, 73.

23. Langer, "Mindfulness versus Positive Evaluation," in C. R. Snyder and Shane J. Lopez, eds., *Oxford Handbook of Positive Psychology*, 2nd ed. (New York: Oxford University Press, 2009), 279–293, at 283.

24. Langer, "Mindfulness versus Positive Evaluation," 291.

25. Langer, *On Becoming an Artist*, 73.

26. Langer, *Mindfulness*, xix.

27. Quoted from Cara Feinberg in her interview with Langer, "The Mindfulness Chronicles: On 'the Psychology of Possibility,'" *Harvard Magazine*.

28. Langer, "Mindfulness versus Positive Evaluation," 289.

29. Langer, "Mindfulness versus Positive Evaluation," 283.

30. Langer, "Mindfulness versus Positive Evaluation," 283, 229.

31. Langer, *Mindfulness*, 17–18.

32. See David N. Perkins, "The Engine of Folly," in Robert J. Sternberg, ed., *Why Smart People Can Be So Stupid* (New Haven, CT: Yale University Press, 2002), 64–85, at 80.

33. See Mike W. Martin, *Love's Virtues* (Lawrence, KS: University Press of Kansas, 1996).

34. Richard H. Thaler and Cass R. Sunstein, *Nudge: Improving Decisions about Health, Wealth, and Happiness* (New Haven, CT: Yale University Press, 2008), 43.

35. Thayer and Sunstein, *Nudge*, 43.

36. Thayer and Sunstein, *Nudge*, 43. See also Brian Wansink, *Mindless Eating: Why We Eat More Than We Think* (New York: Bantam, 2006).

37. Langer, *Mindfulness*, 196.

38. In an essay on self-deception, Langer mentions Dewey's views on habits in understanding selves: Benzion Chanowitz and Ellen J. Langer, "Self-Protection and Self-Inception," in

Mike W. Martin, ed., *Self-Deception and Self-Understanding: New Essays in Philosophy and Psychology* (Lawrence: University Press of Kansas, 1985), 117–135.

39. In a similar vein, Robert J. Sternberg models intelligence as having three aspects: analytical, creative, and practical or common sense skills. *Successful Intelligence* (New York: Plume, 1997).

40. John Dewey, *Human Nature and Conduct: An Introduction to Social Psychology* (New York: Modern Library, 1957 [1922]), 235.

41. John Dewey, "Experience, Knowledge and Value: A Rejoinder," in Paul Arthur Schilpp and Lewis Edwin Hahn, eds., *The Philosophy of John Dewey*, 3rd ed. (La Salle, IL: Open Court, 1989), 515–608, at 591.

42. See especially Howard Gardner, *Frames of Mind: The Theory of Multiple Intelligences* (New York: Basic Books, 1983); and Howard Gardner, *Creating Minds* (New York: Basic Books, 1993).

43. Dewey, *Human Nature and Conduct*, 246–247. James D. Wallace illuminates Dewey's view of decision making in ethics in *Moral Relevance and Moral Conflict* (Ithaca, NY: Cornell University Press, 1988).

44. Dewey, *Human Nature and Conduct*, 235.

45. Dewey, *Human Nature and Conduct*, 37.

46. Dewey, *Human Nature and Conduct*, 39–41. See also John Dewey, *Theory of the Moral Life* (New York: Holt, Rinehart and Winston, 1960), 39.

47. Dewey, *Human Nature and Conduct*, 163.

48. Dewey, *Human Nature and Conduct*, 187.

49. Dewey, *Human Nature and Conduct*, 181.

50. John Dewey, *How We Think: A Restatement of the Relation of Reflective Thinking to the Educative Process* (Lexington, MA: D. C. Heath and Company, 1933), 30.

51. Dewey, *How We Think*, 120, italics removed. See also 125, 277. Linda Trinkaus Zagzebski provides an insightful discussion of Dewey's truth-centered virtues in *Virtues of the Mind: An Inquiry into the Nature of Virtue and the Ethical Foundations of Knowledge* (New York: Cambridge University Press, 1996), 177–184.

52. See Larry A. Hickman, *John Dewey's Pragmatic Technology* (Bloomington, IN: Indiana University Press, 1990).

53. See Murphy, *The Theory of Practical Reason*, 255–270.

54. Diversity among pragmatists is well represented in two recent anthologies: Susan Haack, ed., *Pragmatism, Old and New: Selected Writings* (Amherst, NY: Prometheus Books, 2006); and Robert B. Talisse and Scott F. Aikin, eds., *The Pragmatism Reader: From Peirce through the Present* (Princeton, NJ: Princeton University Press, 2011).

55. John Dewey, *A Common Faith* (New Haven, CT: Yale University Press, 1934).

56. John Dewey, *Democracy and Education* (New York: Macmillan, 1916), 310. See also 50, 55, 100. See also John Dewey, *Experience and Education* (New York: Collier Books, 1963 [1938]), 49.

57. Dewey, *Democracy and Education*, 236.

58. Dewey, *Democracy and Education*, 79.

59. Dewey, *Democracy and Education*, 76. See also 154–155.

Chapter Eight

Mindful Valuing and Psychotherapy

Value-based mindfulness, by definition, always involves values that guide our sense of what matters and should be attended to. Usually the values remain in the background and are not explicitly attended to. *Mindful valuing*, however, makes values the primary object of attention, as themselves what matters—whether they are specified as one's current values (personal-mindfulness) or as sound values (virtue-mindfulness). Values are salient in moral and religious reflection, for example, and they may be equally center stage during psychotherapy. Psychotherapists typically highlight the values of mental health, but they understand health in broad and holistic ways that easily conceal moral values. As an illustration I discuss Albert Ellis's early version of cognitive behavioral therapy, with briefer mention of recent Acceptance and Commitment Therapy (ACT). As a contrast to Ellis's reduction of morality to self-interest, I then discuss stoicism, a tradition that influenced Ellis but that is more explicit about moral values. I begin with a case study of mindful valuing in response to a physical health crisis, using skills that are both philosophical and therapeutic.

MINDFULNESS IN VALUING

At age thirty-five philosopher Havi Carel was diagnosed with a rare lung disease afflicting one in 400,000 women. The disease had already destroyed half her lung capacity. Her physician said the disease would steadily worsen, giving her at most ten years to live. In *Illness: The Cry of the Flesh*, Carel recounts the shock and terror she experienced, followed by depression, despair, and helplessness. In response she resolved to regain happiness and increase control over her life by cultivating a cluster of virtues—courage, hope, humility, patience, honesty, self-respect, authenticity, and compassion.

In doing so she applies moral and philosophical skills aimed at mindful valuing. She also develops a version of what Martha C. Nussbaum calls "a practical and compassionate philosophy—a philosophy that exists for the sake of human beings, in order to address their deepest needs, confront their most urgent perplexities, and bring them from misery to some greater measure of flourishing."[1]

Mindful valuing could not alter Carel's physical *disease*, but it could affect her *illness*—that is, her experience of the physical disease in terms of emotions, attitudes, and beliefs. Thus, although the disease decreases her physical control, she retains her mental freedom to employ mindful valuing in responding to the disease:

> I can, for example, control my thoughts (to some extent); I can control my reactions; I can cultivate the happy aspects of my life and I can say no to distressing thoughts and actions. I can choose what to do with the time I have and I can reject thoughts that cause me agony. I can learn to think clearly about my life, give meaning even to events beyond my control and modify my [value-laden] concepts of happiness, death, illness and time.[2]

Freedom of mind is a familiar theme in discussions of mindfulness. Thoreau intends it when he affirms our ability "to carve and paint the very atmosphere and medium through which we look, which morally we can do."[3] Jon Kabat-Zinn presupposes it when he emphasizes the need to choose a personal vision in practicing meditation, as well as choices to temporarily suspend routine valuing during meditation. And Ellen J. Langer presupposes it when she encourages choices to be open to new information and viewpoints in order to counter restrictive mind-sets. As Carel understands it, mental freedom is not a license to be irrational, immoral, and self-destructive. Instead, it is moral autonomy. It is the freedom and capacity to think and choose rationally. It includes a subjective sense of freedom, that is, an awareness of our capacities and skills in exercising reason. And it includes capacities of mindful valuing—to reflect with care on values, on which values contribute to a good life, and on how best to implement those values.

These values include humility and realism. Carel emphasizes the need to *accept* aspects of her disease that she cannot control. Acceptance is not passive hopelessness. Instead, it begins with truthfulness about the painful facts about her disease, including the very real threats of disability and death. Truthfulness fosters what is sometimes called spiritual or creative resignation, which is the opposite of despair, self-pity, and rage. Truthfulness enables her to identify areas of control that she can build on. She concentrates on what she can do now, rather than dwelling on terrifying losses that lie ahead. She forms new habits of savoring simple pleasures, of finding ways to magnify and multiply them. She stops saving money for retirement so as to use her resources to increase enjoyments for herself and people she loves. In these and other ways, she modifies her value perspective and priorities in desirable ways.

Carel draws on a variety of resources. They include her family, friends, and past experience. They also include her studies in the humanities, in particular modern and classical philosophy. From modern philosophy she invokes phenomenology, a tradition that emphasizes paying close attention to our experience using particular tools of mindfulness.[4] She develops a three-part phenomenological toolkit for coping with disease. Part 1 is to "bracket" our usual valuations—that is, to temporarily suspend or set aside our attitudes and judgments, rather than act on them. Bracketing is akin to Kabat-Zinn's value-suspending mindfulness during therapy-oriented meditation, although here it becomes the first step of active philosophical reasoning about values. Part 2 is to attend closely to our experience, including our habitual ways of valuing ourselves and the world. This assessment includes seeing our experience from multiple perspectives, as Langer emphasized, but Carel adds an emphasis on truthfulness and good judgment that is missing in Langer. Part 3 is to revise valuations in more reasonable directions, and then put the sound values into action in coping with her disease. This coping includes refusing to allow fear to paralyze her. It includes concentrating on areas of her life she can control in order to increase enjoyment, meaning, and moral aspiration.

From classical philosophy Carel invokes Epicurus (341–271 BCE), who teaches that unhappiness is caused by unsound valuations and false beliefs. She points out that it is a mistake to understand Epicurus as a sybarite, a mistake still embedded in language—"epicure" refers to individuals devoted to sensuous pleasures. When Epicurus talks about seeking pleasure he primarily intends lowering pain and suffering, not self-indulgence. He advocates serenity through rational valuing, rational reflection, and self-control. Self-control means disciplining our desires on the basis of truth about what is possible and desirable. For example, the thought of our death causes us distress because we envision ourselves losing something that belongs to us. In truth, we do not possess unlimited life; nor are we guaranteed even an average span of life. Likewise, we mistakenly believe that money and possessions bring happiness, when in fact thrift and moderation create serenity. In general, well-being advances when we mindfully value things in areas we can control, and accept things that are beyond our control. Later I say more about some of these themes as they are developed by the Stoics, who at many points overlap with Epicurus.

A happy note. Serious illness magnifies the role of uncertainty and bad luck in all areas of life, but luck can be good as well as bad. In the second edition of her book Carel reports that experimental drugs are extending her lifespan beyond what doctors initially suggested. She still must cope with a chronic and life-threatening disease, but she has been able to continue working. She reports with joy that she and her husband now have a child.

COGNITIVE BEHAVIORAL THERAPY

Psychotherapy takes many forms, each having its own techniques, concepts, explanatory frameworks, and accounts of what matters as part of therapy.[5] For example, Freudian psychoanalysis uses the technique of *free association*, in which patients closely attend to the flow of their thoughts and feelings, put them into words, and communicate them to the therapist without censorship.[6] This form of mindful self-observation contrasts with Kabat-Zinn's mindfulness-based meditation to reduce stress, which involves suspending value judgments and focusing attention away from the contents of the wandering mind and toward one's breathing or other object. Freud embraces the flow of consciousness as a valuable therapeutic resource, not mere chaotic musings. Patients who free associate are asked to attend to their flow of thoughts and feelings, without suspending the evaluations embedded in them. This flow contains the material used to uncover hidden patterns of thought and behavior, patterns ultimately linked to childhood, that distort healthy attitudes and living in the present.

In classical versions of psychoanalysis, the psychoanalyst mainly listens to the patient's reports about the flow of consciousness. Then, at key junctures, the psychoanalyst might make suggestions, or even explain ideas from the Freudian toolkit, such as the oedipal complex, childhood trauma, and transference. Anthony T. Kronman summarizes the process this way: "the patient is no longer mindlessly acting out a stereotype inherited from the past, sleepwalking through life. He recollects the past *in* his present and thereby achieves a higher degree of wakefulness."[7] In this way, free association plays a role in mindful valuing that, in turn, fosters more mature and healthy ways of thinking and living.

Psychoanalysis was dominant during the first half of the twentieth century, but some time ago it reached its nadir. There are many reasons for its fall from grace, including high cost, questionable effectiveness, and length of treatment. (Kronman was himself in therapy for seven years, and other patients much longer.) Today the shorter courses of cognitive behavioral therapy predominate, at least as therapies that medical insurers are willing to pay for. There are many forms of cognitive behavioral therapy. I discuss one of the earliest, Albert Ellis's Rational Emotive Behavior Therapy (REBT), as popularized in his 1961 self-help book, *A Guide to Rational Living*. I choose REBT not because it is the most effective (it is not), but because it provides a simple illustration of the emphasis on mindful valuing that enters into most cognitive behavioral therapy.

Ellis's goal for patients (and readers) is "a more fulfilling, creative, and less disturbed life by getting in touch with and revising some of your misleading thinking."[8] This goal is mental health, conceived with ample room to conceal moral values, and the same is true of the skills he recommends. The core skills required in revising misdirected valuing are at once psychological, philosophical, and moral: identify irrational thinking, dispute it by arguing with ourselves, replace it with more rational ways of thinking, and act on that rational thinking.[9] Rational self-scrutiny and mindful valuing take place at two levels, general and situational.

At the general level, we identify and assess our core value beliefs, attitudes, and commitments. These core values include standards and ideals we explicitly endorse but especially those we have been acting on without full acknowledgment. Ellis highlights ten false beliefs and harmful attitudes that he repeatedly encountered as a psychotherapist: we desperately need approval from others (as opposed to simply desiring it); we must always be competent and successful (as distinct from competent and achieving in some areas); failures, both our own and other people's, warrant condemnation as wicked ("damning"); frustrating events are always catastrophic ("catastrophizing"); we have no control over our distressing feelings ("helplessness-making"); ordinary dangers warrant obsessive worry; we can escape responsibilities and still have a fulfilling life; bad things from the past must dominate our experience today; the world must be perfect before we can find happiness; and inertia and passivity are the way to attain happiness. This list includes empirical assumptions, for example concerning how to find happiness, which are subject to scientific study. But it also presupposes value judgments about good and bad, and what is reasonable and desirable.

At the situational level, rational self-scrutiny involves identifying and challenging these general beliefs *as* and *when* they enter into particular thoughts, statements, emotions, attitudes, and behavior. Valuing is often conflicted, confused, ambivalent, dogmatic, simplistic, and otherwise indefensible. These flaws need to be challenged in the immediate situations where our value assumptions influence us. They need to be directly engaged in the moment by challenging and reasoning about them, as well as by choosing more effective attitudes and behaviors counter them. Ellis's emphasis on explicit grappling with value judgments in the present is the opposite of Kabat-Zinn's value-suspending mindfulness. Nevertheless the techniques may complement each other. Thus, Kabat-Zinn's value-suspending mindfulness during meditation may provide psychological distance on our unhealthy valuations, thereby preparing us to engage in the contextualized reasoning at the core of Ellis's mindful valuing.

In bridging the general and situational levels, Ellis recommends using *coping statements*, which function as personal mottos. Coping statements provide general guidance and help us quickly identify and respond to irrationalities in our immediate situation and experience. For example, as a countermeasure to the obsessive need for approval from others we might adopt the motto, "Wants are not needs." A fuller coping statement targeted on significant others might be, "I very much *want* John's (or Joan's) attention and love—but that *doesn't* mean that I *need* it!"[10] The italics illustrate how coping statements need to be forcefully stated to ourselves, using emphatic words and simple distinctions. To be effective, they must be applied frequently over substantial periods of time. Coping statements are a subclass of *self-statements* used in reasoning with ourselves, in order to nudge us away from harmful ways of valuing and toward more rational ways. Certainly in moments when we have time, we need to learn to talk to ourselves, silently or otherwise. Those moments might include writing in a journal, but usually a quicker response of reflection is needed. However brief, rational self-dialogue in the moment can be helpful, just as irrational self-messaging is hurtful. For we are language-oriented creatures in how we value ourselves and the world.

Much of Ellis's approach is common sense, refined by psychological experimentation. It is crucial, however, to understand exactly what he means by "rational" and "healthy." Beliefs, emotions, attitudes, and actions are rational, he says, when they promote what we want, all things considered: "By Rational Beliefs we mean those that usually work—produce the results you want—under usual conditions."[11] Yet not all desires are healthy; some are sick and destructive. Rationality and mental health, then, need to be specified in terms of an additional standard. Ellis uses a threefold standard: your survival, health, and happiness. That is, his standard is rational self-interest. It is an enlightened self-interest that appreciates the contributions other people make to our well-being: "To stay alive and to be reasonably happy or satisfied (1) by yourself, (2) in your relationships with other people, (3) by producing and achieving, (4) by being original and creative, (5) by enjoying physical, emotional, and mental activities."[12]

What about moral values? Ellis tends to reduce them to matters of health and self-interest. In his view, moral values are rational when and because they contribute to our good, whether to our survival, health, or happiness. He insists there are no absolute standards of right and wrong, good and bad.[13] By absolutes he means universal standards that have no exceptions, but at times he also seems to mean there are no objectively defensible standards of right and wrong. There are, to be sure, standards of rationality centered on mental health. He understands those standards in terms of self-interested desires for survival and happiness, and beliefs and actions that further those desires. Certainly they exclude standards of moral decency in any form that could generate guilt and blame, attitudes he largely dismisses as unhealthy. Blaming, he insists, is an act of hostility, anger, and negativity. It is irrational and unhealthy. To be fair, he permits criticism of *actions*, but not *persons*. To shift from "my act was bad" to "I am a bad person" is both a logical error and the root of neurosis: "We can actually put the essence of neurosis in a single word: blaming—or damning."[14]

The last claim is implausible, in my view. Although blame easily becomes excessive, within limits it can be integral to strong moral commitment. In renouncing all blame, Ellis makes an implausible absolute value judgment of the sort he otherwise renounces. Furthermore, Ellis's standard of rational self-interest is familiar in psychotherapy, but it is inadequate as a general moral perspective. Consider individuals who derive pleasure and even happiness from harming others, and have sufficient wealth, power, status, and cleverness to avoid social penalties for doing so. Suppose their cruelty and exploitation actually advances their survival and even health. It might be compatible with maintaining a small circle of friends, perhaps even with eliciting the admiration of a large circle of admirers of their power and success. Ellis would have little basis for criticizing the beliefs of such individuals as irrational. Moreover, his emphasis on rational—mindful—valuing needs to allow greater room for the moral virtues. Some versions of cognitive behavioral therapy have moved in that direction, as I illustrate next.

ACCEPTANCE AND COMMITMENT THERAPY

Psychotherapists seek to promote the mental health of their clients. In doing so, however, they might reinforce their clients' reasonable moral convictions as integral to health-promoting mindful valuing. To be sure, therapists are duty-bound to respect their clients' autonomy and rights to shape their value perspectives, rather than imposing their values on clients. They can do so, however, without reducing morality to self-interest, in the way Ellis does. In centering their services on mental health, they can understand mental health as having moral dimensions of basic honesty, decency, and fairness. In particular, therapists who practice ACT, a version of cognitive behavioral therapy, encourage their clients to commit to (permissible) values, including moral values. They might also emphasize cognitive reasoning skills of the sort Ellis highlights. They might even employ value-suspending meditation as one tool.

The acronym ACT is sometimes recast to mean "Accept, Choose Directions, and Take Action." This reformulation is useful, for example, in treating anxiety—currently the most common complaint and symptom therapists confront in patients.[15] Dealing with anxiety requires attunement to what we are thinking and feeling, without panic or self-denigration. Usually it requires abandoning the desire to fully control anxiety, and learning to live with it in creative ways. A standard technique begins by encouraging clients to pinpoint and verbalize anxieties, for example "I am terrified about the talk I must give." This explicit awareness facilitates reflection on the anxiety, creating a space of psychic distancing where rational reflection can occur, as does value-suspending mindfulness. The next two stages, however, involve value-based mindfulness. Choosing Direction means (mindfully) identifying our core values, those we are most committed to. Taking Action means (mindfully) developing a plan of action for carrying on with life, despite anxieties, committing to put the plan into action, and carrying out that commitment. In dealing with anxieties surrounding a promotion or speech, we might find a way to concentrate on preparing and practicing the speech, as well as think through ways to be more confident about our appearance and voice control.

Eric L. Garland and Barbara L. Fredrickson integrate a variety of tools in connection with mindful valuing, including ACT, value-suspending mindfulness during meditation, and positive psychology. They define mindfulness as "placement of attention onto an object while alternatively acknowledging and letting go of distracting thoughts and emotions," where acknowledging and letting go involves appraisals and evaluations.[16] As positive psychologists, they emphasize the positive aspects of human life, rather than focusing just on mental disorders. Although they do not define "positive," they clearly intend criteria such as mental health, well-being, and morality. They provide examples of emotions and attitudes that Fredrickson discusses elsewhere: "joy, gratitude, serenity, interest, hope, pride, amusement, inspiration, awe, and love."[17] These health-promoting values include moral virtues, for example gratitude and love, although in therapeutic settings the moral values are discussed in the language of improved functioning and social engagement. In my terms, the authors integrate clients' value-based mindfulness in scrutinizing their values with an emphasis on positive valuing, as well as periodic use of value-suspending mindfulness during meditation.

Garland and Fredrickson distinguish mindfulness as a mental state, a disciplined practice of entering into this mental state, and a trait or disposition that individuals acquire by engaging in this practice. They hypothesize that all these types of mindfulness promote healthy positive emotions and disrupt harmful spirals of negative emotions. Initially they state their thesis cautiously: "mindfulness might facilitate access to positive emotions with which a person can disrupt a downward spiral and, in turn, nudge the emotional balance toward sustainable positivity."[18] The authors then work toward stronger conclusions: (value-suspending) "mindfulness is a key mechanism that makes reappraisal possible;" "mindfulness is arguably the keystone in the arch of positive reappraisal;" and "mindfulness imparts the individual with the freedom and, therefore, the responsibility for constructing a more purposeful and meaningful existence"—ideas that open the door to assumptions about moral responsibility under the heading of mental health.[19]

As an illustration they describe a patient who, upon being given a diagnosis of cancer, sinks into a vortex of terror, doom, and despair (comparable to Carel's experience). A psychotherapist helps the patient engage in mindfulness meditation, beginning with simple breathing exercises designed to restore a sense of control by temporarily stopping the cascade of negative emotions and appraisals. The intervention nudges the individual toward a sense of feeling lucky to be alive, and gradually a sense of relief and gratitude emerges. Next the therapist encourages the patient to dwell on gratitude, to contemplate and savor emotions of gratitude, and to do so with the aim of fostering deeper gratitude, joy, acceptance, and a sense of control. This "reframing" and "reappraisal" culminates with the patient identifying opportunities for finding meaning in the situation, and for pursuing focused value commitments that foster effective coping and growth.

Garland says he has successfully applied mindfulness-based ACT psychotherapy to a variety of ailments, including anxiety, depression, and addictions. Singly and together, he and Fredrickson are undertaking further clinical studies. Interestingly, they conclude with "an apparent paradox: mindfulness [as psychologists understand it] encourages nonevaluative contact with phenomenological experience . . . whereas positive reappraisal attributes a positively valenced, semantic meaning to experience."[20] In my terms, the apparent paradox is that (temporary) value-suspending mindfulness can promote value-based mindfulness, including mindful positive valuing. It moves patients toward more positive emotional states and evaluations. This positive oriented evaluation process is implicit in Kabat-Zinn and Langer, but the language of positive psychology facilitates stating the moral dimensions of mindful valuing more openly. At the same time, it builds on Kabat-Zinn's discussion of value-laden personal visions. Unlike Kabat-Zinn, Garland emphasizes that positive-value-laden awareness involves some negative evaluations. Thus, receptiveness to opportunities requires distinguishing them from false promises; caring for the good includes carefulness about dangers; passion for excellence is accompanied by disgust for shoddy work; and joy is never far from sadness and suffering.

STOICISM

Ellis acknowledges that he was directly influenced by Epicurus (as was Carel), and he was equally influenced by stoicism.[21] I discuss stoicism because it powerfully illustrates how moral values can explicitly be connected to therapeutic themes without reducing them to narrow self-interest. During its five hundred years of cultural prominence, stoicism generated many important thinkers, in all ranks of society. I discuss Epictetus (55–135 AD), who was a freed slave, with mention of Marcus Aurelius (121–180 AD), a Roman emperor.

The stoics believed that the universe is rational and good. Reason (*logos*) is a cosmic force as well as reflected in human intelligence. This belief seems naïve, even repellent, in light of the bloodbath of the twentieth century, including the horrors of the Holocaust and other genocides. Yet the stoics witnessed horrors of their own, and they were anything but Pollyannaish. They lived in a time of enormous cruelty and suffering. At the same time, they anticipated scientific understanding of the cosmos, human psychology, and human communities. Their ethics blended common sense with uncommon insight into how rational self-control promotes serenity and makes us feel at home in our own skin—and in the universe.

According to Pierre Hadot, "attention (*prosoche*) is the fundamental Stoic spiritual attitude. It is a continuous vigilance and presence of mind, self-consciousness which never sleeps" in the pursuit of virtue.[22] As such, stoic attention is a demanding form of virtue-mindfulness: conscientiously focusing on what matters morally and spiritually. That focus constitutes mindful valuing. It requires reasoning with ourselves and others about the values that should guide us, in general and in our present situation, and putting that reasoning into practice. Hadot adds, "This is the secret of concentration on the present moment: we are to give it all its seriousness, value, and splendor, in order to show up the vanity of all that we pursue with so much worry: all of which, in the end, will be taken away from us by death."[23] Epictetus has a perfectionistic streak. He urges that even "a momentary loss of attention" can undermine character: "If you doze off, all your progress up to that point will be negated. . . . It is no small thing that is being watched over, it equates with honesty, trustworthiness and stability."[24] Yet his perfectionism is mixed with pragmatic flexibility.

"Some things are up to us and some are not up to us."[25] Epictetus transforms this truism into an elemental moral maxim. The maxim enjoins realism: There are limits to what is possible, and it is irrational to exaggerate what is probable. The maxim enjoins humility: There are things we cannot change and should accept, rather than waste energy complaining and worrying about. It elicits hope: There are things we can do, right now, to improve our lives. It calls for responsibility: What we can do includes what we should do, and we should concentrate on the good we can achieve in our immediate situation. And it enjoins clarity and honesty: we are free within limits to control and shape our lives. In turn, like freedom of mind, control combines several things. It refers to a capacity to exercise control. It refers to skills and achievements in exercising control over our lives in tune with sound values. It refers to a subjective sense of control, the awareness and appreciation of our ability to exercise rational self-control. Most important, it refers to opportunity-control: the areas within which we have opportunities to effect change.

Exactly what is up to us? Epictetus's answer reflects his perfectionism and is problematic. He stipulates that what is up to us must be things over which we have *complete* and exclusive control, not mere influence. Those things, he claims, center on our value judgments and whatever flows directly from them: beliefs, emotions, attitudes, desires, and actions. Everything else is "external" to us: "So in life our first job is this, to divide and distinguish things into two categories: externals I cannot control, but the choices I make with regard to them I do control."[26] Externals include not only world events, but also our bodies, health, sickness, death, possessions, public offices, wealth, reputation, actions of others. Epictetus proclaims that our bodies, health, and wealth are "none of our affair" or concern, let alone the well-being of family and friends whom we love.[27] Hence we should not desire them or even evaluate them—they just are.

These sweeping generalizations are implausible, and so is his all-or-nothing view of control.[28] In places he softens them, but he never satisfactorally revises it. He says, for example, that although health is not a good per se, how we act regarding health can be a good. Thus, we can enjoy our health, and that enjoyment is a good.[29] This gerrymandered way of talking serves to reinforce his underlying ideal of invulnerability: We should concentrate on areas where we can have complete and exclusive control, which comprise our inner life rather than things influenced by the world. Epictetus's ideal might be enticing if we make peace of mind paramount: "Don't hope that events will turn out the way you want, welcome events in whichever way they happen: this is the path to peace."[30] But as a general policy it is constricting. It shuts off too many aspects of good lives that can never be under our complete control, everything from relationships of love to improving the world.

To use another example, Epictetus's all-or-nothing view of control undergirds his implausible attitude toward death. He proclaims that death is not a bad thing, and neither is the death of people we love. The bad thing lies in how we evaluate death: "What upsets people is not things themselves but their judgments about the things. For example, death is nothing dreadful . . . but instead the judgment about death that it is dreadful—*that* is what is dreadful. So when we are thwarted or upset or distressed, let us never blame someone else but rather ourselves, that is, our own judgments."[31] Epictetus is right to emphasize that we respond to the world through valuing. Everything that generates fear, dread, anger, hope, or any other emotion, does so in light of our values. He is not right, however, that complete lack of fear about death is the only rational attitude. Whether we have in mind our own death or the death of people we love, there are very good reasons to fear some deaths, and some ways of dying—for example, premature deaths (prior to having a chance to find self-fulfillment), and painful deaths.

If we abandon Epictetus's perfectionism and absolutism, his search for invincibility, and his faith in a completely rational universe, what remains in his contribution to mindful valuing? A great deal—including much that enters into REBT, ACT, and countless additional versions of psychotherapy. It remains true that we need to regularly reflect on what is in our control and what is not. It is especially important to focus on things we can control when confronting problems that threaten to overwhelm us. Major disease is one such problem, as Carel illustrates. Serious addiction is another example. Grappling with addiction typically requires a combination of fortitude and hope, as expressed in the stoic-inspired Serenity Prayer used in Twelve-Step Programs (and its secular analogs): "God grant me the serenity to accept the things I cannot change; courage to change the things I can [and should]; and wisdom to know the difference."[32]

Certainly Epictetus is correct that we have substantial abilities to modify our attitudes in reasonable directions. In confronting difficulties, there are usually "two [or more] handles" or attitudes, one by which we can carry a burden and the other not, and we can shift from the latter to the former.[33] Irrational attitudes lead to ranting and railing against things beyond our control, as well as depression and anxiety about the worst possible outcomes. Rational attitudes focus on accepting what we cannot change and concentrating on what we can do to make things better. Doing so is difficult. We must uncover harmful value judgments and replace them with healthier ones. To do so we reason with ourselves—talk and argue with ourselves, so as to nudge ourselves toward a more decent and healthy life. As a teacher, Epictetus repeatedly says "Look at it this way," "Try putting the question this way," "Talk to yourself, train your thought and shape your preconceptions."[34] This rational self-dialogue and self-argument, based on moral attention (*prosoche*), needs to become habitual, conscientious, and in-the-moment. When it does, moral vigilance merges with mindful living in the present—where the present is linked to the past and future rather than severed from them.

Epictetus offers a variety of additional examples, including some used by Ellis. For example, he discusses the performance anxiety of a musician or public speaker.[35] Epictetus asks the anxious person to pinpoint the evaluations underlying this distress. He discovers that the person is seeking applause, approval, and acceptance. Those things are not exclusively in his control, and hence are outside the proper domain of his freedom. In effect the performer is trying to own something that belongs to the audience, and thereby failing to respect their property: namely, their right to respond freely to the performance in the manner they choose. Moreover, the performer's extreme anxiety reveals a lack of proper focus on things that are in his control and for which he is responsible: his preparation prior to the performance, his concentration on what is required by excellence during the performance, basing his self-esteem on his caring about developing and expressing his talents, etc. In general terms, the overly anxious performer is preoccupied with status, social standing, recognition, rewards, and reputation, all of which are externals that are beyond his exclusive control. Quite likely, the performer also suffers from dishonesty and envy by grasping for honors that belong to the best performer. The remedy is to focus on what can be controlled: performing with one's highest skill based on thorough preparation.

Marcus Aurelius famously illustrates the kind self-help applications enjoined by Epictetus. In the *Meditations*, Marcus seems to speak to us personally: "Everything you're trying to reach—by taking the long way round—you could have right now, this moment. If you'd only stop thwarting your own attempts. If you'd only let go of the past, entrust the future to Providence, and guide the present toward reverence and justice."[36] In fact, he intended the "you" to be himself. His writing was not intended for publication. It was a spiritual exercise, as Hadot calls it, employing precise and motivational writing designed to challenge, control, and comfort himself.[37] Interrogating himself and sometimes giving himself a moral pep talk, Marcus applies many of Epictetus's themes to himself, including status anxiety, self-esteem and self-respect issues, death, and pain. He returns repeatedly to ways of thinking that help him cope and carry on with his duties as emperor. A recurring technique is to meditate on the brevity of any human life and the fear of death, conjoined with the obsession to gain fame and praise. He reflects on the most famous and successful members of every profession, all of whom are dead. He also finds it reassuring to affirm that everything is in flux. To some readers these reflections seem morbid, but Marcus occasionally adds positive words about the goodness in the universe, how it continually renews itself, and above all about the good he can do: "The first step: Don't be anxious. Nature controls it all. And before long you'll be no one, nowhere—like Hadrian, like Augustus. The second step: Concentrate on what you have to do. Fix your eyes on it. Remind yourself that your task is to be a good human being.... [Act] with kindness. With humility. Without hypocrisy."[38] This self-talk and these coping statements are integral to Albert Ellis's version of psychotherapy.

COHEN'S SYNTHESIS

There are striking differences between psychotherapies aimed at patients' self-interest and stoics' moral-oriented therapies, but there are equally striking similarities. It is natural to ask, in concluding, whether a contemporary practical ethics might be integrated with cognitive behavioral therapies attuned to ongoing scientific research.[39] Elliot D. Cohen outlines such a synthesis. Cohen's "Logic-Based Therapy" is presented in *The New Rational Therapy*, a book influenced by Ellis, who wrote a preface for it. Like Ellis, Cohen does not explicitly rely on the term "mindfulness," but he emphasizes the same in-the-present rational thinking about valuing that Ellis does. What is new and important is that Cohen broadens therapists' self-interested emphasis to include the moral virtues. And he does so systematically, rather in the piecemeal ways found in Carel, Garland, and Fredrickson.

Cohen is a pioneer in philosophical counseling: professional counseling that employs philosophical ideas, approaches, and traditions as tools for helping people cope with difficulties. These difficulties usually have a mental-health dimension, certainly where anxiety, depression, and other ailments are involved. But essentially they are difficulties having irrational and unreasonable aspects, as Ellis highlights. And rationality and reason overlap with moral matters that reach beyond narrow self-interest.

Different moral traditions establish their own canons of the virtues. But there are many virtues that can be integrated while also being selectively emphasized for different purposes. As a practicing counselor, as well as applied philosopher, Cohen discusses a host of cardinal virtues (or clusters of virtues) needed for personal growth (and healing). They include courage, self-respect, respect for others, authenticity, rational self-control, morally good judgment and moral creativity, good judgment and foresightedness, and moral creativity. Respect for scientific explanation and critical thinking is especially important for a rational therapy. And he adds to his list "metaphysical security," which is "the ability to accept imperfections in reality" while maintaining both humility and hope about the realistic prospects for exercising control in the world, in a degree sufficient for a good life.[40]

I mention Cohen's synthesis as illustrative rather than the final word. He explicitly integrates morality and mental health, approaching them as complementary rather than competing in thinking about mindful valuing. Only two of the psychologists I discussed in this chapter, Garland and Fredrickson, employ the term "mindfulness," and they intend value-suspending mindfulness. Cohen illustrates how mindful valuing, in the sense of value-based mindfulness (as I call it), contributes to integrating morality and mental health.

NOTES

1. Martha C. Nussbaum, *The Therapy of Desire: Theory and Practice in Hellenistic Ethics* (Princeton, NJ: Princeton University Press, 1994), 3.
2. Havi Carel, *Illness: The Cry of the Flesh*, revised edition (Durham, UK: Acumen, 2013), 150.
3. Henry D. Thoreau, *Walden* (Princeton, NJ: Princeton University Press, 2004), 90.
4. See especially Carel, *Illness*, xiv–xx, 9–15, 106–110.

5. See Jerome D. Frank and Julia B. Frank, *Persuasion and Healing: A Comparative Study of Psychotherapy*, 3rd ed. (Baltimore, MD: Johns Hopkins University Press, 1991).
6. See for example, Sigmund Freud, *An Autobiographical Study*, trans. James Strachey (New York: W. W. Norton, 1963 [1935]), 75–76.
7. Anthony T. Kronman, *Confessions of a Born-Again Pagan* (New Haven, CT: Yale University Press, 2016), 733.
8. Albert Ellis and Robert A. Harper, *A Guide to Rational Living*, 3rd ed. (Woodland Hills, CA: Melvin Powers Wilshire Book Company, 1977).
9. Ellis and Harper, *A Guide to Rational Living*, 222.
10. Ellis and Harper, *A Guide to Rational Living*, 236.
11. Ellis and Harper, *A Guide to Rational Living*, 39, italics removed. See also 13–14, 28.
12. Ellis and Harper, *A Guide to Rational Living*, 14–15.
13. See Ellis and Harper, *A Guide to Rational Living*, 39, 128.
14. See Ellis and Harper, *A Guide to Rational Living*, 127.
15. Carolyn Daitch, *Anxiety Disorders* (New York: W. W. Norton and Company, 2011), 43–44. See also Georg H. Eifert and J. P. Forsyth, *Acceptance and Commitment Therapy for Anxiety Disorders* (Oakland, CA: New Harbinger, 2005).
16. Eric L. Garland and Barbara L. Fredrickson, "Mindfulness Broadens Awareness and Builds Meaning at the Attention-Emotion Interface," in Todd B. Kashdan and Joseph Cirarrochi, eds., *Mindfulness, Acceptance, and Positive Psychology: The Seven Foundations of Well-Being* (Oakland, CA: Context Press, 2013), 30–67, at 46.
17. Barbara Fredrickson, *Positivity* (New York: Crown Publishers, 2009), 39.
18. Eric L. Garland and Barbara L. Fredrickson, "Mindfulness Broadens Awareness and Builds Meaning at the Attention-Emotion Interface," 32.
19. Garland and Fredrickson, "Mindfulness Broadens Awareness and Builds Meaning at the Attention-Emotion Interface," 47, 58, 59.
20. Garland and Fredrickson, "Mindfulness Broadens Awareness and Builds Meaning at the Attention-Emotion Interface," 57.
21. Ellis and Harper, *A Guide to Rational Living*, 5.
22. Pierre Hadot, *Philosophy as a Way of Life: Spiritual Exercises from Socrates to Foucault*, trans. Michael Chase, ed. Arnold L. Davidson (Oxford: Blackwell, 1995), 84.
23. Pierre Hadot, *Philosophy as a Way of Life*, 229.
24. Epictetus, *Discourses*, in *Discourses and Selected Writings*, trans. and edited by Robert Dobbin (New York: Penguin, 2008), 197.
25. Epictetus, *Handbook of Epicetetus*, trans. Nicholas White (Indianapolis, IN: Hackett Publishing, 1983), 11. Epictetus's writings are actually the record of his talks made by his student, Arrian.
26. Epictetus, *Discourses*, 86.
27. Epictetus, *Discourses*, 221.
28. See Steven Luper's fine critique, *Invulnerability: On Securing Happiness* (Chicago, IL: Open Court, 1996).
29. Epictetus, *Discourses*, 155, 183, 198.
30. Epictetus, *Discourses*, 224.
31. Epictetus, *Handbook of Epicetetus*, 13.
32. Reinhold Niebuhr is usually credited with articulating *The Serenity Prayer*. See Elisabeth Sifton, *The Serenity Prayer* (New York: W. W. Norton, 2003).
33. Epictetus, *Handbook of Epicetetus*, 26.
34. See, for example, Epictetus, *Discourses*, in *Discourses and Selected Writings*, 46 and 201.
35. Epictetus, *Discourses*, 103–106.
36. Marcus Aurelius, *Meditations*, trans. Gregory Hays (New York: Modern Library, 2003), 161.
37. Marcus Aurelius, *Meditations*, 35–53.
38. Marcus Aurelius, *Meditations*, 102.

39. Owen Flanagan insightfully outlines the interface of morality and mental health in *Varieties of Moral Personality: Ethics and Psychological Realism* (Cambridge, MA: Harvard University Press, 1991).

40. Elliot D. Cohen, *The New Rational Therapy: Thinking Your Way to Serenity, Success, and Profound Happiness* (Lanham, MD: Rowman & Littlefield Publishers, 2007), 17.

Part Three

Well-Being

Chapter Nine

Happiness and Virtues

Philosophers have an enduring interest in the wise pursuit of happiness, but positive psychologists have gone much further in creating a cottage industry that studies the mindful pursuit of happiness, or subjective well-being as they call it. The editor of a recent collection of scientific articles asks, "If the quest for an ultimate tool that would consistently increase individual well-being is the holy grail of positive psychology, could mindfulness be the answer?"[1] The editors of another collection depict mindfulness as the platform for promoting happiness and health: "mindfulness skills can make it easier to repair negative moods, enhance positive moods, or increase the amount of positive appraisals about the self, world, and future."[2] Both sets of editors intend (what I call) value-suspending mindfulness—suspending value judgments while paying close attention to immediate experience.[3] Yet they often slide toward value-based mindfulness by making value assumptions about health, rationality, and the virtues.

I first clarify what happiness is—a matter of obvious importance in studying the mindful pursuit of happiness. Next I sample a few areas where positive psychologists have studied mindfulness in connection with happiness. The virtues comprise one of those areas, an area that draws together philosophical and psychological interests. I conclude with the paradox of happiness, which contrasts two general strategies for mindfully pursuing happiness.

WHAT IS HAPPINESS?

Mike Leigh's film *Happy-Go-Lucky* is a witty and wise depiction of happiness. Poppy (played by Sally Hawkins), is an elementary school teacher who is undeniably happy. She has a happy temperament: cheerful and not given to excessive depression, anxiety, and anger. She also loves her life, as she testifies in a key scene. Accompanied by her friend Zoe, she visits her sister Helen, who believes that happiness centers on acquiring conventional goods—a husband, a house, and lots of money. Ironically, Helen possesses all these goods and yet is not nearly as happy as Poppy. From insecurity more than love, Helen challenges whether Poppy is happy, given that she possesses none of these conventional goods.

HELEN: "I just want you to be happy, that's all."

POPPY: "I am happy."

HELEN: "I don't think you are."

POPPY: "I am. I love my life. Yeah, it can be tough at times. That's part of it, isn't it? I've got a great job, brilliant kids [i.e., wonderful students], lovely flat. I've got her to look at [referring to her friend Zoe]. I've got amazing friends. I love my freedom. I'm a very lucky lady, I know that."[4]

Poppy responds to difficulties with resilience and moral concern. For example, when one of her students bullies another child on the playground, she promptly aids the bullied child and then also attempts to help the bully. She learns about the bully's abusive family and brings in a counselor to work with him. On another occasion her bicycle is stolen. She quickly adjusts to the theft and decides to learn how to drive a car. Her driving instructor turns out to be a hateful and dangerous man, himself a bully. Rather than becoming spiteful she learns from the encounter to be more careful. As she says, and as the film confirms, she loves her life despite such occasional difficulties. Taking that cue, I will understand our lives as happy insofar as we love them, valuing them in ways manifested with manifold enjoyments and a robust sense of meaning.[5]

Happiness cannot be defined in terms of universal sources of pleasure and meaning. When advertisers proclaim that happiness is a particular new car or watch, we know they are not defining happiness. At most they are making (dubious) claims about things that might contribute to the happiness of some individuals, in order to entice them to buy their products. In a different vein, Charles Schulz also claims to have defined happiness in his *Peanuts* comic strip when he drew Lucy hugging Snoopy and exclaiming "Happiness is a warm puppy."[6] But hugging a puppy obviously does not define happiness, even though it contributes to the happiness of many individuals, and even though it serves as a poignant metaphor for love, which *is* a major source of happiness for most people. In general, happiness cannot be equated with any of its specific sources and ingredients.

In characterizing happiness as *subjective well-being*, psychologists remind us that happiness is about attitudes and emotional dispositions, in contrast with *objective well-being* which consists in possessing things such as power, celebrity, money, and pets.[7] They also remind us that if we want to know if someone is happy, and how happy, it makes sense to ask them. The answer they give is not always decisive, for it is quite possible to deceive ourselves about how happy we are, as does Helen. But their answer is a good starting point, assuming that they understand the question and do not deliberately lie. Beyond that, however, subjective well-being is understood in different ways by psychologists.

Some psychologists define subjective well-being entirely in terms of pleasure. According to these *hedonistic definitions*, we are happier in the degree that our lives are replete with pleasures: the more pleasure the more happiness.[8] Yet it seems quite possible to have much pleasure without being happy, as is true of many drug addicts and other kinds of pleasure junkies. It is also possible to be happy with relatively low levels of pleasure, as with some ascetics. Other psychologists understand subjective well-being as overall contentment with life. According to these *life-satisfaction definitions*, we are happy in the degree we live with an attitude of satisfaction with our life, regardless of how much pleasure we experience. Yet, it seems possible to be contented with our life and yet have such a low level of enjoyment that we are more resigned than happy. Still other psychologists adopt *hybrid definitions* that interpret subjective well-being as a combination of pleasure, life satisfaction, and a sense of meaning. For example, Sonja Lyubomirsky defines happiness as "the experience of joy, contentment, or positive well-being, combined with a sense that one's life is good, meaningful, and worthwhile."[9] I too favor a hybrid definition. In my view, we are happy insofar as we love our life overall, valuing it with ample enjoyments and a robust sense of meaning. Admittedly this definition is vague, but then so is the word "happiness." In any case, it is sufficiently clear as a working definition to be in tune with hybrid definitions such as Lyubomirsky employs.

My definition of subjective well-being intimates why we value happiness so dearly, for we value each of its dimensions—myriad pleasures, a sense of meaning, and loving our life (rather than detesting or merely enduring it). To be sure, happiness is not the entirety of a good life, for good lives are also morally decent, authentic, healthy, and fulfilling. Nevertheless, happiness is a cherished good that interweaves with all other dimensions of good lives. In particular, for most of us a life that we love includes moral decency. We might even be willing to place limits on our pursuits of happiness in order to secure justice, honesty, striving for excellence, compassion and the happiness and well-being of people we love.[10]

Nearly everyone desires happiness, and nearly everyone finds it desirable (valuable). As William James observes, "How to gain, how to keep, how to recover happiness, is in fact for most men at all times the secret motive of all they do, and of all they are willing to endure."[11] Of course, sometimes we fail to pursue happiness intelligently, reasonably—and mindfully. Certainly the pursuit of happiness can be complicated. For one thing, obtaining things we believe will make us happy may in fact bring misery—witness buyer's regret. As a familiar maxim says, happiness is not getting what we want; it is wanting what we get, or already have. For another thing, we easily fail to fully appreciate and cultivate—to be mindful of—areas of our lives that make vital contributions to our happiness. Positive psychologists are illuminating many of these areas.

POSITIVE PSYCHOLOGY

Christened in 1998, positive psychology is a movement that emphasizes positive experiences, traits, relationships, institutions, and values. Earlier humanistic psychologists, such as Abraham Maslow and Carl Rogers, also studied the positive aspects of life, but they lacked the experimental rigor of positive psychologists. Positive psychologists attract strong funding for their studies, and a wide audience. They also conduct experiments on a breathtaking range of topics, as outlined by Martin E. P. Seligman.

> The field of positive psychology at the subjective level is about positive subjective experience: well-being and satisfaction (past); flow, joy, the sensual pleasures, and happiness (present); and constructive cognitions about the future—optimism, hope, and faith. At the individual level it is about positive personal traits—the capacity for love and vocation, courage, interpersonal skill, aesthetic sensibility, perseverance, forgiveness, originality, future-mindedness, high talent, and wisdom. At the group level it is about the civic virtues and the institutions that move individuals toward better citizenship: responsibility, nurturance, altruism, civility, moderation, tolerance, and work ethic.[12]

The eponymous term *positive* is ambiguous. Especially in connection with subjective experience, it might mean what *feels good*, that is, what is pleasurable. Thus, joy and serenity are positive emotions because they feel good, and depression and anxiety are negative moods because they feel bad. Instead, positive might mean *positivity*, in the sense of being upbeat and optimistic, a tone that permeates positive psychology. Or it might mean what is *healthy*, understanding health holistically and expansively. Many "negative" emotions that do not feel good are nevertheless healthy, and express healthy desires, for example justified instances of regret, resentment, and fear. Positive might also mean *valued* or desired by an individual or group. And it can even mean *genuinely valuable* or desirable (worthy of being desired), that is, *good* in terms of moral virtues and other sound values in good lives.[13]

These ambiguities make it easy to slide from facts to values, from feelings to values, and from desired to desirable. Likewise, when mindfulness is discussed in connection with positive states, it is easy to shift from value-suspending mindfulness to value-based mindfulness, and from personal-mindfulness to virtue-mindfulness. These ambiguities and shifts need to be borne in mind in discussing positive psychologists' contributions to the mindful pursuit of happiness. These contributions include the following areas, some of which were touched on in earlier chapters: meditation, savoring, flow, caring relationships, emotional self-regulation, and the virtues. As I proceed I take note of different senses of "mindfulness" employed in psychological studies of these areas.

To begin with, mindfulness-based *meditation* is extensively studied in connection with how mindfulness increases happiness by reducing stress and improving coping.[14] Meditation researchers generally understand mindfulness as value-suspending mindfulness (chapter 6). Practiced regularly, meditation helps many of us detach from the sources of anxiety and other distress, at least temporarily, so they do not overwhelm us and so that we can better understand them. Even intense negative feelings come to be seen as transient, rather than permanent sources of suffering.[15] Meditation that employs temporary value-suspending mindfulness, together with focusing on an immediate present that is buffered from wider horizons of value and time, can help counter the shame and guilt generated by self-condemnation. It can also reduce the fear, anger, and hatred generated by unduly negative judgments about other people. More positively, regularly engaging in meditation can increase a sense of control, a sense of freedom to shape our lives, and increased enjoyment and meaning, all of which contribute to happiness.

Savoring is fully experiencing, dwelling on, intensifying, or fostering pleasures.[16] Typically it involves mindfulness, but this time the mindfulness is value-based personal-mindfulness rather than value-suspending mindfulness—we value what we savor. Positive psychologists (echoing Thoreau, Goethe, and Brenda Ueland) celebrate taking time to smell the roses, in contrast with being so earnestly goal-oriented that we postpone pleasure to a distant future. Savoring is not limited to taking pleasure in our immediate situation. It also includes taking delight in and deriving meaning from our previous accomplishments, and pleasure in anticipating future events. In this way, savoring can frame the present in light of a valued past and future, rather than an isolated present moment. The mindfulness involved in savoring is value-based, where the relevant values include pleasure, happiness, and the values embedded in desirable activities and relationships.

Flow is widely studied in connection with happiness and mindfulness, both taken separately and together. As Mihaly Csikszentmihalyi defines it, flow is immersion in purposive activities in ways that seamlessly integrate skills, goals, and information feedback, so as to generate enjoyment and a sense of meaning. Persons act on clear goals that express their values, engage their skills so as to match challenges, and obtain immediate feedback. Action and awareness merge as they focus concentration on what they are doing, without distractions, including distractions from worries. Csikszentmihalyi specifies that flow frees us from unduly negative judgments about ourselves (and others). He depicts this liberation as a side-effect of immersion in activities that suppresses our usual self-preoccupation.[17]

> Information that keeps coming into awareness is congruent with goals, psychic energy flows effortlessly. There is no need to worry, no reason to question one's adequacy. But whenever one does stop to think about oneself, the evidence is encouraging: "You are doing all right." The positive feedback strengthens the self, and more attention is freed to deal with the outer and inner environment.[18]

Flow tends to increase happiness and skillful accomplishment simultaneously: "If the surgeon's mind wanders during an operation, the patient's life is in danger. Flow is the result of intense concentration on the present, which relieves us of the usual fears that cause depression and anxiety in everyday life."[19] As this example illustrates, the mindfulness in flow is value-based, in contrast with value-suspending mindfulness during meditation.[20] What we might call *flow-mindfulness*—the mindfulness characteristic of the task-attention involved in flow experiences—is thus a form of personal-mindfulness. Flow involves positive valuations of our goals for the specific activities we engage in during flow. In addition, flow might combine a focus on the present with an orientation to longer-term goals, such as goals of careers and marriages. In both ways, the centrality of valued goals plays a key role in flow-mindfulness, in contrast with the value-suspending mindfulness during meditation, which buffers the present from the past and future. Insofar as our values are sound, flow-mindfulness becomes virtue-mindfulness. Insofar as the soundness of the values is undecided, flow-mindfulness constitutes personal-mindfulness. Although Csikszentmihalyi refers to all flow as "optimal experience," he stops short of saying it always involves sound values. Thus, he allows that criminals might be in states of flow (using flow-mindfulness) in carrying out wrongdoing:

> The flow experience, like everything else, is not "good" in an absolute sense. It is good only in that it has the potential to make life more rich, intense, and meaningful; it is good because it increases the strength and complexity of the self. But whether the consequence of any particular instance of flow is good in a larger sense needs to be discussed and evaluated in terms of more inclusive social criteria.[21]

Caring relationships, like flow activities, are not always good, at least not in all respects. Nevertheless, insofar as "caring" is value-laden and suggests mutual benefits, caring relationships often involve virtue-mindfulness that contributes to happiness. Positive psychologists repeatedly confirm that caring relationships contribute to happiness. They do so in many ways, by structuring and enriching lives over time and in the moment. Barbara Fredrickson says that love is promoted by mindfully fostering the daily accumulation of "micro-moments of positivity" which blend pleasure with meaning.[22] Some varieties of love are mostly unilateral, for example love for an infant—although the infant's smile and touch expresses some reciprocity. Reciprocity is essential, however, in most relationships among adults, certainly marriages.

Happy marriages, those rooted in love and commitment, contribute to the happiness of both spouses. Although positive psychologists typically study happy marriages using health-oriented headings—for example, "emotional intelligence"—moral values are clearly involved. Consider John M. Gottman's *The Seven Principles for Making Marriage Work*, perhaps the most widely recommended self-help book for improving relationships. By and large, Gottman's "principles" are actually virtues, or reflections of virtues. And most of his principles involve virtue-mindfulness. His first principle explicitly mentions love: Enhance Your Love Maps, whereby "emotionally intelligent couples are intimately familiar with each other's world" and "pay attention to the details of their spouse's life."[23] Loving individuals are mindful of such details about their partner as mattering—mattering to them because they matter to the partner. Other principles include Nurture Your Fondness and Admiration, for example, by meditating on why you cherish your partner; Turn toward Each Other Instead of Away, by being responsive to your spouse's bids for attention; be more attuned to the sources of conflict and ways of positively dealing with them; and maintain an atmosphere of honest communication about what matters to each other. Gottman emphasizes the little things as mattering, because they become big things as desirable habits that sustain intimate caring relationships, and thereby promote shared happiness. All his principles involve personal-mindfulness, with a general cast of virtue-mindfulness, even though he does not explicitly rely on the word "mindfulness."

Emotion-regulation is monitoring and improving our emotional reactions. It usually embodies elements of virtue-mindfulness. To regulate our emotions implies self-control in suppressing anger, hatred, and other "negative" emotions. Equally important, it involves fostering positive emotions, such as hope and good cheer. To that end, a vital resource is cognitive reappraisal: using good reasoning to rethink our situation in ways that increase enjoyment, decrease discouragement, and enrich our sense of meaning about how our lives are going. This reappraisal leads to, or includes, implementing that rethinking. In the background, there is often an assumption that cognitive reappraisal and emotion-regulation are aimed at healthy goals, which typically include moral decency and rationality.

Albert Ellis understood that cognitive reappraisal centers on mindful valuing. The mindful valuing is obviously an instance of value-based mindfulness, whether personal-mindfulness or virtue-mindfulness. It can be enriched by therapeutically refined skills in selecting the best ways to cope with stressful situations, defuse misery-making anxieties, and find ways to make the best of opportunities. These value-laden themes are frequently concealed beneath psychological vernacular such as "emotional intelligence" and "sensitivity," as in this definition of mindfulness: "Mindfulness concerns a receptive state of mind wherein attention, informed by a sensitive awareness, simply observes what is taking place in the present."[24] Even so, positive psychologists increasingly link the virtues to ideas such as emotion-regulation, cognitive reappraisal, and emotional intelligence. In doing so they can provide helpful therapeutic resources. They might also blur facts and values, descriptive and prescriptive statements, and self-interest and morality.[25]

HAPPINESS AND THE VIRTUES

The contribution of the *virtues* to happiness, and of happiness to the virtues, is a particularly exciting topic in positive psychology. Positive psychologists are refreshingly open about studying moral *character*, in contrast with earlier psychologists' aspirations to engage in value-neutral studies of *personality*. Yet, when mindfulness is mentioned in these studies, it is often unclear what is being discussed: value-suspending mindfulness (the dominant paradigm in psychology) or value-based mindfulness? And when value-based mindfulness is occasionally implied, is it personal-mindfulness or virtue-mindfulness?

What Jonathan Haidt calls the virtue hypothesis—"Cultivating virtue will make you happy"—is "alive and well, firmly ensconced in positive psychology."[26] It is ensconced, that is, as a statistical generalization (not a universal statement) about the general tendency of virtue to augment happiness. How can psychologists study the virtues without departing from their empirical framework of description and explanation, rather than evaluation?[27] As scientists, they generally study what most people *believe* is good, as distinct from what actually is good (morally or otherwise). In particular, psychologists survey and summarize what most people believe to be virtues. Then they study how the virtues, thus understood, contribute to health and happiness (and vice versa). Results of the experiments are tabulated as statistical generalizations, which are then refined by new tests. Yet sometimes these statistics are used normatively, as the basis for claims about what is good, usually under the rubric of mental health (and well-being). These claims can build bridges between science and the humanities.

To illustrate, consider the virtue of gratitude, in particular as it opposes the "deadly sin" of envy. Gratitude has several major dimensions: thankfulness to particular individuals who contribute to our lives from motives of concern for our well-being; more broadly, appreciation of the good things in our lives; and the virtue shown in the disposition to be thankful and appreciative on appropriate occasions and in justified ways. Ethicists and moralists have long explored the ways in which gratitude contributes to happiness, for example by countering painful attitudes of envy. As a sin or vice, envy is not jealousy; it is hating other people for what they have (and usually wanting it for ourselves). In this sense, Iago envies Othello. Envy tends to be painful, to ourselves and as perceived by others. To admit to envy implies acknowledging a painful lack in ourselves, perhaps an overall emptiness and failure to secure a life for ourselves we can enjoy and love. To acknowledge our envy of the rich, for example, is to acknowledge our failure to secure a satisfying degree of wealth.[28] Envy tends to pervade consciousness, shunting attention away from the good we have. Henry Fairlie even speculates that envy is a product of self-hatred:

> The envious man does not love himself, although he begins with self-love. He is not grateful for, or happy in, what he is or what he has. The sin is deadly, less because it destroys him, than because it will not let him live. It will not let him live as himself, grateful for his qualities and talents, such as they are, and making the best and most rewarding use of them. His disparagement of others is a reflection of his disparagement of himself; he regards himself with as much malice as he regards them.[29]

Philip C. Watkins identifies multiple pathways by which mindful experiences and expressions of gratitude contribute to happiness.[30] Dispositions to experience appropriate gratitude tend to (a) increase happiness-promoting feelings of self-esteem from receiving gifts and the perceived goodwill of others toward us; (b) strengthen our sense of satisfaction with our life as containing much good; (c) counteract the effects of habituation, whereby we take things for granted; (d) deflect attention from feelings of deprivation generated by comparing what we have to what others have; (e) strengthen our ability to delay gratification because we are more satisfied with what we already have; (f) appreciate more in our lives because as we learn to appreciate little things more; (g) improve how we deal with stress, because we bring a sense of well-being to situations; (h) promote greater readiness to remember good things from the past; (i) counter our general tendencies to be self-absorbed; (j) add additional social benefits, in that other people admire people who appreciate what they have and dislike envious and petty people; etc.

Of course, gratitude is only one of many important virtues. Like many philosophers before them, psychologists seek a unifying framework for thinking about the virtues. Working with Christopher Peterson, Seligman claims to have identified six general virtues found (endorsed) in all cultures: wisdom, courage, humanity, justice, temperance, and transcendence. Each of these general virtues (or "strengths") encompasses several more specific virtues (or "skills"). Wisdom includes creativity, curiosity, open-mindedness, love of learning, and perspective. Courage includes bravery, persistence, integrity, and vitality. Humanity includes love, kindness, and social intelligence. Justice includes citizenship, fairness, and leadership. Temperance includes forgiveness/mercy, humility, prudence, and self-regulation. And transcendence includes appreciation of beauty and excellence, gratitude, hope, humor, and spirituality.[31] Peterson and Seligman offer this schema as a hypothesis, subject to revision and refinement in light of ongoing cultural studies. They often seem to imply, however, that they are not merely reporting facts. They present themselves as studying what is virtuous, not merely believed to be virtuous; what is desirable, rather than simply desired by most people in most cultures. In doing so, they easily slide from scientific description and explanation to making normative claims about sound values. In particular, the slide is found when mindfulness is discussed in connection with the virtues.

For example, Ryan M. Niemiec and Judith Lissing have developed mindfulness-based strengths practice.[32] Officially they define mindfulness as value-suspending: "being present to what is happening in the unfolding moment to moment experience, without pre-conceptions or judgments."[33] They encourage their clients/patients to employ mindfulness-based meditation as a key tool for systematically cultivating virtues such as love, honesty, hope, and gratitude aimed at improving relationships and solving problems at work. In effect, they employ temporary value-suspending mindfulness to promote virtue-mindfulness.

BALANCING OPTIMISM AND TRUTHFULNESS

Morality involves cultivating a host of virtues, and these virtues interact with each other. Virtue-mindfulness plays a crucial role in balancing and resolving tensions among the virtues in pursuing happiness. Consider the mindful balancing of optimism and truthfulness, a topic that engages both philosophers and psychologists. Optimism is a topic of enduring philosophical interest, and early on Seligman made it a central area of study in positive psychology.[34] As a virtue, optimism is not the blissed-out rosiness conveyed in the lyrics of Bobby McFerrin's Reggae song "Don't Worry, Be Happy," nor

Johnny Mercer's one-sided call to "accentuate the positive, eliminate the negative."[35] Optimism does involve accenting what is good, but a realistic optimism would acknowledge the bad as well. Positive psychologists admit as much, although they are somewhat less eager to acknowledge they are making moral judgments when they draw lines delineating truthful optimism.

For example, Ellen J. Langer and Christell T. Ngnoumen contend that mindfulness is the "essence" of happiness, and they stipulate that "a mindful attitude involves identifying the positives in a situation," and favoring them over negative interpretations of events, while still taking account of negativities.[36] Again, Barbara L. Fredrickson says we should remain open to the negative in order to counter it: "Perhaps counterintuitively, being open to negativity is healthier than being closed off from it," and a "scientifically tested way to curb negativity's momentum is practicing mindfulness."[37] These scientists make empirical claims but they also embed value assumptions under the heading of "positivity," which they build into mindfulness—thereby tacitly using some version of value-based mindfulness. In any case, truthfulness in acknowledging the challenging, even tragic aspects of human experience is compatible with realistic optimism, and hence requires exercising good judgment and balanced perception. Exploring these tensions and compatibilities between truthfulness and optimism requires a robust conception of virtue-mindfulness, a concept that draws on philosophical as well as psychological understanding of the virtues.

William James earlier explored the tensions between and mindful integration of optimism and truthfulness. James was a leading psychologist, as well as a distinguished philosopher, and retrospectively he qualifies as a positive psychologist. He contrasts healthy-mindedness and sick-mindfulness, and argues that we need elements of both. Healthy-mindedness is "the tendency which looks on all things and see that they are good."[38] It ranges from the embarrassingly superficial ("moon-struck with optimism") to practical-oriented "concrete therapeutics."[39] By itself, however, "healthy-mindedness is inadequate as a philosophical doctrine" because it neglects important aspects of life, aspects that "may after all be the best key to life's significance, and possibly the only openers of our eyes to the deepest levels of truth."[40] As a corrective to one-sided healthy-mindedness, he says somewhat awkwardly, we need at least a modicum of "sick-mindedness": the tendency to worry about disease, death, evil, and other unsavory aspects of life, and in doing so to experience suffering, fear, tragedy, and other negative emotions. He might have expressed his view more clearly by defining "healthy-mindedness" as the balanced and truthful *emphasis* on the good over the bad, rather than a blanket celebration of good.

Robert Nozick, a philosopher who consulted with positive psychologists, comes closer to articulating a moral balance between optimism and truthfulness. He does so in a manner that is compatible with the work of positive psychologists while being far more explicit about morally sound values. In his view, we value positive emotions because they feel good, whether joy or self-esteem or love. But we also value them because they are truthful and reflect reality, including painful emotions such as outrage against injustice. We want emotions attuned to reality, just as we want beliefs to be true. We value contact with reality, in addition to how things feel, because that contact enables us to cope and also makes us better persons—more truthful.

Nozick develops these points by invoking his famous thought experiment of an experience machine. Imagine a sophisticated virtual-reality device that directly fires our neurons in ways that make us believe we are responding to real events. Indeed, imagine that once attached to the machine we fully believe we are experiencing real events. We can program the machine in advance to provide complex series of experiences and emotions, such as climbing Mount Everest, writing a novel, and being in love (all the while kept alive by life support systems). Many of us might choose to enter the machine for brief periods of recreation or learning, but very few of us would enter the machine permanently. Why not? Because we value contact with reality. We desire and consider it desirable to have our beliefs and emotions compatible with the way the world actually is.

Nozick formulates a concept of (what I call) virtue-mindfulness in balancing truthfulness and optimism. He formulates an additional "reality principle," one that complements the general reality principle that calls for being in contact with reality: "we should pay attention to the things around us in proportion to their importance, not simply to the things but to the aspects that make them important."[41] He emphasizes that selective attention is an elemental form of evaluating. It is also crucial to personal autonomy, which enables us to shape our emotional lives in significant ways. Emotions influence what we attend to, and what we attend to influences our emotions. Our emotional lives are complicated, of course. If we attend only to what is positive we will be optimistic at the expense of being superficial and untruthful. If we attend only to the dark side of life, we will be gloomy and despairing, and risk depression. Sometimes we do well to cope by deliberately distracting ourselves from problems. And there is much room for imaginative adventures in the arts, when the sadness we feel in watching a play or film differs from the wholly painful sadness we feel in daily life.

Nozick calls for flexibility and moderation. He rejects (as too strong) the view that contact with reality must be maximized at all times, and he rejects (as too weak) the view that only some degree of contact with reality is desirable. He favors an in-between view: each bit of contact with reality has some value, but that value can be overridden sometimes by other considerations such as happiness. How best to balance potentially conflicting considerations is as complicated here as it is in many other types of value dilemmas. He is receptive to a reality principle "slanted toward focus upon the positive" without "significant detachment" from reality.[42] He also highlights practical skills that facilitate flexibility, such as *"zoom lens* ability": "we need to be able to alter our attention's focus as appropriate, back and forth from the general picture to details, from confirmation to things that don't fit, from the surface to what is deep, from the immediate to the long-term."[43]

Nozick sets the right tone and provides a helpful framework for thinking about mindfulness in balancing truthfulness and optimism, and tacitly other virtues. Appealing to good judgment, he articulates the need for nuanced value judgments that integrate optimism with maintaining contact with reality. Such value judgments illustrate the promise of integrating positive psychology and humanistic philosophy in understanding the virtues. They do so, however, by being clear that philosophical ethics is as much involved as the kind of empirical studies of what people and cultures believe, which positive psychologists study.

PARADOXICAL PURSUITS

Meditation, savoring, flow, caring relationships, and the virtues illustrate major pathways for mindfulness to contribute to happiness. Beyond them, and perhaps unifying them, is there some general strategy for mindfully pursuing a happy life? One suggestion, much discussed in the history of philosophy, is that we should pursue happiness indirectly. According to the paradox of happiness, to get happiness we should forget about it. We should concentrate instead on important relationships, activities, ideals, and other things beyond ourselves. Then, with any luck, happiness will come as a by-product.

The happiness paradox is not a logical contradiction, nor even a seeming contradiction. It is a paradox in the sense that it is counter intuitive and deeply surprising, for we usually believe that important things (like happiness) should be pursued directly, by keeping our eye on the prize.[44] The paradox cautions against being preoccupied with happiness. Doing so is self-defeating. It undermines rewarding relationships and meaningful activities that are vital for happiness and require an outward orientation. As John Stuart Mill wrote, "Those only are happy (I thought) who have their minds fixed on some object other than their own happiness; on the happiness of others, on the improvement of mankind, even on some art or pursuit, followed not as a means, but as itself an ideal end. Aiming thus at something else, they find happiness by the way."[45]

Mill spoke from experience. At age twenty, following a demanding home-schooling from his father, he suffered a major depression. He had single-mindedly devoted his life to the utilitarian ideal of maximizing the general good—the happiness of all people affected by our actions. But when he asked himself whether achieving that ideal, or simply seeing it completely realized, would make him happy, he realized it would not. The realization shattered him. At least, that is what he believed. I suspect that his depression probably had multiple causes, and his philosophical self-questioning was only the immediate catalyst. In any case, for most of a year he struggled just to cope, experiencing little pleasure and with no sense of meaning. Gradually his depression lifted, and enjoyment and a sense of meaning returned.

The experience led him to articulate a new strategy for mindfully pursuing happiness, and a new version of utilitarianism. He had been educated to equate happiness with large quantities of pleasure. His depression and recovery led him to believe instead that quality of pleasures, more than quantity, matters for happiness. By quality he meant value. He became convinced that the more valuable, "higher" pleasures derive from love, friendship, learning, beauty, meaningful work, and virtuous character, all of which require an element of submission to values and avoiding self-preoccupation. Furthermore, these other things need to be valued and pursued for themselves rather than mainly from ulterior self-interested motives, in order for them to produce higher pleasures.

Elsewhere Mill offers an additional explanation for why direct focus on our happiness is self-defeating. This direct focusing leads us to grasp for things not in our control.

> [P]aradoxical as the assertion may be, the conscious ability to do without happiness gives the best prospect of realizing such happiness as is attainable. For nothing except that consciousness can raise a person above the chances of life by making him feel that, let fate and fortune do their worst, they have not the power to subdue him; which, once felt, frees him from the excess of anxiety concerning the evils of life and enables him, like many a Stoic in the worst times of the Roman Empire, to cultivate in tranquility the sources of satisfaction accessible to him.[46]

Mill's reflections on the mindful pursuit of happiness are insightful. They are also flawed. For one thing, he conflates two claims: (1) Happiness derives from caring about things beyond ourselves, which we *believe* and *feel* to be valuable, and (2) Happiness derives from commitments to *genuinely* valuable things. This blurring of facts and values is of the same sort found in much positive psychology. For another thing, he neglects the need for periodic reviews—*mindful* reviews—of how happy we are, and why we are happy or unhappy. He also neglects the wide variations in how individuals might best pursue happiness. For example, it might make sense for some individuals to undertake a "project" to raise their level of happiness.

Consider Gretchen Rubin's yearlong project to increase her level of happiness, as recounted in *The Happiness Project*. Rubin has a privileged life. She is a graduate of Yale Law School, a successful writer, a mother of two lovely children, and married to a wealthy hedge fund manager (who is the son of Robert Rubin, the former Treasury Secretary). Despite "having it all," she found herself suffering from a "midlife malaise—not as severe as Mill's crisis of depression, but nonetheless a marked and recurrent sense of discontent."[47] In response, she does exactly what Mill cautions against—she focuses directly on her happiness. For twelve months she explores, experiments with, and systematically seeks to increase her happiness level. In each area of her life she actively cultivates new ways to increase enjoyment and meaning, devoting a full month to each area: her work, family, friends, hobbies, purchases, etc. Critics might charge her with self-indulgence, with being an ultraprivileged individual who further indulges herself in a self-oriented pursuit of happiness. She worries about that charge, and returns to it several times. Her main defense is that she sets her project within a context of personal growth that includes dimensions of caring for others—her family, friends, and people in need.[48] In this way, she believes, she avoids the kind of self-absorbed pursuit of happiness that Mill identified as self-defeating. Probably she does avoid it. She seems to be happier because of the project she undertook, and also a person of good character.

I have a different concern about Rubin's project, one connected with the ambiguity surrounding "positive" mental states, specifically the difference between what is desired and what is desirable. Rubin's discussion of values repeatedly lapses into subjectivity, into what she desires and *feels* to be valuable.[49] She takes for granted that the main point of life is to pursue and find happiness. She then understands happiness in terms of feeling good, especially feeling good about yourself. As for moral values, she tends to reduce them to feelings—to "feeling right" about what she does. She also highlights how feeling happy motivates moral conduct: "when I felt happy, I was more likely to be lighthearted, generous, creative, kind, encouraging, and helpful," and when she felt unhappy she is less caring toward others.[50] Mill emphasized that values should be sound, and recognized as "ideal ends" that make claims on us. Rubin reverses this. She reduces values to feelings. She is not alone, of course. The belief that values are mere preferences and feelings permeates much of society and psychology. To their credit, at least some positive psychologists try to block wholesale subjectivism concerning the virtues, by understanding them as widely held ideals of character.

Mill, Rubin, and positive psychologists agree on one thing. Happiness is enormously important, yet it needs to be pursued through other things that bring enjoyment and meaning—in degrees sufficient to create a life we love. For most of us those things include moral ideals and virtues, but they include a variety of additional things as well. That was true for Mill. His depression was precipitated when he realized that his utilitarian goals, around which he had centered his idealistic youth, were not enough for his happiness. He asked himself, in all honesty, whether the complete achievement of the ideal of maximum good in the world would make him happy. "And an irrepressible self-consciousness distinctly answered, 'No!' At this my heart sank within me: the whole foundation on which my life was constructed fell down."[51] The irony is that at the time he was following much the same advice as he offers a year later, following his depression. He was committed to a goal beyond himself: the ideal of the greatest good for the greatest number of people. In effect, he came to realize that commitment to goods beyond ourselves is necessary but not sufficient for happiness. For the goods need to engage us, and for most of us the goods require more than simply moral values.

The mindful pursuit of happiness requires discovering and fostering an appropriate *cluster* of goods beyond ourselves, moral and nonmoral, which bring sufficient enjoyments and meaning to create a life we love. The configuration of happiness-making ingredients is highly personal, although we can learn from the statistical generalizations about sources and ingredients of happiness discovered by positive psychologists. Sources and ingredients interact, sometimes creating tensions: among moral and nonmoral goods, as well as among specific virtues like optimism and truthfulness. As a result mindfulness in pursuing happiness requires good judgment in myriad situations, not simply once and for all decisions about strategies and fixed goals. Fortunately we have evolved as creatures with healthy capacities to adjust to change. We have also evolved as creatures who can integrate a wide variety of motives in order to create a satisfying—even joyous—life.[52]

In sum, mindfulness, including different types of mindfulness, contributes to happiness in many ways studied by positive psychologists, as well as by philosophers. Positive psychologists easily slide from statistical facts about what makes people happy to making moral judgments. This is especially true when they discuss tensions among different virtues and even different categories of value. Happiness, mental health, and morality are distinct categories of value that can be in tension, even though they overlap and are interwoven in complicated ways.[53] Regarding mindfulness, what is most important in a situation is often less about mental health than moral judgment about how to weigh, for example, honesty against compassion, and justice against mercy. More is not always better with regard to any given virtue, and the virtues need to be balanced in ways that require good moral judgment.[54] This is one of the points where positive psychology can be complemented and enriched by philosophical inquiry, indeed by all areas of the humanities.

NOTES

1. Itai Ivtzan, "Mindfulness in Positive Psychology: An Introduction," in Itai Ivtzan and Tim Lomas, eds., *Mindfulness in Positive Psychology: The Science of Meditation and Well-Being* (New York: Routledge, 2016), 1–12, at 1.

2. Joseph Ciarrochi, Todd B. Kashdan, and Russ Harris, "The Foundations of Flourishing," in Todd B. Kashdan and Joseph Ciarrochi, eds., *Mindfulness, Acceptance, and Positive Psychology: The Seven Foundations of Well-Being* (Oakland, CA: Context Press, 2013), 1–29, at 11.

3. Ivtzan, "Mindfulness in Positive Psychology: An Introduction," 5; and Ciarrochi, Kashdan, Harris, "The Foundations of Flourishing," 3.

4. *Happy-Go-Lucky*, Miramax, produced by Simon Channing Williams, directed and screenplay written by Mike Leigh (2008).

5. See Mike W. Martin, *Happiness and the Good Life* (New York: Oxford University Press, 2012).

6. See David Michaelis, *Schulz and Peanuts: A Biography* (New York: HarperCollins, 2007), 343.

7. See Ed Diener and Robert Biswas-Diener, *Happiness* (Malden, MA: Blackwell Publishing, 2008), 4.

8. See, for example, Richard Layard, *Happiness: Lessons from a New Science* (New York: Penguin Press, 2005), 12.

9. Sonja Lyubomirsky, *The How of Happiness: A Scientific Approach to Getting the Life You Want* (New York: Penguin, 2007), 32. See also Daniel Kahneman, "Objective Happiness" in Daniel Kahneman, Ed Diener, and Norbert Schwarz, eds., *Well-Being* (New York: Russell Sage Foundation, 1999), 3–25.

10. Robert Nozick, *The Examined Life* (New York: Simon and Schuster, 1989), 99. See also Daniel M. Haybron, *The Pursuit of Unhappiness* (New York: Oxford University Press, 2008), 123.

11. William James, *The Varieties of Religious Experience* (New York: Modern Library, 1902), 77

12. Martin E. P. Seligman, "Positive Psychology, Positive Prevention, and Positive Therapy," in C. R. Snyder and Shane J. Lopez, eds., *Handbook of Positive Psychology* (New York: Oxford University Press, 2002), 3–9, at 3.

13. See Christopher Peterson, *A Primer in Positive Psychology* (New York: Oxford University Press, 2006), 4.

14. Lyubomirsky, *The How of Happiness*, 240–41.

15. R. A. Baer, "Self-Focused Attention and Mechanisms of Change in Mindfulness-Based Treatment," *Cognitive Behaviour Therapy, 38*(S1) (2009): 15–20.

16. See Fred Bryant and Joseph Veroff, *Savoring: A New Model of Positive Experience* (Mahway, NJ: Erlbaum, 2006).

17. See Tarli Young, "Additional Mechanisms of Mindfulness: How Does Mindfulness Increase Well-Being?" in Ivtzan and Lomas, eds., *Mindfulness in Positive Psychology*, 156–172.

18. Mihaly Csikszentmihalyi, *Flow: The Psychology of Optimal Experience* (New York: Harper Perennial, 1990), 39.

19. Mihaly Csikszentmihalyi, *Creativity: Flow and the Psychology of Discovery and Invention* (New York: HarperCollins Publishers, 1996), 112.

20. Sue Jackson fails to emphasize this point in "Flowing with Mindfulness: Investigating the Relationship Between Flow and Mindfulness," in Ivtzan and Lomas, eds., *Mindfulness in Positive Psychology: The Science of Meditation and Wellbeing*, 141–155.

21. Csikszentmihalyi, *Flow*, 70.

22. Barbara L. Fredrickson, *Love 2.0: Creating Happiness and Health in Moments of Connection* (New York: Plume, 2014).

23. John M. Gottman, with Nam Silver, *The Seven Principles for Making Marriage Work* (New York: Three Rivers Press, 1999), 48.

24. Netta Weinstein, Kirk W. Brown, and Richard M. Ryan, "A Multi-Method Examination of the Effects of Mindfulness on Stress Attribution, Coping, and Emotional Well-Being," *Journal of Research in Personality, 43*, (2009): 374–385, at 374.

25. An insightful general critique of this blurring in contemporary psychology and other sciences is developed by James Davison Hunter and Paul Nedelisky in *Science and the Good:*

The Tragic Quest for the Foundations of Morality (New Haven, CT: Yale University Press, 2018).

26. Jonathan Haidt, *The Happiness Hypothesis: Finding Modern Truth in Ancient Wisdom* (New York: Basic Books, 2006), 158 and 170.

27. See Mike W. Martin, "Happiness and Virtue in Positive Psychology," *Journal for the Theory of Social Behaviour, 37* no. 1 (2007): 89–103.

28. Nelson W. Aldrich, Jr., *Old Money* (New York: Alfred A. Knopf, 1988), 67.

29. Henry Fairlie, *The Seven Deadly Sins Today* (Notre Dame, IN: University of Notre Dame Press, 1979), 67–68.

30. Philip C. Watkins, "Gratitude and Subjective Well-Being," in Robert A. Emmons and Michael E. McCullough, eds., *The Psychology of Gratitude* (New York: Oxford University Press, 2004), 167–192.

31. Christopher Peterson and Martin E. P. Seligman, eds., *Character Strengths and Virtues: A Handbook and Classification* (Washington, DC: American Psychological Association, and New York: Oxford University Press, 2004).

32. Ryan M. Niemiec and Judith Lissing, "Mindfulness-Based Strengths Practice (MBSP) for Enhancing Well-Being, Managing Problems, and Boosting Positive Relationships," in Ivtzn and Lomas, eds., *Mindfulness in Positive Psychology*, 15–36.

33. Niemiec and Lissing, "Mindfulness-Based Strengths Practice (MBSP) for Enhancing Well-Being, Managing Problems, and Boosting Positive Relationships," 15.

34. See Martin E. P. Seligman, *Learned Optimism* (New York: Alfred A. Knopf, 1991).

35. "Ac-Cent-Tchu-Ate the Positive," lyrics by Johnny Mercer, music by Harold Arlen (1944).

36. Christelle T. Ngnoumen and Ellen J. Langer, "Mindfulness: The Essence of Well-Being and Happiness," in Ivtzan and Lomas, eds., *Mindfulness in Positive Psychology* 97–107, at 99.

37. Barbara Fredrickson, *Positivity* (New York: Crown Publishers, 2009), 166.

38. James, *The Varieties of Religious Experience*, 86.

39. James, *The Varieties of Religious Experience*, 94.

40. James, *The Varieties of Religious Experience*, 160.

41. Robert Nozick, *The Examined Life: Philosophical Meditations* (New York: Simon and Schuster, 1989), 119.

42. Nozick, *The Examined Life*, 121.

43. Nozick, *The Examined Life*, 122.

44. More exactly, there are multiple paradoxes of happiness. See Mike W. Martin, "Paradoxes of Happiness," *Journal of Happiness Studies, 9*, no. 2 (2008): 171–184. Reprinted in Antonella Delle Fave, ed., *The Exploration of Happiness: Present Perspectives* (New York: Springer, 2013), 31–46.

45. John Stuart Mill, *Autobiography* (New York: Penguin, 1989), 117.

46. John Stuart Mill, *Utilitarianism* (Indianapolis, IN: Hackett Publishing, 1979), 16.

47. Gretchen Rubin, *The Happiness Project* (New York: HarperCollins, 2009), 2.

48. Rubin, *The Happiness Project*, 215, 282–85.

49. See Mike W. Martin, *Memoir Ethics: Good Lives and the Virtues* (Lanham, MD: Lexington Books, 2016), 102–104.

50. Rubin, *The Happiness Project*, 285.

51. Mill, *Autobiography*, 112.

52. See Mary Midgley, *Beast and Man: The Roots of Human Nature*, revised ed. (New York: Routledge, 1995), 331.

53. See Owen Flanagan, *Varieties of Moral Personality: Ethics and Psychological Realism* (Cambridge, MA: Harvard University Press, 1991), 315–332.

54. R. Biswas-Diener, T. B. Kashdan, and G. Minhas, "A Dynamic Approach to Psychological Strength Development and Intervention," *Journal of Positive Psychology, 6* (2011): 106–118.

Chapter Ten

Mindful Work in Balanced Lives

To work mindfully is to pay attention to what matters concerning work (value-based mindfulness), where the values are those of an individual (personal-mindfulness) or sound values (virtue-mindfulness). The values include work responsibilities, ideals of craftsmanship and professionalism, organizational standards, and personal career commitments, all of which contribute to meaning and fulfillment. They also include the values defining balanced lives. Virtue-mindfulness has always been essential to good work—work that is excellent and morally valuable. Its importance has increased given the increasing demands of contemporary work.[1] Psychologists who discuss mindful work typically intend value-suspending mindfulness, at least officially. But I argue that they presuppose moral values and camouflage them under expansive concepts of mental health. I begin with a case study of virtue-mindfulness.

WORKING MINDFULLY

Warren Buffett is one of my heroes.[2] Students chuckle when I mention that in classes on business and professional ethics, no doubt enjoying the incongruity of a modestly paid and somewhat shabbily dressed philosopher admiring one of the world's richest people. I suggest to them that Buffett cares about wealth for admirable reasons and uses it for desirable purposes. Even as a child during the 1930s depression, he was preoccupied with making money. He held a variety of jobs, most successfully delivering newspapers. He saved what he earned and bought a farm while still in high school. By then he earned more than his teachers, and he saw no need to attend college. But encouraged by his father, he earned a bachelor's and a master's degree in business that prepared him to undertake investment partnerships. He remained a lifelong learner and teacher. In his early years he taught a few classes and later gave regular talks to college students. He also educated investors through newsletters and media appearances. In doing so he mixes homespun stories with lucid explanations and epigrams: "Be fearful when others are greedy, and be greedy when others are fearful";[3] and "Bear in mind—this is a critical fact often ignored—that investors as a whole cannot get anything out of their businesses except what the businesses earn."[4]

Buffett was asked at a dinner party to name the primary factor leading to his success. He immediately replied *focus*. (So did his friend Bill Gates, who attended the same dinner.) By focus he meant "the intensity that is the price of excellence. . . . It meant single-minded obsession with an ideal."[5] The skill and commitment to focus on what matters in his work developed with education and experience. After achieving financial security in his twenties, he continued to concentrate on growing his wealth, benefiting himself but also his family, investors who trusted him with their money, employees of organizations he owns, and wider communities to which he contributes. Eventually he oriented his career around the entrepreneurial ideal of creating an organization, Berkshire Hathaway. Doing so enabled him to express his interests, derive meaning and happiness from his work, and work with people he respected—something particularly important to him. It also enabled him to promote the public good.

Buffett has no interest in psychologists' discussions of mindfulness-based meditation. His studies in psychology extend little beyond what he learned in Dale Carnegie courses on public speaking and leadership. Of course he engages in meditation in the colloquial sense of contemplating and reflecting on his work. He enjoys studying corporate financial statements and deliberating about how to buy stocks (very) low and sell (very) high. Initially he purchased stock in companies that generated outsized returns on modest investments. Later, influenced by his colleague Charlie Munger, he purchased high-quality companies at reasonable prices. He and Munger decide how best to macro-allocate resources and choose managers for the companies owned by Berkshire Hathaway, and then they delegate authority to the managers to run the businesses.[6] Within wide limits they forgive mistakes made by the managers, but they do not tolerate damage to the company's reputation.

Such details about Buffett's business practices may seem a digression, or at most a preface to discussing mindful work. They are not. They are integral to understanding what virtue-mindfulness is, in his line of work. So are additional details about Buffett's values, temperament, and character. Mindful work includes ethics and integrity, as much as business acumen and competitiveness in profit-making within the bounds of law. It also enters into decisions about whether to stay with a particular job or to change jobs. And it requires focus, passion, and commitment. Buffett tried retiring twice, knowing he had vastly more wealth than he needed. He quickly grew bored and returned to work with renewed enthusiasm. Well into his eighties, he jokes about continuing to work for several years after he dies.

Mindful work also pertains to decisions about what to do with money earned. Buffett has pledged the vast majority of his wealth to philanthropy, illustrating how mindfulness about work and wealth extends to helping others. Rather than leaving all his wealth to his children, which he feared would undermine their initiative and responsibility, he decided to give his children enough money to do whatever they want to do, but not so much that they can do nothing. He also encourages his children to be philanthropists, and established foundations for each of them to run in serving to their favorite causes. Because he feels less qualified in philanthropy than finances, he deeded the bulk of his fortune to the Bill and Melinda Gates Foundation, which he considers an exceptionally effective and well-run organization. In addition, he and Bill Gates developed the Giving Pledge, signed by nearly two hundred of the world's billionaires, to donate at least half of their wealth to philanthropic causes.[7]

As Buffett illustrates, mindfulness in work is not a stand-alone value. It needs to be understood in light of a host of additional values that define excellent, ethical, and meaningful work in specific contexts. Which values, and whose values? Organizations typically answer that it is the values of the organization, which workers are expected to embrace and promote. These goals are connected to the specific products and services organizations provide, as well as to the basic function of the organization: to promote profit for shareholders, to serve a wider range of stakeholders including customers and local communities, or to promote social goods as in the case of not-for-profit organizations. In addition, many organizations employ professionals who are bound by the codes of ethics of their professional societies. Enlightened organizations also acknowledge a role for workers' personal ideals that contribute to meaning and monetary gain.[8] "Mindful managers" and "enlightened capitalists," as James O'Toole writes, try to respect all stakeholders in their companies, including "customers, employees, shareholders, suppliers, host communities, the broader society, and the natural environment."[9]

In sum, mindful work, understood as virtue-mindfulness concerning work, is paying attention to what matters concerning work, in light of personal and sound values. Paying attention combines focus and alertness, perspective from connecting the present to the past and future, and skill and creativity that advances excellence in work. Understood in this manner, mindfulness at work is not a newly minted psychological technique centered on value-suspending meditation. It is an enduring and essential aspect of good work in good lives.

BALANCED LIVES

Balance is a recurring theme in discussions of mindful work. It is also a complicated topic that bears on many different values in good lives. In a *descriptive* sense, balance refers to the actual configuration of activities, relationships, aspirations, time-allocations, and other elements in a person's life. In a *normative* sense, balance refers to configurations that are reasonable and desirable in terms of sound values in good lives.[10] The descriptive sense is relevant to mindfulness, in that we need to become mindful of actual configurations as a first step in moving toward more desirable configurations. The normative sense is primary, however. Psychologists who discuss mindful work highlight the values of mental health. Yet moral values are frequently concealed in their concepts of mental health, including values such as love, fairness, authenticity, happiness, a sense of meaning, and self-fulfillment.

Balance is discussed in a variety of work-related contexts, but three examples suffice to indicate its complexity, and also to illustrate different concepts of mindfulness used in discussing it: work-family, money and other goods, and the use of personal digital technologies. *Work-family balance*, to begin with, is integrating work commitments with family responsibilities in desirable ways. Critics fault Buffett on this score. They contend that he was excessively preoccupied with work at the expense of his family. His children report being raised primarily by his wife, Susan. In addition his marriage was damaged by his excessive focus on work. After their children were grown, Susan moved to San Francisco, where she pursued a love relationship with her tennis coach, and also became a philanthropist and activist in confronting the AIDS epidemic. She remained married to Buffett, however, and joined him on important occasions such as annual shareholder meetings for Berkshire Hathaway. Buffett admits that the damage to his marriage was the biggest regret of his life.[11]

It is easy to identify imbalance once overall bad consequences are caused by work patterns, as with the damage to Buffett's marriage. Identifying imbalances before then is more difficult. Desirable ways of balancing work and leisure cannot be specified in advance and in the abstract, for all families at all times. Normative, mindful balance requires ongoing good judgment in integrating the important things in our personal and professional lives. It also requires mutually respectful discussions and fair negotiations among family members affected. Another complication is that balance among commitments and configurations can be viewed at a given time or instead over a lifetime, and the two viewpoints might yield different conclusions. *Diachronic balance* concerns allocations of time and commitments over a long period of time, perhaps a lifetime. *Synchronic balance* concerns allocations of time and commitment at a given stage or state of our lives, such as the present (flexibly defined). At a given moment we might be lopsided in one direction or another, but in ways that make good sense over a lifetime. Thus, we might devote most attention to our education during college years, more time to work during subsequent years, and little or no work during retirement.

Money-balance is the pursuit and use of money in mindful ways. These ways are generally understood in terms of moderation, but moderation cannot be specified in absolute quantities of money. Moderation concerns reasonable allocations of time and effort, in light of individual interests and talents, and other relevant values. For someone like Buffett, moderation in pursuing wealth implies obeying the law and not unfairly exploiting people, but it does not entail abandoning the search for great wealth at some arbitrary number of dollars. The sensible pursuit and use of money is a reasonable goal for everyone, and in that pursuit we should exercise good judgment. Yet the extent of financial ambition is a highly personal matter.

Self-help books on mindful work attempt to be more specific about balance and moderation, but they generally leave large areas of vagueness. Typically they invoke values of spiritual aspirations as well as financial and personal needs. A good example is Jonathan K. DeYoe's *Mindful Money*. DeYoe is a certified private wealth advisor who also pursued graduate studies in Buddhism. Although he does not define mindfulness, he slides between personal-mindfulness and virtue-mindfulness. Minimally, virtue-mindfulness implies honesty. It includes acknowledging and accepting important truths and values concerning work, bearing them in mind and acting on them in situations where they are relevant. In places he invokes a Buddhist-inspired concept of virtue-mindfulness. According to it, moderation in pursuing wealth requires overcoming material "attachments," in the pejorative sense of excessive emotional obsessions with money. DeYoe dilutes this injunction into an acceptance of life in a system of capitalism: "Mindfulness asks us to be keenly aware of where we are right now, and where we are is always Here and nowhere else. . . . In fact, accepting things as they truly are, rather than the illusion of how we wish them to be, is considered the very key to what Buddhists call enlightenment."[12]

Most of DeYoe's book deals with good judgment in earning, saving, investing, and spending. Thus, he debunks illusory get-rich-quick schemes. He draws on psychological studies suggesting that personal relationships, a sense of meaning, and virtues like generosity and gratitude contribute more to happiness than great wealth. Only a third of his book contains specific investment advice. The advice is sensible enough: pay off high-interest debt, begin saving 10–15 percent of your income as early as possible, invest in a diversity portfolio in tax-deferred retirement plans and later in additional taxable investments, adopt a long-term horizon and be patient, and infuse the present with a long-term plan to build wealth. The key point is that mindfulness about money is based on values, directly or indirectly. Those values combine purely economic aims with moral and spiritual aspirations.

Tech-balance is balancing time and involvement in using personal digital devices—such as cell phones, digital games, Facebook, and email.[13] Frequently tech-balance is approached in terms of addiction: Does the excessive use of personal digital technologies amount to a mindless behavioral addiction, akin to compulsive gambling? Adam Alter contends it does. Most individuals need to "be more mindful about how they are allowing tech to invade their life. Next they should cordon it off. I like the idea, for instance, of not answering email after six at night."[14] In opposition, Rohan Gunatillake contends that contemporary life requires almost constant connectedness. In *Modern Mindfulness*, he recommends more personalized apps that facilitate shorter and more convenient times for meditation (which is how he thinks of mindfulness), and he has designed and markets mindfulness apps such as "the buddhify app," designed to facilitate a "mobile style mindfulness."[15]

David M. Levy proposes an appealing middle ground in *Mindful Tech: How to Bring Balance to Our Digital Lives*. Levy, who is a computer scientist teaching in the Information School at the University of Washington, shifts the focus away from addiction, leaving that topic to psychiatrists, although he has no doubts that "some people become dependent on their digital devices or apps in ways that are deeply dysfunctional."[16] They need "honest [self-] observation, a commitment to make changes in the service of greater health, and caring support of others around us."[17] The central issue is balance, which he defines as the reasonable allocation of time and energy between the "Fast World" of digital technologies and the "Slow World" of activities, relationships, and other areas that are more "contemplative"—his word for *mindful*.

At one point Levy formulates a concept of personal-mindfulness, quoting words from one of his student's essays: "What mindfulness really is to me is the ability to direct your attention where you want it to go—to have a choice. . . . When we are mindful we choose to pay attention to what is explicitly important to us; being mindful begins to reveal our values in a way wandering lost through the digital landscape can never do."[18] This personal-mindfulness requires integrating two forms of attention: self-awareness of our feelings and thoughts and "task attention" that is oriented outward to our activities in using digital technologies.[19] Moments of self-awareness, for example, serve to alert us to how our minds are wandering but also how we are engaged obsessively in ways that undermine a balanced life. Levy develops an extensive set of activities and practices designed to improve mindful application of digital skills. Although value-suspending meditation is involved in some of the exercises he develops, it is not his primary emphasis. Instead, most of the exercises involve observing, recording, reflecting on, and discussing with others how we are using specific devices. Then, in light of what we discover, we develop personal guidelines for improving our use of the devices.

Although ultimately Levy leaves the task of developing tech-use guidelines to each of us, he invokes two overarching values that make a claim on us: mental health and the effective use of the technologies. Under the rubric of mental health he tacitly conceals moral values. He also shifts from personal-mindfulness to virtue-mindfulness. Thus, he seeks to improve the "quality of life in the digital age" by "using our attention wisely" as we interact with digital technologies.[20] He speaks of "digital craft" and the skill used to perform that craft, where skill includes matters of health, well-being, and moral decency. Texting while driving, for example, is not merely a personal choice based on personal-mindfulness. It is dangerous to others and to ourselves; it is morally wrong, except perhaps in emergencies; and it "ought to be banned or at least severely limited."[21] Levy also discusses more nuanced examples of being disrespectful of others by using laptops for recreational purposes during business meetings and college classes.

As these examples illustrate, writers on balance tend to shift between personal-mindfulness and virtue-mindfulness, and sometimes allude to the value-suspending mindfulness found in therapeutic meditation. Similar shifts and blends enter into discussions of meditation as an organizational resource.

MEDITATION AS AN ORGANIZATIONAL TOOL

Meditation has become a familiar resource for organizations, including for-profit and nonprofit corporations. It is used to improve mental health through stress management and to enhance work performance. Thus, its rationale combines workers' well-being with advancing organizational needs. I begin with an example where value-suspending mindfulness during meditation is blended with Buddhist-inspired concept of value-based mindfulness.

Phil Jackson used meditation early in his basketball career.[22] He discovered that practicing Zen meditation calmed his hyperactive personality and made him more focused during games. In his eyes, meditation also contributed to his personal growth as he rebelled against the pressures of organized religion, after being raised by parents who were both ministers. Later he taught meditation to the NBA teams he coached. In doing so he pioneered meditation as a coaching tool for his players, who included Michael Jordan of the Chicago Bulls, and Shaquille O'Neal and Kobe Bryant of the Los Angeles Lakers.

Jackson teaches his players breathing-anchored meditation: sit up; focus on your breathing, as you slow and steady it; let thoughts drift by, observing them without evaluation or reaction; return to focusing on your breathing. This value-suspending mindfulness during meditation advanced several organizational goals: alleviating stress, improving attention on the court, contributing to bonding as team members rather than independent stars, and in all these ways helping to win games and championships. Jackson adopts "The ring" as a team motto. It combines the symbolism of NBA championship rings that signify status and achievement with the psychological symbolism of the self as caring about other team members. As he explains, "Obviously, we're not talking romantic love here or even brotherly love in the traditional Christian sense. The best analogy I can think of is the intense emotional connection that warriors experience in the heat of battle."[23]

Although he officially emphasizes value-suspending mindfulness during meditation, Jackson comfortably slides to value-based mindfulness. He advocates spiritual values of compassion and caring. He also frames athletic competition as a journey, rather than a mere means to winning. In doing so he borrows from Buddhist thinkers who fuse being in the moment with remembering what is important: "'Mindfulness is remembering to come back to the present moment,' writes Zen teacher Thich Nhat Hanh."[24] Remarkably, Jackson rewrites Buddhism's Noble Eightfold Path in basketball terms. His entry for the "right mindfulness" step is "coming to every game with a clear understanding of our plan of attack, including what to expect from our opponent," along with "playing with precision, making the right moves at the right times, and maintaining constant awareness throughout the game, whether you're on the floor or on the bench."[25]

Jackson's approach to mindfulness and meditation is intuitive and anecdotal. In contrast, some organizational psychologists conduct more systematic studies of how value-suspending mindfulness contributes to good work. In doing so they integrate goals such as stress relief, improved concentration, and workers' desires for increasing enjoyment and a sense of meaning. For example, Michael F. Steger and Eve Ekman define mindfulness as "a type of cultivated awareness that emerges through deliberately paying attention to experiences as they occur in the present moment, in real-time, while understanding their temporary nature."[26] According to their studies, mindfulness-based meditation reduces stress in workers in several ways. It circumvents the negative appraisals that foster stress, both self-appraisals and employers' appraisal of our job performance.[27] It helps individuals discern more clearly and immediately when signs of stress arise, including physiological signs of muscle tension and incipient headaches. And it lessens the frustration and feelings of helplessness in demanding work that lead to withdrawal of empathy. Overall, "Mindfulness practices have been found to reduce stress, depression, and anxiety, and to increase activation in brain regions responsible for regulating attention and positive affective states, including empathy and pro-social emotions."[28] These results have particular importance for care providers, for example in health care, and for teachers. Their work can generate high levels of stress and burnout, whether owing to long hours, modest pay, administrative pressure, or the challenges of helping people in desperate need.

Steger and Ekman allude to moral values indirectly, concealing them under "pro-social emotions." Yet meditation easily becomes a tool serving narrow organizational goals, blinkered from broader moral concerns about the role of organizations in society. An illustration is meditating in a pleasant garden setting at a biological weapons factory might induce a sense of personal well-being about producing a harmful product. Yet there are many more everyday instances where meditation masks moral problems and functions more like a band aid than a cure.

David Gelles, a business writer for the *New York Times*, is attuned to such concerns, but nevertheless celebrates the mindfulness movement at the workplace. In *Mindful Work*, he rotates among personal-mindfulness, virtue-mindfulness, and value-suspending mindfulness. But an early passage indicates a value emphasis: "Mindfulness is about being fully present. It is about attending to the here and now, without being lost in thoughts about the past, or fantasies about the future. It is a quality of being that embodies kindness, curiosity, and acceptance."[29] Gelles explores mindful meditation as a tool in coping with stress and increasing happiness, but also in improving organizations. He expresses optimism that meditation can change organizations by making them more humane, paving the way for a kinder and gentler version of capitalism.

As one of many case studies, he depicts Janice Marturano, initially General Mill's deputy general counsel and subsequently a high level executive in highly intense mergers and acquisitions. After one event left her exhausted, she followed a friend's advice and attended a six-day retreat conducted by Jon Kabat-Zinn. She returned with a resolve to practice meditation, and after several months found her resilience had returned and she could better cope with work-related stress. Noticing the change, her colleagues encouraged her to teach meditation techniques to other corporate leaders, which led to corporate-sponsored retreats for General Mills executives and over a thousand additional employees. Gelles reports that the program has improved, perhaps transformed, the corporate culture at General Mills. He does not supply hard data about increased productivity or reduced medical bills for stress-related illness. Instead his support comes in the form of inspiring anecdotes and informal surveys. For example, when layoffs came along at General Mills as part of its normal business cycle, coworkers were more empathetic and supportive of one another.

Although Gelles tries to balance optimism with caution, ultimately he veers toward idealism about mindfulness-based meditation. He hopes that the widespread use of meditation will transform capitalism: "Workplaces can become more humane, products can become more sustainable, consumers can make better choices. And slowly, mindfulness can start to change the culture, and capitalism, one dollar at a time."[30] I am less sanguine than Gelles. Mindful meditation improves some corporate cultures, but I suspect it is most effective in corporations that already have a humane culture and are devoted to community goods, as are many not-for-profit corporations. As an economic system, however, capitalism aims at generating profits, and it is driven by competition and by what Joseph Schumpeter famously called "the perennial gale of creative destruction."[31] Most for-profit companies that experiment with mindfulness programs will demand payoffs in terms of company profits. They will also tailor even their understanding of mindfulness to corporate needs, which of course include keeping workers happy in promoting corporate goals, as well as good publicity.

Gelles replies to concerns about corporate co-opting of mindfulness by abruptly shifting to an honorific concept of virtue-mindfulness. He acknowledges that mindful work within a capitalist system tends to degenerate into base forms used for undesirable purposes. But he insists that such uses are not *true* mindful meditation. True mindfulness aims at insight and tends to produce kindness and compassion.[32] Indeed, at one point he even criticizes Kabat-Zinn's mindfulness-based stress reduction (MBSR): "By my lights, MBSR isn't perfect. It's a bit too focused on individual outcomes and doesn't do enough to encourage students to be kind or address issues like their environmental impact on the world."[33] Gelles's shifts between value-suspending mindfulness and virtue-mindfulness indicate a lack of clarity about the role of values in understanding mindful work. I conclude with one more illustration of this unclarity, this time returning us to the verbal bête noire, "nonjudgmental."

A NONJUDGMENTAL REPRISE

In discussing mindful work, as elsewhere, psychologists blur different senses of *nonjudgmental*: not judgmental in the pejorative sense of "judgmental" (by avoiding unduly negative and excessively blame-oriented), not negative (by suspending all negative value judgments), not judging (by suspending all value judgments), and accepting or affirming (by making positive value judgments). Blurring these meanings leads to blurring value-based and value-suspending mindfulness. It eclipses the centrality of values in mindfulness, and then smuggles them in the back door.

Consider Oberdan Marianetti and Jonathan Passmore's essay on mindful work prominently published in the *Oxford Handbook of Positive Psychology and Work*. They specify that mindfulness involves three elements: nonjudgmental attention, inclusive experience, and authentic experience. *Nonjudgmental attention*, they specify, means *not judging*: observing our thoughts, feelings, and situation "without an intention to change them, approve or disapprove of them, like or dislike them."[34] The other two elements, however, veer toward values. Thus, *inclusive experience* means we are aware of the full range of what is happening in our present experience, which presumably includes the value dimensions of that experience. *Authentic experience* means a combination of truthfulness (honesty) and truth (accurate discernment) in recognizing what we are experiencing. The values might specify what is important in our work, perhaps in terms of its excellence and ethics. They might allude to the meaning of work in terms of everything from the skills and relationships it involves to the salary and wealth it produces. In this way, authenticity and inclusiveness are in tension with, even at odds with the first element, nonjudgmental attention.

In one passage, however, the authors shift to a definition of mindfulness as nonjudgmental attention, *tout court*. They contend that, so defined, mindfulness fosters authenticity and inclusiveness (now regarded as effects rather than as part of the definition of mindfulness): "Mindfulness, the purposeful, non-judgemental focus on the present . . . fosters a more inclusive and authentic vision of 'reality.'"[35] It is unclear how this fostering occurs. I suspect the authors simply assume that mindful individuals are already committed to at least some sound values.

Value assumptions remain in the background throughout their essay. Here are three examples. First, adapting a case study from Kabat-Zinn, they describe a manager of a large manufacturing firm who goes to a stress clinic to help him deal with work-related stress that is causing dizzy spells and a sense that his life is out of control. He takes an eight-week program of MBSR, in which he practices meditation based on value-suspending mindfulness. The program reduces his obsession with controlling all aspects of work, and helps him accept his emotions without being overrun by anxiety. He returns to work better able to monitor his stress levels, relax before stress overwhelms him, delegate problems, and communicate more calmly and clearly. In discussing the example, the authors make no mention of Kabat-Zinn's emphasis on having a "vision" of why the meditation is being practiced—that is, the values that guide the meditative practice.

Second, the authors describe cabinetmakers, pressured by deadlines, who fail to notice their chisel has been blunted, thereby causing their work to both slow and to lessen quality of the work. They aver that the cabinetmakers would have spotted the problem if they had used greater mindfulness. Agreed—*if* we use a concept of value-based mindfulness, as paying attention to what matters in light of relevant values about quality work in their situation. In discussing the example, the authors apparently shift from value-suspending mindfulness (during meditation) to value-based mindfulness (involved in craftsmanship). They also reference Ellen Langer's concept of flexibility-mindfulness: "the continuous creation of new categories; openness to new information; and an implicit awareness of more than one perspective."[36] As argued in chapter 7, Langer repeatedly assumes value judgments in discussing newness, creativity, and mental health.

Third, the authors suggest that mindfulness contributes to flow experiences, or that flow experiences just are instances of mindfulness. In flow we become immersed in our present activities, concentrating not on ourselves but instead on exercising skill in response to challenges in the situation, with clear goals and immediate feedback. Meaning-giving values are essential, as Mihaly Csikszentmihalyi underscores: "The task at hand draws one in with its complexity to such an extent that one becomes completely involved in it. There is no distinction between thought and action, between self and environment. The important thing is to execute each move as well as possible, because lives may depend on it."[37] Csikszentmihalyi's says flow presupposes that we experience work as in tune with our attitudes and values, but it also requires adjusting our attitudes to the work we undertake, and to its normative requirements. This emphasis on values is lost in Marianetti and Passmore's emphasis on value-suspending mindfulness, or concealed by terms like "inclusive" and "authentic."

In short, Marianetti and Passmore illustrate how psychologists officially define mindfulness as value-suspending awareness, then invoke unacknowledged values. We do better to begin with a value-based conception of mindful work. Doing so immediately raises questions about which values are at stake. Are the values the de facto values of a specified organization or person? Or are the values presented as sound—as not being immoral, irrational, and unhealthy? If the latter, is the implicit concept of virtue-mindfulness secular, Buddhist, or some other religious concept?[38] In any case, the crux of mindful work is rarely value-suspending mindfulness, but instead value-based mindfulness. Mindful work centers on how work connects work to personal ideals, professional ideals and norms, organizational ideals, patterns of consumption and leisure, philanthropy, the uses of digital technology, and additional issues about the uses of income and wealth.

NOTES

1. For example, recall the discussion in chapter 4 of Ronald Epstein, *Attending: Medicine, Mindfulness, and Humanity* (New York: Scribner, 2017).

2. The following portrait is drawn from Alice Schroeder, *The Snowball: Warren Buffett and the Business of Life*, updated version (New York: Bantam Books, 2009); and Roger Lowenstein, *Buffett: The Making of an American Capitalist* (New York: Random House, 2008).

3. Warren Buffett, "Buy American. I Am," *New York Times* (October 16, 2008). http://www.nytimes.com/2008/10/17/opinion/17buffett.html.

4. Warren Buffett, "Mr. Buffett on the Stock Market" (a Buffett speech converted into an article by Carol Loomis), in Carol Loomis, ed., *Tap Dancing to Work: Warren Buffett on Practically Everything, 1966–2012* (New York: Portfolio/Penguin, 2012), 166–75, at 172.

5. Schroeder, *The Snowball*, 523.

6. Carol Loomis, "The Inside Story of Warren Buffett," in Carol Loomis, ed., *Tap Dancing to Work: Warren Buffett on Practically Everything, 1966–2012*, 62–75, at 72.

7. See David Callahan, *The Givers: Wealth, Power, and Philanthropy in a New Gilded Age* (New York: Alfred A. Knopf, 2017), 19–28.

8. See Mike W. Martin, *Meaningful Work: Rethinking Professional Ethics* (New York: Oxford University Press, 2000).

9. James O'Toole, *Enlightened Capitalists: Cautionary Tales of Business Pioneers Who Tried to Do Well by Doing Good* (New York: HarperCollins, 2019), xx, xxi.

10. See Mike W. Martin, "Balancing Work and Leisure," in *The Value of Time and Leisure in a World of Work*, ed. Mitchell R. Haney and A. David Kline (Lanham, MD: Lexington Books, 2010), 7–24.

11. Schroeder, *The Snowball*, 388.

12. Jonathan K. DeYoe, *Mindful Money: Simple Practices for Reaching Your Financial Goals and Increasing Your Happiness Dividend* (Novato, CA: New World Library, 2017), 25.

13. For a fuller discussion, see Mike W. Martin, "Mindful Technology," in Emanuele Ratti and Thomas A. Stapleford, eds., *Science, Technology and the Good Life: Perspectives on Virtue in Modern Science and Technology*, Oxford University Press, forthcoming.

14. Adam Alter, quoted by Claudia Dreifus, "Why We Can't Look Away from Screens," *New York Times* (March 7, 2017), D7. See also Adam Alter, *Irresistible: The Rise of Addictive Technology and the Business of Keeping Us Hooked* (New York: Penguin Press, 2017).

15. Rohan Gunatillake, *Modern Mindfulness: How to Be More Relaxed, Focused, and Kind While Living in a Fast, Digital, Always-On World* (New York: St. Martin's Griffin, 2017), especially, 1–27.

16. Levy, *Mindful Tech*, 198.

17. Levy, *Mindful Tech*, 199.

18. Quoting a former student, David M. Levy, *Mindful Tech: How to Bring Balance to Our Digital Lives* (New Haven, CT: Yale University Press, 2016), 26–26.

19. See, for example, Levy, *Mindful Tech*, 4, 28, 40.

20. Levy, *Mindful Tech*, 3, 167.

21. Levy, *Mindful Tech*, 178.

22. Phil Jackson and Hugh Delehanty, *Eleven Rings: The Soul of Success* (New York: Penguin Books, 2014).

23. Jackson and Delehanty, *Eleven Rings*, 3–4.

24. Jackson and Delehanty, *Eleven Rings*, 137.

25. Jackson and Delehanty, *Eleven Rings*, 220–221.

26. Michael F. Steger and Eve Ekman, "Working It: Making Meaning with Workplace Mindfulness," in Itai Ivtzan and Tim Lomas, eds., *Mindfulness in Positive Psychology: The Science of Meditation and Well-Being* (New York: Routledge, 2016), 228–242, at 234.

27. Steger and Ekman, "Working It: Making Meaning with Workplace Mindfulness," 236.

28. Steger and Ekman, "Working It: Making Meaning with Workplace Mindfulness," 234–235.

29. David Gelles, *Mindful Work: How Meditation Is Changing Business from the Inside Out* (Boston, MA: Houghton Mifflin Harcourt, 2016), 23. See also 4, 27, 57.

30. Gelles, *Mindful Work*, 252–253.

31. Joseph A. Schumpeter, *Capitalism, Socialism, and Democracy* (New York: Harper and Bros., 1947), 84, 87.

32. Gelles, *Mindful Work*, 218–227.

33. Gelles, *Mindful Work*, 81.

34. Oberdan Marianetti and Jonathan Passmore, "Mindfulness at Work: Paying Attention to Enhance Well-Being and Performance," in *Oxford Handbook of Positive Psychology and Work*, ed. P. Alex Linley, Susan Harrington, and Nicola Garcea (New York: Oxford University Press, 2010), 189–200, at 196.

35. Marianetti and Passmore, "Mindfulness at Work: Paying Attention to Enhance Well-Being and Performance," at 189.

36. Ellen J. Langer, *The Power of Mindful Learning*, 2nd ed. (Boston, MA: Da Capo Press, 2016), 4; see also 49–63.

37. Mihaly Csikszentmihalyi, *Good Business: Leadership, Flow, and the Making of Meaning* (New York: Viking, 2003), 40.

38. See *Mindfulness in the Marketplace: Compassionate Responses to Consumerism*, ed. Allan Hunt Badiner (Berkeley, CA: Parallax Press, 2002.

Chapter Eleven

Authenticity and *Seize the Day*

"The past is no good to us. The future is full of anxiety. Only the present is real—the here-and-now. Seize the day" (62).[1] This advice bewitches Tommy Wilhelm, the protagonist in *Seize the Day*, Saul Bellow's comic, compassionate, and cautionary novella about mindfulness and authenticity in good lives. Wilhelm hopes the advice will provide a quick fix to his financial and family problems, and free him from his agonizing regrets and fears. More than that, he hopes it will reveal his authentic self—if only he can figure out what that means. The novel sets in opposition four value perspectives on authentic selves and good lives, and thereby on what ultimately matters in living mindfully in the moment. Wilhelm's perspective is largely hedonistic, although he is capable of humanitarian feelings and for the first time is seeking a deeper self-understanding. His father, Dr. Adler (a physician), holds a conventional perspective centered on family and financial responsibilities, an outlook largely shared by Wilhelm's estranged wife, Margaret. Dr. Tamkin (a self-proclaimed psychologist), who offers Wilhelm the seize-the-day advice, understands the authentic self as a blend of instinct and selfless love. And the novel's narrator, partly reflecting Bellow's personal views, intimates that the authentic self is a unity of responsibility, self-development, and self-expression in a good life.

WILHELM'S WORRIES

Seize the Day takes place during a single day, with extensive references to Wilhelm's past mistakes. All events occur in and around Hotel Gloriana, where most of the characters reside. Dr. Tamkin has lived in the hotel for a year. Dr. Adler is a permanent resident living in retirement. Wilhelm is a temporary resident who has come to ask Adler for money, with the additional hope of receiving emotional support. Although Margaret is not a resident of the hotel, she connects to it via phone calls with Wilhelm.

Wilhelm's immediate crisis centers on finances and family. Nearly bankrupt, he recently entrusted his last $700 to Dr. Tamkin, whom he rightly suspects of investing it unwisely. Several months earlier, in a fit of spite, Wilhelm quit his ten-year job selling children's furniture because he thought he deserved the promotion his boss gave to a relative. At age forty-four, he fears his lack of a college degree will hamper his search for a new job, although he has yet to make an effort to find a job. In his youth he had dropped out of college after two years hoping to become an actor, and to escape what he viewed as the constricted lives of most ordinary people. Despite failing a screen test he moved to Hollywood where he wasted eight years working as an extra in films, when he worked at all. He now seeks a divorce from Margaret but he desperately wants to visit their two sons who live with her. She refuses both the divorce and the visitation until he sends more money for child support. At the moment he cannot pay his hotel bill, let alone provide additional child support.

Wilhelm's deeper crisis centers on meaning and identity. He lacks any stable sense of who he is, which might provide a basis for self-respect. Although he prides himself on his fine clothes and genuine charm, his body looks to him like a "fair-haired hippopotamus," with a large face, wide mouth, and stump teeth (4). Usually he succeeds in pumping himself up with surges of self-esteem, but he is equally prone to bouts of self-hatred: "Ass! Idiot! Wild boar! Dumb mule! Slave! Lousy, wallowing hippopotamus!" (52). His past misfortunes torture him. He is terrified about where his life is going. And he struggles desperately to cope in the present.

The two crises are connected. The finance-family crisis is the catalyst for grappling with the meaning-identity crisis, and in turn the meaning-identity crisis deepens his reflections on the finance-family crisis. He is having great difficulty thinking about both tangles of problems. When he reflects on the past he does little more than nurse old wounds and assign blame, whether to Adler, Margaret, himself, or fate. He knows he has made mistakes, but he is convinced his failings resulted primarily from bad luck. In a melancholy moment he consoles himself by contemplating how little freedom any of us have to change our lives (21). Another time he reassures himself that he has worked hard by exerting himself. Yet he senses he hasn't worked hard in some other important way—perhaps by failing to cultivate passion and commitment to excellence in his career (4). Money strikes him as a force beyond his control. It flows in good times and mysteriously dries up in bad times (36). He is mindful about it only when he experiences desperate need for it (88). Usually he barely lives within his means, without saving for the future (105). He fantasizes about escaping "the world's business" of money making (32). At the same time, he regards himself as superior to people like his father, whom he mocks for worshipping money, all the while remaining comically oblivious to his own obsession with money.

When he looks to the future he believes he tries to make reasonable decisions about how best to proceed. Yet he has little track record to give him confidence. Truth be told—and it is told by the novella's narrator—he has a long record of poor judgment in making major decisions. At times he acts impulsively, as when he quit his job. More often, as in deciding to become an actor, he engages in lengthy deliberation and then makes poor decisions: "After much thought and hesitation and debate he invariably took the course he had rejected innumerable times" (19). His major decisions have been mindless—not in the sense of avoiding thought, but in the sense of manifesting poor judgment about what matters most. It is as if reasoning just wears him out, and he ultimately acts independently of it. This is especially true when much is at stake and his desires render him ripe for mistakes (54).

ADLER AND MARGARET ON FAMILY AND MONEY

Wilhelm sees only three ways to resolve his immediate financial crisis: persuade Adler to give him money, convince Margaret to ease her demands for child support, or win big in the stock market by investing with Tamkin. As for getting Adler to help, he knows the odds are against him. For decades he and his father have been waging a psychological war. Adler is a wealthy retired physician who can easily afford to give money to Wilhelm, and also to Wilhelm's sister who is also pestering him for financial support. But Adler has adopted a firm policy not to give money to his grown children. Doing so, he is convinced, would result in endless subsidies to adults who fail to responsibly earn a living. Adler was disgusted when Wilhelm dropped out of college and squandered his youth in Hollywood. He was appalled when Wilhelm abandoned his marriage and later quit his job. He has a litany of additional complaints about Wilhelm's slouching and slovenliness, failure to practice Judaism properly, abuse of prescription pills, and histrionics about personal problems that Adler regards as petty, at least compared to the serious ailments he treated during his career. He is also annoyed that Wilhelm ignored his cautions about Tamkin's untrustworthiness.

Dr. Adler views himself as prudent about money and loving toward his son. Wilhelm views him as selfish and unloving, even though he knows Adler paid for his college education, financially supported Margaret and their children while he served in the military, and is likely to leave him money in his will. Son and father have difficulty communicating on virtually everything, especially money, family, work, religion, and education. At breakfast and again later in the day, Wilhelm pleads with Adler for a gift or loan, asking with a modicum of surface humility and a mountain of underlying contempt. When challenged by Adler for quitting his job, Wilhelm insists that quitting was "a question of morale," a matter of self-esteem and self-confidence. Adler corrects him: "Don't you mean a moral question?" (33). Wilhelm hastily grants it is that too, but he probably has in mind his employer's nepotism and injustice in firing him, rather than accepting moral responsibility as Adler intends. When Adler reminds him of his financial responsibilities to his family, Wilhelm bitterly replies that he has met his obligations for two decades without asking anyone for help. That reply is only partly true. Although he had not asked Adler for money until now, he had not met his financial obligations to his family by prudently saving for future contingencies. In any case, Wilhelm dodges Adler's call for mindfulness about his financial and family responsibilities in the here-and-now.

Wilhelm's second envisioned solution to his financial problems, convincing Margaret to lower her demands, is equally unpromising. Margaret shares Dr. Adler's assessment of Wilhelm as being irresponsible. In a phone conversation later in the day she calmly tells Wilhelm to "stop thinking like a youngster" who believes it possible to constantly start over again (108). Wilhelm deflects the criticism by demanding that Margaret get a job, at least part-time work. Margaret insists she must stay home to care for their two children, aged fourteen and ten. With characteristically poor judgment, Wilhelm blurts out that their children are not babies and can take care of themselves while she works (109).

Margaret and Adler share a tough-love approach to Wilhelm, albeit with minimal love.[2] In turn, Wilhelm sees them as selfishly motivated by money, power, revenge, and moralistic self-satisfaction, although at times he grudgingly acknowledges they have some basis for their views. In any case, he desperately needs help, financially and emotionally, and neither of them will offer that help. He sees few resources left in grappling with his crises. Beyond his flawed judgment, he relies somewhat on prayers for God's mercy, and fragments of poetry remembered from college classes. He has yet to accept the need for a new job search. Dr. Tamkin is his last hope, or so he believes.

TAMKIN'S TRUE SOUL

Tamkin presents himself as a savvy investor, selfless healer, perceptive psychologist, and "psychological poet" (65). In addition, Wilhelm regards him as a savant who talks about the "deeper things of life" (78). He speaks "a kind of truth" that helps some people, and he seems to care about Wilhelm more than his own father does (60). Tamkin's core advice, offered with buoyant enthusiasm to Wilhelm and to anyone else who listens, is to forget the past and the future, and simply live in the present. The advice promises a quick fix that resonates with Wilhelm's impulsive nature, although he has little idea what it means. As it turns out, neither does Tamkin.

Regarding money, the recommendation to live in the moment is notoriously bad advice for most investors. Trying to time the ups and down of the stock market usually produces bad outcomes: panic selling when the market drops, followed by staying too long on the sidelines as the market recovers. But Tamkin assures Wilhelm that he has mastered the "scientific" art of buying low and selling high with precise timing, even in the volatile market of commodity trading (6). Tamkin excites Wilhelm—and probably himself—with patter about the fortune to be made in day-trading in commodities. In fact he is a mediocre investor on a good day, and today is not a good day. He foolishly invested Wilhelm's seven hundred dollars in commodities, specifically in futures of lard stocks, which are dropping as rapidly as their name suggests. Tamkin is also a cheat. He manipulates Wilhelm into signing a power of attorney that allows him to control how he invests Wilhelm's money, within an unequal partnership designed to benefit primarily himself. All the while, Tamkin diagnoses speculators in the market as having "money fever," which he depicts as pathological as well as financially self-defeating. Just as politicians have "character neuroses" that make them compulsive liars and power mongers, businessmen are heartless and "spread the plague" of money obsession (60). When Wilhelm nervously asks Tamkin about his own apparent speculation in the financial markets, Tamkin cleverly shifts the topic from his motives to his expertise. He claims to invest because he is good at it. He also claims to invest dispassionately and for amusement, much like a gentleman with extra cash for playing a game. He pretends Wilhelm has the same motivation, despite knowing of his financial desperation.

To further secure Wilhelm's confidence in him, Tamkin readily supports Wilhelm's attitudes to his family. He agrees with Wilhelm that Adler is petty, pathological, and judgmental concerning money and family. He reinforces Wilhelm's hostility to Margaret, making misogynous comments about her and about women in general, whom he blames for making men impotent. He endorses Wilhelm's abandonment of Margaret, using a snappy therapeutic phrase: "don't marry suffering" (94). Tamkin is also quick to back down whenever his advice upsets Wilhelm, in particular when he brings up his relationship with his sons (93). In all these ways he bolsters Wilhelm's self-esteem with a mixture of caring and self-ingratiation designed to benefit from Wilhelm's money and perhaps his admiration. He seems to believe his pop psychology with a dollop of duplicity, and he is a con-man and a comical self-deceiver in ways that are impossible to pry apart. As a self-appointed therapist he shows some genuine caring toward his "patients." But he has ulterior motives of financial self-interest, power, and vanity, none of which he admits to others—or even to himself. He skillfully tailors his account of the truth to his "patients" in order to profit from their money and admiration.

Regarding meaning and identity, Tamkin urges Wilhelm to discover his "true" or "real soul" and to express it in the here-and-now. In his view, what matters in the present moment is to express our feelings, not to respond to legitimate claims on us in our situation. Tamkin explains, plausibly enough, that we define ourselves by what we care about most deeply, and by who we love, although he understands these things mainly in terms of pleasurable feelings rather than commitments. He also explains that we are divided creatures. We have conflicting loves that define different "souls" in us. Some loves, and hence some souls, are objectionable in that they are selfish, egotistical, vain, or cruel (66). They constitute pretender souls that sap energy from our true soul, making us sick and causing suffering for ourselves and others.

What is our true soul? Tamkin endorses two views, each in the name of science. One view is implausibly idealistic: our true soul is our better self that loves the truth and loves other people selflessly (67). Tamkin claims to be authentic in exactly this way; he claims to prize the truth and selflessly nudge others toward greater health and happiness. The other view is crassly reductionist: our true soul consists of animal instincts, which include the anything-but-selfless desires for sex and for self-regard (93). Perhaps he believes these views are compatible because he assumes our instincts include a predominance of selfless love. Echoing Rousseau, he says this selfless love is distorted by social pressures that cause greed and narcissism, impose sexual restrictions, and generate shame and guilt (66). Echoing Freud, Tamkin blames unrealistic expectations and social restrictions for suppressing sexual instincts and thereby causing neurosis.[3] He diagnoses Wilhelm and other residents of Hotel Gloriana as suffering from disorders rooted in irrational guilt and unconscious distortions of natural desires (59). And he celebrates people who "free themselves from morbid guilt feelings and follow their instincts" (93). In doing so he implies that all guilt and shame are unhealthy, and all instinctive conduct is healthy—equally implausible generalizations.

Tamkin approaches moral problems in terms of mental health, as do many contemporary therapists. But although he claims to practice science-based psychotherapy, his specific therapeutic recommendations are clownish. For example, he says he taught Greek to a patient in order to keep him in the present, thereby steadying him so he does not flee his problems by traveling to other countries (63). Tamkin's recommendations largely serve his self-interest. For example, on one occasion, following lunch together, Wilhelm requests that they return to the brokerage house to check on their investment. Tamkin knows the market is going against them, and he tries to stall Wilhelm. Conveniently for Tamkin, they encounter Mr. Rappaport, an old and partly blind acquaintance who asks for help getting to the cigar store. Wilhelm resists helping Rappaport, but Tamkin insists that living in the here-and-now requires Wilhelm to act with kindness, rather than being obsessed with money (96). The ruse enables Tamkin to hurry to the market to make investment decisions by himself. At every turn, Tamkin slyly exploits Wilhelm's naïveté and selfless impulses by deflecting his attention to what is *not* most important in the here-and-now.

Exactly what does Tamkin mean by living in the moment, whether in investing or in expressing one's true soul? Does he intend *value-based mindfulness*: attending to what matters in our situation, in light of values? Or does he intend *value-suspending mindfulness*: a value-neutral awareness of our immediate situation, perhaps used to calm the mind by diminishing self-hatred, guilt feelings, anger, fear, and other negative emotions? It may seem unlikely he would draw such a distinction, but in fact he comes close to doing so. Thus, he recommends value-suspending mindfulness to calm Wilhelm and thereby distract him from value-based mindfulness about their sinking investments. When Wilhelm anxiously asks to withdraw his money from the market—a move involving value-based mindfulness—Tamkin tries to change the topic by suggesting Wilhelm is neurotic. Then, seeing Wilhelm angered by the distraction, Tamkin switches to recommending value-suspending mindfulness to lower his anxiety. He begins with a poetic image: nature knows only the present, which is like a beautiful huge wave that we should allow to carry us. To go with the flow we need only pick any element in the present moment and focus on it: "And say to yourself here-and-now, here-and-now, here-and now. 'Where am I?' 'Here.' 'When is it?' 'Now.' Take an object or a person. Anybody. 'Here and now I see a person'" (85–86). Tamkin fails to provide any meaningful context for value-suspending mindfulness during meditation, such as how naming items in our immediate experience might help defuse their emotional valences. In this way, Tamkin uses value-suspending mindfulness to undermine value-based mindfulness, and certainly to generate confusion. Wilhelm is flabbergasted. He discerns no calming benefits of value-suspending meditation, and he rightly suspects Tamkin is trying to distract him from his all-too-present concerns about his investments.

Regarding value-based mindfulness, does Tamkin mean *personal-mindfulness*: attending to what matters to us in our situation, in light of our current values? Or does he mean *virtue-mindfulness*: attending to what matters in our situation in light of sound values that we care about and implement with good judgment? Perhaps he intends both, in some unspecified combination. As a self-proclaimed therapist, he supports his patient/clients as they act on their autonomous values. As a self-proclaimed guru, however, he intends virtue-mindfulness, given his emphasis on expressing our true soul in the moment. Because we have multiple values that sometimes conflict, importance requires integrating, balancing, and setting priorities among values, and among valuable things. It requires doing so with good judgment and self-control, each of which Wilhelm has in short supply, and both of which Tamkin purports to instill in him.

Tamkin exemplifies the therapeutic trend in ethics—the tendency to approach moral matters in terms of mental health.[4] This social trend was well underway when Bellow published *Seize the Day* in 1956, a decade before Philip Rieff declared "the triumph of the therapeutic."[5] At its best, the trend creatively integrates morality and mental health. At its worst, it degrades morality and replaces it with a crass version of mental health. Tamkin recommends something closer to the degraded and crass version, but it has surface appeal to Wilhelm. Interestingly, Bellow was briefly in Reichean therapy when he began writing *Seize the Day*.[6] Bellow's biographer suggests that Wilhelm's "assessment of Tamkin is not far from Bellow's assessment of [Wilhelm] Reich, at the time: 'He spoke of things that mattered, and as very few people did this he could take you by surprise, excite you, move you.'"[7] Tamkin could also muddle your mind, which in Wilhelm's case was easy enough to do.

WILHELM'S SOUL SEARCHING

Wilhelm is awed by Tamkin's notion of the true soul and tries to apply the idea to himself. In doing so he seeks self-excuse as much as self-understanding. If his past mistakes resulted from false selves, then he—as his true self—is not blameworthy. Wilhelm readily identifies and names several pretender souls. "Wilky," his parents' nickname for him, is his childish and dependent self. "Tommy Wilhelm," the name he gave himself in Hollywood, is his unrealistic freedom-loving self. "Velvel," the name his loving grandfather called him, is his embodied identity, the self residing in his hippopotamus-like body that has difficulty breathing when under stress (68).[8] He reasons that his true soul is none of these selves. Instead, it is a purely spiritual entity. This idea confuses him, and he postpones further reflection.

Later, at the brokerage house, it occurs to him that his true self might connect with an unusual experience he had several days earlier. He had been walking through an underground corridor on his way to buy tickets for a baseball game. Normally he hated that tunnel, but this time he paused to read the graffiti on the walls. In that moment he experienced a vision of sorts: "All of a sudden, unsought, a general love for all these imperfect and luridlooking people burst out in Wilhelm's breast" (81). At the time this experience was quickly forgotten. In recalling it while at the brokerage house, Wilhelm links it to Tamkin's view that nearly everyone has a mental illness. He links it as well to a remark made at breakfast by one of Adler's friends, something about the general difficulty of distinguishing sanity from madness. Perhaps, Wilhelm ruminates, everyone is sick. Perhaps even Tamkin is a lunatic (79). Perhaps everyone on the streets of New York is a suffering outcast, trapped in their private language and unable to communicate. Perhaps the inability to distinguish our craziness from our insanity is hell on earth. Suddenly it occurs to him there is a deeper level of truth, beyond suffering. There is some larger body that unites everyone around elemental truths that everyone can grasp. His earlier experience of this unity in the underground corridor might be a clue to who he is—"Truth, like" (81).

Once again his reasoning stalls, and he forgets the experience. Nevertheless it sets the backdrop for a further spiritual, perhaps mystical, experience that culminates his day, and the novel.[9] Just prior to the experience, he had been given painful rejections by Adler, Margaret, and Tamkin. After making a final desperate plea for help, his father labels him a slob and yells at him to leave him alone. Wilhelm then calls Margaret and pleads for understanding. She tells him to grow up and hints he deserves his suffering. Enraged, Wilhelm walks into the street where he thinks he sees Tamkin, but loses him in a large crowd attending a funeral. He tries to find shade to protect him from the heat, but the crowd pushes him into a funeral line. Stepping aside when he nears the open coffin, he sees the dead stranger close up and begins to cry. His tears increase as he thinks of his children and his inability to help them. He thinks briefly about Olive, his new lover with whom he has vague hopes of starting life anew. Finally his tears flow "past words, past reason," until they flood into an ecstasy of funeral music, flowers, and lights, moving him "toward the consummation of his heart's ultimate need" (114).

The ending is ambiguous. What is Wilhelm's ultimate need, the knowledge of which might unlock his true soul?[10] Presumably the need is more than escaping his immediate money problems, but is it to escape "the world's business" of money seeking (32)? Probably the need includes a release from suffering, which he prayed for at the beginning of his day (22), but would that release merely return him to a comfortable and pleasurable life (74)? The need also includes being loved by his children, father, and Olive, but does it also include a wider loving engagement with humanity? There is no chance Wilhelm will undertake a heroic life, much less become a mystic. But given his genuine capacities for empathy, we might hope he is not doomed to remain a *schlemiel*.[11] One thing is clear. The intensity of the culminating spiritual experience, with all its emotional honesty and power, does not guarantee a better life for him. Perhaps the experience will be short-lived and leave a minor trace, as did his earlier experience in the underground tunnel. To bring about any real change, the ecstatic experience needs to stimulate commitments that might form the core of an authentic identity, understanding authenticity in a deeper way than Tamkin proposes.

AUTHENTICITY

The ideal of expressing our true self by living in the present is doubly inspirational. On the one hand, it reminds us that life is short and precious; it must not be squandered with excessive regrets about the past and fears and fantasies about the future. On the other hand, it appeals to the ideal of authenticity, of being who we really are rather than engaging in self-posturing. Yet that ideal is treacherous when it too narrowly rivets attention on a buffered here-and-now, in disregard of a wider horizon of time and value. A blinkered focus on the present can undermine caring and commitments, which require seeing the present in light of the past and future. That blinkered focus results in a fragmented identity, rather than one worth calling authentic.

Like mindfulness, authenticity can mean many things, even contradictory things. In my view, authenticity is a hybrid virtue that combines self-honesty, autonomy, and self-respect.[12] *Self-honesty* is truthfulness with ourselves. It implies trying to get at important truths about ourselves, as well as avoiding undesirable forms of self-deception—where self-deception takes myriad forms such as willful ignorance (intentionally avoiding inquiries one suspects would reveal unpleasant truths about oneself), systematic ignoring of relevant truths, emotional detachment when emotional engagement is called for, engaging in self-pretense, and rationalization (biased reasoning).[13] As such, self-honesty is not a stand-alone virtue, any more than mindfulness is. To be honest and mindful is to pay attention to *important* matters, where importance is understood in terms of a full spectrum of additional moral values and additional values that enter into a good life for us.[14]

Although Wilhelm's effort to understand himself contains elements of honest struggle, primarily it reflects his habitual self-deception. He continues to see himself as victim, rather than squarely admitting that his mistakes and the poor reasoning that led to them. He is not fully honest about his responsibilities in matters of money and family. In the eyes of Bellow, Wilhelm is a *schlemiel*: "I sympathize with Wilhelm but I don't like him. . . . I saw him as a misfit wooing his hard-nosed father with corrupt platitudes of affection, or job-lot, bargain-sale psychological correctness. I thought he was one of those people who make themselves pitiable to extract your support."[15] Given Bellow's ambivalence toward his character, it is remarkable that he manages to elicit our empathy and compassion for Wilhelm. He does so in part by having the narrator keep the focus on Wilhelm's suffering and search for meaning, telling the story mostly through Wilhelm's eyes while seamlessly adding wider perspective to create irony and humor.[16]

Autonomy is making choices by exercising reason and self-control. Through autonomy we create a self, making choices for which we are responsible, rather than passively imbibing influences from society. We form identifications with and commitments to persons, groups, traditions, and activities. At least in major decisions, Wilhelm's reasoning is ineffective. Not only does the reasoning fail to manifest good judgment. It even fails to guide his choices. His emotions play a stronger role in his decisions, though impulsively as in spitefully quitting his job before securing other employment. In his midforties he still has not resolved his childish anger toward his father and wife.

The personal identity created through autonomous decisions need not be, and usually is not, an idealized self. For Wilhelm, it is probably not the idealized self he longs for in his concluding spiritual experience. Much less is it the idealization that Tamkin offers: the fantasy of a self that is simultaneously fully instinctual and selflessly loving. Perhaps it is not even the idealized moral self hinted at in Shakespeare's stirring injunction, "This above all, to thine own self be true."[17] In any case, all idealized self-concepts carry risks. They can easily degrade into the view that because we are our ideal self, we are not ultimately responsible for the harm caused by our pretender selves. Idealized self-concepts can also foster unhealthy dissociations: I am only part of what is in me. A better therapist than Tamkin might emphasize that mental health requires integrating all basic tendencies ("loves") in ways that are both responsible and personally satisfying. Such a therapist would also know that ideal selves are rarely the ones that act in an isolated present.

Self-respect is the virtue of properly valuing oneself, without the excess of narcissism and the defect of self-abasement. Potentially Wilhelm could find a reliable basis for increased self-respect in his genuine capacities for empathy, compassion, and spiritual unity with even strangers. But most of all he needs to stop hating himself. To do so he needs to forgive himself for past mistakes, or at least learn to live with them without self-torture. Self-forgiveness is based on self-understanding. It is based on remembering and honest acknowledgment. It acknowledges wrongdoing, with remorse and accepting responsibility. At times Wilhelm senses as much (22), but in the main he is charmed by Tamkin's advice to forget mistakes, rather than to remember and forgive himself for them. Worse, he refuses to acknowledge that he is responsible for his mistakes, preferring instead to see himself as a victim rather than a perpetrator of harm (69). Even in his prayers to God, he only confesses regrets, not responsibility for wrongdoing. His brief attempts of self-forgiveness are not accompanied by a resolve to change (21).

In sum, Tamkin offers sham advice when he urges Wilhelm to focus on a present severed from the past and future, rather than connected to a meaningful past and future. In doing so he disregards commitments undertaken in the past and extending into the future, commitments that can ground a coherent and authentic identity, commitments grounded in values that guide what we pay attention to in our present situation. A wholesale refusal to identify ourselves with the past might be possible for some individuals,[18] but for Wilhelm it is neither possible nor desirable. He knows he needs to forgive himself for his past mistakes and wrongdoing, and self-forgiveness presupposes acknowledging his past as part of who he is. Living in the present will not remove all his regrets, but it might temper the pain they cause. Nor will it banish his fears about the future, though with any luck it might help him summon courage and hope in confronting genuine dangers. Yet it might nudge him toward greater attention to what matters in his situation, with intelligence and commitment, remembrance and foresight, gratitude and delight.

NOTES

1. Parenthetical page references in this chapter are to: Saul Bellow, *Seize the Day* (New York: Penguin 1996).
2. See Robert F. Kiernan, *Saul Bellow* (New York: Continuum, 1989), 57–75.
3. Freud's therapeutic critique of Judeo-Christian morality is found, among other places, in *Civilization and Its Discontents*, trans. James Strachey (New York: W. W. Norton, 1989).
4. See Mike W. Martin, *From Morality to Mental Health: Virtue and Vice in a Therapeutic Culture* (New York: Oxford University Press, 2006).
5. Philip Rieff, *The Triump of the Therapeutic* (Chicago, IL: University of Chicago Press, 1966).
6. See Daniel Fuchs, "Bellow and Freud," in *Saul Bellow in the 1980s*, ed. Gloria L. Cronin and L. H. Goldman (East Lansing: Michigan State University Press, 1989), 27–50. Reich is now largely forgotten (or ridiculed), but at the time he was a respected explorer of a sexual politics. See E. V. Wolenstein, *Psychoanalytic Marxism* (London: Free Association Books, 1993), 90.
7. Zachary Leader, *The Life of Saul Bellow: To Fame and Fortune, 1915–1964* (New York: Alfred A. Knopf, 2015), 507. Bellow based Tamkin on a man he knew about who was "a scatterbrain, a poseur" and a "foolish grotesque" advisor, as quoted by Leader, 765–765, n50. Tamkin is also a corrupt Jewish counselor, as S. Lillian Kremer argues in "Seize the Day: Intimations of Anti-Hasidic Satire," in *Small Planets: Saul Bellow and the Art of Short Fiction*, ed. Gerhard Bach and Gloria L. Cronin (East Lansing: Michigan State University Press, 2000), 157–167. Gilead Morahg discusses Tamkin as a catalyst for Wilhelm's growth in "The Art of Dr. Tamkin," in *Modern Critical Views: Saul Bellow*, ed. Harold Bloom (New York: Chelsea House Publishers, 1986), 147–159.
8. See Sarah Blacher Cohen, *Saul Bellow's Enigmatic Laughter* (Urbana: University of Illinois Press, 1974), 90–114.
9. Wilhelm's two experiences are mystical in the wide sense introduced by William James in *The Varieties of Religious Experience* (New York: Modern Library, 2002), 370–372.
10. See Ellen Pifer, *Saul Bellow against the Grain* (Philadelphia: University of Pennsylvania Press, 1990), p. 95.
11. See Jules Chametzky, "Death and the Post-Modern Hero/Schlemiel: An Essay on *Seize the Day*," in *New Essays on Seize the Day*, ed. Michael P. Kramer (New York: Cambridge University Press, 1998), 111–123, at 122; and John Jacob Clayton, "Alienation and Masochism," in *Modern Critical Views: Saul Bellow*, ed. Harold Bloom (New York: Chelsea House Publishers, 1986), 65–85, at 68.
12. See Mike W. Martin, *Memoir Ethics: Good Lives and the Virtues* (Lanham, MD: Lexington Books, 2016), 57–69.
13. I develop this conception of self-honesty in *Self-Deception and Morality* (Lawrence: University Press of Kansas, 1986).
14. On connections between authenticity and additional values, see Charles Taylor, *The Ethics of Authenticity* (Cambridge, MA: Harvard University Press, 1992).

15. "'I Got a Scheme!': The Words of Saul Bellow," interview of Saul Bellow by Philip Roth, *The New Yorker* (April 25, 2005), 83. Cited by Zachary Leader, *The Life of Saul Bellow*, 509.
16. James Wood, *How Fiction Works* (New York: Farrar, Straus and Giroux, 2008), 35–37.
17. Shakespeare, *Hamlet*, I.iii.
18. See Galen Strawson, "Against Narrativity," *Ratio*, SVII (2004): 428–452, at 433.

Chapter Twelve

Mindfulness Movement Critics

The mindfulness movement—the social trend celebrating the contribution of mindfulness to good lives—is a confluence of ideas, ideals, and practices. This complexity makes the movement difficult to assess overall. *External* critics, who observe the movement as outsiders, sometimes dismiss it as a hodgepodge of fads, yet the movement has deep as well as shallow currents. *Internal* critics, who participate in the movement, highlight its positive aspects, while decrying its distortions. They typically denounce what they see as false ideas and superficial ideals while calling for a return to the "true" meaning of mindfulness. Their true-false contrasts, which take various forms, bear on questions I explored in this book.

What is mindfulness? How should we understand the striking diversity in how it is defined and studied by scientists and scholars, as well as within popular culture? In particular, how does mindfulness during therapy-oriented meditation relate to mindfulness in pursuing everyday activities and relationships? Is mindfulness a value and a virtue, and how does it connect with other values? In general, what is the contribution of mindfulness to good lives? After summarizing my responses to these questions, I relate what I have said to the concerns of several internal critics.

RECAP

One of my primary aims has been to make sense of the bewildering variety of concepts of mindfulness. These concepts include ideas about careful attention to what matters that are developed without relying on the word "mindfulness," for example Thoreau's notion of wakefulness and Csikszentmihalyi's concept of attention during flow. I pursued this aim by highlighting the role of values in understanding mindfulness. I began with a familiar everyday concept of value-based mindfulness as paying attention to what matters in light of values—and awareness of, heeding, remembering, attunement to, taking into account important or interesting elements of a situation or in general. This concept branches according to the reference point used in specifying relevant values. Personal-mindfulness is attending to what matters to an individual in light of their values, whether or not the values are defensible. Virtue-mindfulness is paying attention to what matters in light of sound values, those values that are not immoral, irrational, or unhealthy.

This trio of concepts—value-based mindfulness, personal-mindfulness, and virtue-mindfulness—forms bridges to the more specialized concepts of mindfulness in psychology, religion, and philosophy. All three concepts are skeletal until fleshed out with substantive value perspectives concerning what matters in particular situations. Ultimately, those value perspectives reflect conceptions of good lives. In addition, value perspectives on mindfulness might recommend specific practices to cultivate mindfulness. They might highlight particular modes of attention, such as inward focus on our experience or outward focus on activities and relationships. And they might indicate when and how the present should be narrowed and buffered from the past and future, or instead broadened and connected to wider horizons of time and value. In general, as Mary Midgley observes, "Understanding is relating; it is fitting things into a context."[1] The contexts into which thinkers fit mindfulness reflects their interests and value perspectives, and hence there can be multiple ways to understand mindfulness.

I sampled a wide variety of thinkers who understand mindfulness with different interests, including different value perspectives or different value emphases. The values (and thinkers) include authenticity (Henry David Thoreau, Saul Bellow, Oberdan Marianetti/Jonathan Passmore), balance (Jonathan K. DeYoe, David M. Levy), beauty (Christophe André, Brenda Ueland), calm and control (Jon Kabat-Zinn, the stoics), intelligent and creative problem solving (Goethe, Ellen J. Langer, John Dewey), mental health and morality (most thinkers I discussed), happiness (Mihaly Csikszentmihalyi), kindness and curiosity (Shamash Alidina, among others), meaningful work (Phil Jackson, David Gelles, Michael F. Steger, Eve Edman), optimism and positivity (positive psychologists, including Eric L. Garland and Barbara L. Fredrickson), peace and compassion (Buddhism), professional responsibility (Ronald Epstein), rational valuing and therapy (Sigmund Freud, Albert Ellis, Elliot D. Cohen). In each instance I applied my trio of concepts in understanding a thinker's definition of mindfulness as it pertains to their interests and values. The following list provides a rough summary, dividing concept/conceptions that are explicitly value-centered and those which specify value-suspending mindfulness. (I include Thomas Joiner and Eric Harrison who are discussed below.)

Value-Based Mindfulness: Attending to What Matters, in Light of Values

Alidina: purposeful attention infused with kindness, curiosity, and acceptance.

André: heightened attention to works of art in light of aesthetic values.

Buddhist right-mindfulness: bearing in mind and acting attentively on Buddhist values.

Cohen: ethical and rational thinking in valuing, including while assessing our present situation.

Csikszentmihalyi's flow-mindfulness: attentiveness during flow.

Dewey's intelligence: value-infused decision making using good judgment.

Ellis's rational valuing: reasoning and living based on healthy valuing.

Epstein's attending: conscientious, ethical, and excellent work in a profession.

Freud's free association: attending to one's thoughts and feelings, including value-laden and past-oriented ones, and honestly communicating them to a therapist.

Garland and Fredrickson: placing attention on an object while acknowledging, evaluating, and letting go of distractions.

Gelles: being fully present in the moment, with kindness, curiosity, and acceptance.

Harrison: alert perception and reasonable evaluation of experience and situations.

Jackson: remembering to be present in the moment, specifically during competitive sports.

Langer's flexibility-mindfulness: inventiveness and openness to new information and viewpoints when making decisions.

Levy's wise contemplation: integrating self-awareness and task attention to express our values and to achieve reasonable balances in using personal digital technologies.

Marianetti/Passmore: awareness that is authentic, inclusive, and nonjudgmental.

Steger and Edman: awareness from paying attention in the moment, as while working.

Stoic attention: moral vigilance and conscientiousness.

Dr. Tamkin (in Saul Bellow's novella): expressing one's authentic self in the here-and-now.

Thoreau's wakefulness: heightened awareness of what matters in pursuing a good life.

Ueland's microscopic truthfulness: self-expression combined with appreciation of goodness and beauty.

Value-Suspending Mindfulness: Nonjudgmental Attending and Awareness

Kabat-Zinn and most psychologists: nonjudgmental attention to and awareness of present experience.
Joiner: moment-to-moment nonjudgmental awareness, emphasizing outward orientation.

My second aim has been to argue that psychologists frequently presuppose values when they study mindfulness, including moral values embedded in holistic concepts of mental health. These values should be made transparent—both in designing and interpreting experiments, and in writing books for the public that celebrate mindfulness in good lives. Some internal critics of the mindfulness movement speak of *the* psychological concept of mindfulness, as if there is a univocal concept shared by all psychologists, a concept the critics criticize in light of their favored moral or spiritual concept. Instead I emphasized the variety of psychological concepts of mindfulness developed in different contexts with different aims in mind. For example, perhaps most psychologists understand mindfulness as inward-directed, on our personal experience, but Langer and Csikszentmihalyi understand mindfulness as outward-oriented attention during activities and problem solving. Again, most psychologists discuss the values connected with mindfulness as subjective preferences and feelings. To their credit, positive psychologists seek firmer foundations for morality in widespread beliefs about the virtues, yet they too devote too little attention to possibilities of rational reflection in justifying moral beliefs and in reasonably balancing conflicting moral values.

I devoted special attention to Jon Kabat-Zinn and Ellen J. Langer, because they generated large and influential literatures on mindfulness. Regarding Kabat-Zinn's concept of value-suspending mindfulness—nonjudgmental attention to and awareness of our immediate experience—I highlighted the ambiguities surrounding "nonjudgmental." Officially, Kabat-Zinn defines "nonjudgmental" as suspending value judgments and reactions based on them. At least on the surface, his value-suspending mindfulness is the direct opposite of value-based mindfulness. At a deeper level, however, value-suspending mindfulness can be viewed as a special instance of value-based mindfulness, in which what matters for relieving stress and promoting health is to temporarily suspend value judgments during meditation. In addition values are present in the background of meditation as integral to the "personal vision" that provides the motives and rationale for practicing meditation. Selected values also enter more explicitly into loving-kindness meditation and other Buddhist-inspired meditative practices, contrary to Kabat-Zinn's official emphasis on suspending all value judgments during mindfulness-based meditation.

Regarding Ellen J. Langer, I interpreted her concept of flexibility-mindfulness in problem solving as value-based, in that it centers on the values of inventiveness and openness to new ideas and viewpoints. Her concept is at most an anemic version of virtue-mindfulness, for it fails to mention the additional sound values that enter into decision making. Although she regards all values as subjective and relative, in discussing examples she assumes a host of additional background values that she does not treat as arbitrary, including moral decency, mental health, and rationality. Because of her value assumptions, I recommended reconstructing flexibility-mindfulness as a more robust version of virtue-mindfulness, such as used by John Dewey under the heading of "intelligence."

Psychotherapists encourage their client/patients to employ value-based, personal-mindfulness in valuing in healthy and self-interested ways. As an illustration I discussed Albert Ellis, who discusses mindfulness without using the word. In places Ellis seems to advocate replacing everyday morality with mental health. Yet in practice he presupposes values of rationality and moral decency under an expansive concept of mental health. Positive psychologists like Martin Seligman and Mihaly Csikszentmihalyi, and Barbara L. Fredrickson, and Acceptance and Commitment Therapists like Eric L. Garland (who collaborated with Fredrickson), are more explicit in discussing virtues in good lives. They remain strongly influenced by Kabat-Zinn's value-suspending mindfulness, but they open the door to richer varieties of virtue-mindfulness.

My overarching aim has been to understand the role of mindfulness as a virtue in good lives, drawing on psychology, philosophy, popular culture, and literature. In my view, to study mindfulness is largely to study how it implements values in our immediate situation, while remembering that the values attached to wide horizons of meaning and time in good lives. Value-based mindfulness is always dependent on additional values, in light of which we identify what is important and deserving of attention. Certainly virtue-mindfulness must be understood in light of value perspectives on good lives. And even the value-suspending mindfulness involved in therapeutic meditation can contribute to good lives when conjoined with enriched conceptions of virtue-mindfulness.

As quickly as we unfold our value perspective on mindfulness, we risk potential disagreement and hopefully invite dialogue—about good lives and about what matters and should be attended to. I used Thoreau as an extended illustration, but issues about sound values ran throughout the book. Just as values are central in understanding mindfulness, the topic of mindfulness is relevant to value discussions, but mindfulness does not settle value disagreements. Good lives have kaleidoscopic variety, and the values that enter into good lives need to be understood in a pluralistic manner, without falling into crass relativism.

Finally, along the way I commented on the wider social implications of the mindfulness movement. In my view, the movement contains much good and some bad. On the positive side, it offers a variety of resources in grappling with a troubled and troubling world that is increasingly stressful, frenetic, fragmented, and confusing. Those resources are largely therapeutic, yet they also include ways to help us sharpen responses to excellence, beauty, and moral conscientiousness. On the negative side, I rejected beliefs that value-suspending mindfulness is anything like a wide-ranging panacea. I also objected to most psychologists' tendency to reduce values to matters of mere subjective feelings, a reduction that degrades moral discourse in popular culture. At the same time, I am heartened by recent positive psychology that takes the virtues seriously. I also expressed my hope that the mindfulness movement will enrich morality by connecting it with mental health research. I conclude with a few additional comments about the mindfulness movement in light of several of its internal critics.

INTERNAL CRITICS

Internal critics participate in the mindfulness movement while objecting to its distortions, excesses, and fluff. They proceed in the spirit of Michael Walzer's suggestion: "criticism is most properly the work of 'insiders,' men and women mindful of and committed to the society whose policies or practices they call into question—who *care about* what happens to it."[2] Internal critics typically contrast true mindfulness (authentic, genuine, desirable concepts) and false mindfulness (ersatz, superficial, distorted, debased concepts). These true-false contrasts take many forms, three of which I discuss as illustrations: Buddhist critics; Thomas Joiner, who is a psychologist who critiques other psychologists; and Eric Harrison, who is a secular and entrepreneurial practitioner of meditation.

Buddhist critics, to begin with, advocate right-mindfulness as anchored in Buddhist values while critiquing psychological concepts of mindfulness as narrowly self-interested. Buddhism takes many forms, but a primary theme is that right-mindfulness is based on compassion, kindness, love, humility, truthfulness, and peace. As such, right-mindfulness implies attunement to sound spiritual ideals; it is a robust version of what I call virtue-mindfulness. Buddhist critics charge that right-mindfulness has been diluted by psychologists who develop concepts of mindfulness severed from spiritual values, replacing right-mindfulness with value-suspending mindfulness, or tethering mindfulness to superficial understandings of mental health. The critics see mindfulness in popular culture as largely a set of expedient therapeutic techniques for promoting pleasure, consumerism, and work performance within capitalist economies.

A concise and much-cited Buddhist critique of this sort is presented in a 2013 blog entry "Beyond McMindfulness," written by Ron Purser (a professor of management) and David Loy (a Zen teacher). Purser and Loy coined "McMindfulness" as a derogatory name for false versions of mindfulness that are at odds with right-mindfulness rooted in Buddhist ideals. They write, "Rather than applying mindfulness as a means to awaken individuals and organizations from the unwholesome roots of greed, ill will and delusion, it is usually being refashioned into a banal, therapeutic, self-help technique that can actually reinforce those roots."[3] Buddhist right-mindfulness (*samma sati*), they explain, emphasizes humility, discipline, peace, compassion, kindness, and selfless love. It is guided by desirable intentions and motives, as centered on moral self-restraint and spiritual discipline. In contrast, false, secular wrong-mindfulness (*miccha sati*) constantly emphasizes the self—self-esteem, self-love, self-serenity, self-compassion, self-forgiveness. When mindfulness is not reduced to value-suspending for stress relief, it is reduced to personal-mindfulness for purposes of narcissism and greed within consumerist capitalism. To be clear, Purser and Loy are not saying there is one concept of mindfulness that can be applied in two different ways, for good or bad purposes. Rather, they are saying there are two concepts of mindfulness: a Buddhist-inspired version of virtue-mindfulness, and a psychological concept of mindfulness involving the distortion of sound values.

Purser and Loy do not speak for all Buddhist scholars, of course. Buddhist scholars and practitioners differ considerably among themselves about exactly how to understand Buddhist ideals and truths.[4] Some Buddhists are doctrinaire and fundamentalist. Others are ecumenical and cosmopolitan in spirit, and might accept or even welcome many secularizations of mindfulness. Most notably, the Dalai Lama has spent a lifetime connecting Buddhism to a wider spiritual and scientific landscape. Again, Bhikkhu Bodhi is not alarmed by secularization per se. He cautions against secular reductions of mindfulness to mental activities such as attention, which can serve either moral or immoral purposes. But in an ecumenical spirit, he welcomes selective borrowing and reworking of Buddhist ideas insofar as it contributes to alleviating suffering, assuming researchers are clear and respectful of Buddhist spiritual traditions.[5] Both the Dalai Lama and Bhikkhu Bodhi welcome the rich interplay that can occur among concepts and conceptions of mindfulness.

The second internal critique is developed by psychologist Thomas Joiner. In his perceptive but also perplexing book, *Mindlessness: The Corruption of Mindfulness in a Culture of Narcissism*, Joiner bewails the distortions of mindfulness by members of his profession, as well as within popular culture. According to him, true mindfulness is "moment-to-moment non-judgmental awareness of one's environment and subjective state."[6] By *nonjudgmental* he means nonevaluative—being dispassionate, and suspending all value judgments, including both positive and negative evaluations of ourselves. In this sense, even positive evaluation of ourselves and others is "judgmental." As he writes in a rather jarring passage, "It is worth noting how *judgmental* positive self-regard is."[7] In my terms, then, Joiner officially defines mindfulness as value-suspending.

Joiner also understands true mindfulness as mainly focused outwardly on the world rather than inwardly on ourselves, although it includes elements of self-awareness. He briefly praises Langer for her outward focus on problem solving, but otherwise he criticizes his peer psychologists for excessive inward-turning in thinking about mindfulness.[8] He also gently critiques Kabat-Zinn who, though not trained as a psychologist, has had an enormous influence among psychologists. Joiner admires Kabat-Zinn for promulgating nonjudgmental mindfulness (what I call value-suspending mindfulness), but he says Kabat-Zinn goes too far in the direction of celebrating the self—too much self-compassion, self-acceptance, self-love; too much "love affair" with the beauty of ourselves.[9]

Joiner contends that nonjudgmental mindfulness is a valuable concept that has become degraded in the mindfulness movement: "a noble and useful idea—mindfulness—[has been] sullied by a culture of superficiality, mediocrity, and especially, selfishness."[10] This noble and useful idea has been morally degraded into a false mindfulness, which unduly elevates the individual, eclipses the full richness of the world, and undermines moral responsibility and virtue. The degradation has been so extensive that Joiner worries that even authentic mindfulness, noble and useful as it is, might be an "imperfect idea" that "contains the seeds of its own undoing, even without the conspiring force of a culture of self-regard."[11]

Joiner's seeming ambivalence—both celebrating and expressing qualms about nonjudgmental mindfulness—is one of many tensions running through his book. To begin with, exactly why does he think nonjudgmental and outward-oriented mindfulness a "noble and useful idea"? He offers two explanations (and justifications). First, mindfulness facilitates and perhaps constitutes "awareness of the richness, subtlety, and variety of the present moment—importantly, *all* of the present moment, not just the self."[12] "Not just the self" underscores Joiner's insistence that authentic mindfulness is not primarily self-oriented. Second, mindfulness is a therapeutically and rationally useful idea, for it enables us "to pause, reflect, and gain distance and perspective."[13] In offering these two explanations, Joiner shifts from value-suspending mindfulness to value-based mindfulness. The "richness" of the present moment implies value and worth, thereby suggesting that he has shifted to value-based mindfulness. Again, "perspective" suggests a wise or at least useful understanding, based on reasonable value judgments, if not during meditation at least as part of its framework that provides the rationale for meditating. In this way, he slides toward his version of virtue-mindfulness.

Joiner repeatedly smuggles in values in understanding mindfulness. He comes close to admitting as much toward the end of his book. There he calls for "selfless and authentic mindfulness, combined with a selfless stoicism gazing outwardly intently enough on virtue" to celebrate "responsibility and duty."[14] Is he saying that authentic mindfulness (per se) is a selfless (altruistic?) and desirable ideal? If so, he is tacitly abandoning his initial concept of value-suspending mindfulness and shifting to a more robust concept of virtue-mindfulness. Or do the words "combined with" perhaps hint that authentic mindfulness is value-suspending and takes on value only when yoked together with other virtues and responsibilities, thereby reinforcing his earlier qualms about it being (by itself) a flawed concept? This obscurity surfaces frequently in the book. Officially, he specifies that authentic mindfulness is nonevaluative (value-suspending). But, contradicting himself, he hints that mindfulness is fully authentic only when it is attached to sound values—to proper (humble) valuing of the self and proper valuing of other people. Again, in discussing savoring he says that authentic mindfulness is part of a "three-pronged package of mindfulness, reappraisal, and savoring."[15] That is, value-suspending mindfulness acquires its worth (and authenticity?) only when it is part of a wider configuration of values, including "reappraisal" in the form of rational valuing in particular contexts. It then becomes a version of what I call virtue-mindfulness.

In perhaps his most provocative criticism, Joiner contends that the mindfulness movement has degraded psychology and other health professions: "faux mindfulness has been the key conduit, the Trojan horse, through which the larger culture's turn toward the self has infected the mental health field and profession."[16] Apparently he means that psychologists' preoccupation with value-suspending and inward-oriented mindfulness is the main influence in fostering the narrow celebration of the self in health psychology. I question that claim. At most the mindfulness movement reflects and extends the turn toward the self that began much earlier in psychology. The 1960s self-esteem movement, for example, was at least as potent in turning toward the self. Much earlier, Freud's therapeutic attack on moral ideals as unrealistic and unhealthy was a major influence.[17] And in turn, there have been far deeper social forces that influence the preoccupation on the self more than the community in psychology has. We might hope that positive psychology will embrace concepts of value-based mindfulness, to balance psychologists' emphasis on value-suspending mindfulness.

In short, Joiner's critique of the mindfulness movement cries out for reframing. Value-suspending mindfulness is not by itself a "noble idea," however useful it might be as a therapeutic tool. If anything, the noble idea is virtue-mindfulness: attending to what matters in light of sound values. Some of Joiner's values are attractive (though somewhat idealistic) and might be developed using a concept of virtue-mindfulness. But my main point is conceptual, rather than recommending revisions to his framework. Rather than clarifying mindfulness, Joiner is yet another example of psychologists celebrating value-suspending mindfulness while assuming background values that should be made transparent and salient.

The third internal critique is offered by Eric Harrison in *The Foundations of Mindfulness: How to Cultivate Attention, Good Judgment, and Tranquility*. Harrison renounces most of the doctrines of traditional Buddhism and Asian spiritual traditions, including detachment and world-denying, preoccupation with suffering, and karma and reincarnation.[18] At the same time, he greatly admires the Buddha as a philosopher and psychologist, and embraces his ethics of truth and compassion. He draws on the Buddha's core concept of right-mindfulness which, he contends, centers on a truthful search for understanding and sound evaluation.[19] To this extent, it is compatible with, but deepens the colloquial meaning of mindfulness: "to pay attention to what you are doing to avoid mistakes or improve performance."[20] This deepened mindfulness differs sharply from modern psychological concepts of value-suspending mindfulness. "It makes a huge difference whether we see mindfulness as a discriminating, choice-making function or as a passive, meditative state of mind."[21] Restated in my terms, it makes a huge difference whether we understand mindfulness as virtue-mindfulness or instead as value-suspending mindfulness. Value-suspending mindfulness can be used for good or bad purposes. Worse, value-suspending mindfulness amounts to an "abnegation of thought and action" based on values.[22] Value-suspending mindfulness plays a role only during meditation, when we temporarily suspend our usual activities and value-based reactions.[23] Those meditative episodes are not at all the primary, most important kind of value-based reactions that we constantly make in daily life. Even to focus attention involves a value judgment that what we are attending to is worth our time.

I agree with much of Harrison's illuminating critique of the mindfulness movement, although I differ with him in details and emphasis. For example, Harrison tends to emphasize self-reflective mindfulness. He encapsulates his view, and his interpretation of the Buddha's view, this way: "you are mindful if you know what you are doing and can describe it to yourself."[24] He tends to depict mindfulness as a switching from the routine attention involved in most everyday activities to a special mode of self-reflection, in which we ask ourselves what we are doing and whether it is worth doing.[25] In contrast I emphasize virtue-mindfulness as involving skills of attending to what matters, where what matters might be ourselves but is often things other than ourselves. Thus, virtue-mindfulness can consist in engaging in activities in a thoughtful manner, whether or not this involves extensive self-reflection. Harrison insightfully recommends reorienting the mindfulness movement to value judgments and reactions based on them, and moving away from its value-suspending emphasis. Of course, what matters most is that the values are sound. It makes a huge difference whether value-based mindfulness is virtue-mindfulness or merely personal-mindfulness. Harrison's critique would be more forceful if he explicitly worked with this distinction, but it is clear enough that he presupposes something like it. Even *sati*, he says, can be employed for desirable or undesirable aims.[26]

To conclude, the thinkers who explore mindfulness invariably approach it with particular interests and value concerns. The same is true of critics of the mindfulness movement. The critics I have mentioned—Harrison, Joiner, and the Buddhists—all draw attention to what they see as valuable aspects of the mindfulness movement, while introducing a critical edge. Critical does not mean wholly or unduly negative; it does not mean judgmental in the pejorative sense. Instead it means seeking clarity, understanding, and fair assessment of an important movement. I have tried to proceed in a similar spirit in exploring how mindfulness contributes to good lives.

NOTES

1. Mary Midgley, *Beast and Man: The Roots of Human Nature*, revised ed. (New York: Routledge, 1995), 18.
2. Michael Walzer, *The Company of Critics: Social Criticism and Political Commitment in the Twentieth Century*, 2nd ed. (New York: Basic Books, 2002), xi.
3. Ron Purser and David Loy, "Beyond McMindfulness," blog post, *Huffington Post* (July 1, 2013), https.//www.huffpost.com/entry/beyond-mcmindfulness_b_3519289.
4. See J. Mark G. Williams and Jon Kabat-Zinn, eds., *Mindfulness: Diverse Perspectives on Its Meaning, Origins and Applications* (London: Routledge, 2013); and Robert Meikyo Rosenbaum and Barry Magid, *What's Wrong with Mindfulness (and What Isn't): Zen Perspectives* (Somerville, MA: Wisdom Publications, 2016).
5. Bhikkhu Bodhi, "What Does Mindfulness Really Mean? A Canonical Perspective," in Williams and Kabat-Zinn, eds., *Mindfulness: Diverse Perspectives on Its Meaning, Origins and Applications*, 19–39, at 35–36.
6. Thomas Joiner, *Mindlessness: The Corruption of Mindfulness in a Culture of Narcissism* (New York: Oxford University Press, 2017), 39. See also 1.
7. Joiner, *Mindlessness*, 16. See also, 13, 55.
8. Joiner, *Mindlessness*, 20.
9. Joiner, *Mindlessness*, 18, 24.
10. Joiner, *Mindlessness*, 1.
11. Joiner, *Mindlessness*, 4, 34.
12. Joiner, *Mindlessness*, 1.
13. Joiner, *Mindlessness*, 42.
14. Joiner, *Mindlessness*, 185.
15. Joiner, *Mindlessness*, 55.
16. Joiner, *Mindlessness*, 139.
17. See Philip Rieff, *The Triumph of the Therapeutic* (Chicago: University of Chicago Press, 1966, 1987).
18. Eric Harrison, *The Foundations of Mindfulness: How to Cultivate Attention, Good Judgment, and Tranquility* (New York: The Experiment, 2017), 3, 165–166.
19. Harrison, *The Foundations of Mindfulness*, 8, 15 104–105.
20. Harrison, *The Foundations of Mindfulness*, 8.

21. Harrison, *The Foundations of Mindfulness*, 308.
22. Harrison, *The Foundations of Mindfulness*, 164.
23. Harrison, *The Foundations of Mindfulness*, 311–313.
24. Harrison, *The Foundations of Mindfulness*, 110, italics removed.
25. Harrison, *The Foundations of Mindfulness*, 111, 154.
26. Harrison, *The Foundations of Mindfulness*, 151.

Bibliography

Aldrich, Nelson W., Jr. *Old Money*. New York: Alfred A. Knopf, 1988.
Alidina, Shamash. *Mindfulness for Dummies*. Second edition. Chichester, UK: John Wiley and Sons, 2015.
Alter, Adam. *Irresistible: The Rise of Addictive Technology and the Business of Keeping Us Hooked*. New York: Penguin Press, 2017.
Améry, Jean. *On Aging: Revolt and Resignation*, trans. John D. Barlow. Bloomington: Indiana University Press, 1994.
André, Christophe. *Looking at Mindfulness: Twenty-Five Paintings to Change the Way You Live*, trans. Trista Selous. New York: Blue Rider Press, 2014.
Aristotle. *Nicomachean Ethics*. Revised edition. Trans. J. A. K. Thomson and H. Tredennick. Harmondsworth, UK: Penguin, 1976.
Armstrong, John. *Love, Life, Goethe: Lessons of the Imagination from the Great German Poet*. New York: Farrar, Straus and Giroux, 2006.
Aurelius, Marcus. *Meditations*, trans. Gregory Hays. New York: Modern Library, 2003.
Austin, J. L. *How to Do Things with Words*. Second edition. Edited by J. O. Urmson and Marina Sbisá. Cambridge, MA: Harvard University Press, 1975.
Badiner, Allan Hunt, ed. *Mindfulness in the Marketplace: Compassionate Responses to Consumerism*. Berkeley, CA: Parallax Press, 2002.
Baer, R. A. "Self-Focused Attention and Mechanisms of Change in Mindfulness-Based Treatment." *Cognitive Behaviour Therapy* 38:S1 (2009): 15–20.
Batchelor, Martine. "Meditation and Mindfulness," 157–64 in *Mindfulness: Diverse Perspectives on Its Meaning, Origins and Applications*. Edited by Mark G. Williams and Jon Kabat-Zinn. New York: Routledge, 2013.
———. "Meditation: Practice and Experience," 27–47 in *The Psychology of Meditation: Research and Practice*. Edited by Michael A. West. New York: Oxford University Press, 2011.
Baumeister, Roy. "Pragmatic Prospection," 157–89 in *Homo Prospectus*. Edited by Martin E. P. Seligman, Peter Railton, Roy F. Baumeister, and Chandra Sripada. New York: Oxford University Press, 2016.
Bellow, Saul. *Seize the Day*. New York: Penguin, 1996.
Bishop, S., M. Lau, S. Shapiro, L. Carlson, N. Anderson, J. Carmody, Z. Segal, S. Abbey, M. Speca, D. Velting, and G. Devins. "Mindfulness: A Proposed Definition." *Clinical Psychology: Science and Practice* 11 (2004): 230–41.
Biswas-Diener, R., T. B. Kashdan, and G. Minhas. "A Dynamic Approach to Psychological Strength Development and Intervention." *Journal of Positive Psychology* 6 (2011): 106–18.
Boden, Margaret. *The Creative Mind: Myths and Mechanism*. New York: Parker, 2004.

Bodhi, Bhikkhu. *The Noble Eightfold Path: Way to the End of Suffering*. Onalaska, WA: BPS Pariyatti Editions, 1994.
———. "What Does Mindfulness Really Mean? A Canonical Perspective," 19–39 in *Mindfulness: Diverse Perspectives on Its Meaning, Origins and Applications*. Edited by Mark G. Williams and Jon Kabat-Zinn. New York: Routledge, 2013.
Bortolotti, Lisa, ed. *Philosophy and Happiness*. Hampshire, UK: Palgrave Macmillan, 2009.
Boyce, Barry, ed. *The Mindfulness Revolution: Leading Psychologists, Scientists, Artists, and Meditation Teachers on the Power of Mindfulness in Daily Life*. Boston, MA: Shambhala, 2001.
Broudy, Harry S. *Enlightened Cherishing: An Essay on Aesthetic Education*. Urbana: University of Illinois Press, 1994.
Bryant, Fred, and Joseph Veroff. *Savoring: A New Model of Positive Experience*. Mahway, NJ: Erlbaum, 2006.
Buffett, Warren. "Mr. Buffett on the Stock Market," 166–75 in *Tap Dancing to Work: Warren Buffett on Practically Everything, 1966–2012*. Edited by Carol Loomis. New York: Portfolio/Penguin, 2012.
Burdick, Alan. *Why Time Flies: A Mostly Scientific Investigation*. New York: Simon and Schuster, 2017.
Butler, Joseph. *Fifteen Sermons Preached at the Rolls Chapel*. Edited by W. R. Matthews. London: G. Bell and Sons, 1964.
Cafaro, Philip. *Thoreau's Living Ethics: Walden and Pursuit of Virtue*. Athens: University of Georgia Press, 2004.
Callahan, David. *The Givers: Wealth, Power, and Philanthropy in a New Gilded Age*. New York: Alfred A. Knopf, 2017.
Cameron, Laurie J. *The Mindful Day: Practical Ways to Find Focus, Calm, and Joy from Morning to Evening*. Washington, DC: National Geographic, 2018.
Carel, Havi. *Illness: The Cry of the Flesh*. Revised edition. Durham, UK: Acumen, 2013.
Chabris, Christopher, and Daniel Simons. *The Invisible Gorilla*. New York: Crown Publishers, 2010.
Chametzky, Jules. "Death and Post-Modern Hero/Schlemiel: An Essay on *Seize the Day*," 111–23 in *New Essays on Seize the Day*. Edited by Michael P. Kramer. New York: Cambridge University Press, 1998.
Chanowitz, Benzion, and Ellen J. Langer. "Self-Protection and Self-Inception," 117–35 in *Self-Deception and Self-Understanding: New Essays in Philosophy and Psychology*. Edited by Mike W. Martin. Lawrence: University Press of Kansas, 1985.
Cheever, Susan. *American Bloomsbury*. New York: Simon and Schuster, 2006.
Ciarrochi, Joseph, Todd B. Kashdan, and Russ Harris. "The Foundations of Flourishing," 1–29 in *Mindfulness, Acceptance, and Positive Psychology: The Seven Foundations of Well-Being*. Edited by Todd B. Kashdan and Joseph Ciarrochi. Oakland, CA: Context Press, 2013.
Clayton, John Jacob. "Alienation and Masochism," 65–85 in *Modern Critical Views: Saul Bellow*. Edited by Harold Bloom. New York: Chelsea House Publishers, 1986.
Cohen, Elliot D. *The New Rational Therapy: Thinking Your Way to Serenity, Success, and Profound Happiness*. Lanham, MD: Rowman & Littlefield Publishers, 2007.
Cohen, Sarah Blacher. *Saul Bellow's Enigmatic Laughter*. Urbana: University of Illinois Press, 1974.
Collingwood, R. G. *The Principles of Art*. New York: Oxford University Press, 1958.
Conway, Jill Ker. *The Road from Coorain*. New York: Vintage Books, 1989.
Cowley, Malcolm. "How Writers Write," 3–21 in *The Paris Review Interviews*, First Series. Edited by Malcolm Cowley. New York: Penguin Books, 1960.
Csikszentmihalyi, Mihaly. *Creativity: Flow and the Psychology of Discovery and Invention*. New York: HarperCollins, 1996.
———. *Flow: The Psychology of Optimal Experience*. New York: Harper and Row, 1990.
———. *Good Business: Leadership, Flow, and the Making of Meaning*. New York: Viking, 2003.
Daitch, Carolyn. *Anxiety Disorders*. New York: W. W. Norton and Company, 2011.

Dallmayr, Fred. *Mindfulness and Letting Be: On Engaged Thinking and Acting.* Lanham, MD: Lexington Books, 2016.
Dann, Kevin. *Expect Great Things: The Life and Search of Henry David Thoreau.* New York: Penguin Random House, 2017.
Darley, John M., and C. Dan Batson. "From Jerusalem to Jericho: A Study of Situational and Dispositional Variables in Helping Behavior." *Journal of Personality and Social Psychology* 27 (1973): 29–40.
De Waal, Edmund. *The Hare with Amber Eyes.* New York: Farrar, Straus and Giroux, 2010.
Dewey, John. *A Common Faith.* New Haven, CT: Yale University Press, 1934.
———. *Democracy and Education.* New York: Macmillan, 1916.
———. *Experience and Education.* New York: Collier Books, 1963[1938].
———. "Experience, Knowledge and Value: A Rejoinder," 515–608 in *The Philosophy of John Dewey.* Third edition. Edited by Paul Arthur Schilpp and Lewis Edwin Hahn. La Salle, IL: Open Court, 1989.
———. *How We Think: A Restatement of the Relation of Reflective Thinking to the Educative Process.* Lexington, MA: D. C. Heath and Company, 1933.
———. *Human Nature and Conduct: An Introduction to Social Psychology.* New York: Modern Library, 1957[1922].
———. *Theory of the Moral Life.* New York: Holt, Rinehart and Winston, 1960.
DeYoe, Jonathan K. *Mindful Money: Simple Practices for Reaching Your Financial Goals and Increasing Your Happiness Dividend.* Novato, CA: New World Library, 2017.
Diener, Ed, and Robert Biswas-Diener. *Happiness.* Malden, MA: Blackwell Publishing, 2008.
Dillon, Robin S., ed. *Dignity, Character and Self-Respect.* New York: Routledge, 1995.
Donoghue, Denis. *The American Classics: A Personal Essay.* New Haven, CT: Yale University Press, 2005.
Doris, John M. *Lack of Character: Personality and Moral Behavior.* New York: Cambridge University Press, 2002.
Doris, John M., and the Moral Psychology Research Group. *The Moral Psychology Handbook.* New York: Oxford University Press, 2010.
Dreifus, Claudia. "Why We Can't Look Away from Screens," D-7 in *New York Times*, March 7, 2017.
Edel, Leon. *Henry D. Thoreau.* Minneapolis: University of Minnesota Press, 1970.
Eifert, Georg H., and J. P. Forsyth. *Acceptance and Commitment Therapy for Anxiety Disorders.* Oakland, CA: New Harbinger, 2005.
Ellis, Albert, and Robert A. Harper. *A Guide to Rational Living.* Third edition. Woodland Hills, CA: Melvin Powers Wilshire Book Company, 1997.
Engeström, Yrjö, and David Middleton. "Introduction: Studying Work as Mindful Practice." 1–14 in *Cognition and Communication at Work.* Edited by Yrjö Engeström and David Middleton. New York: Cambridge University Press, 1998.
Epictetus. *Discourses and Selected Writings*, trans. and edited by Robert Dobbin. New York: Penguin, 2008.
———. *Handbook of Epictetus*, trans. Nicholas White. Indianapolis, IN: Hackett Publishing, 1983.
Epstein, Ronald. *Attending: Medicine, Mindfulness, and Humanity.* New York: Scribner, 2017.
Fairlie, Henry. *The Seven Deadly Sins Today.* Notre Dame, IN: University of Notre Dame Press, 1979.
Feinberg, Cara. "The Mindfulness Chronicles: On 'the Psychology of Possibility.'" *Harvard Magazine.* September–October 2010. http://harvardmagazine.com/2010/90/the-mindfulness-chronicles.
Feinberg, Joel. "Absurd Self-Fulfillment," 297–330 in Joel Feinberg, *Freedom and Fulfillment: Philosophical Essays.* Princeton, NJ: Princeton University Press, 1992.
Fernyhough, Charles. *The Voices Within: The History and Science of How We Talk to Ourselves.* New York: Basic Books, 2016.
Fields, Rick. *How the Swans Came to the Lake: A Narrative History of Buddhism in America.* Third edition. Boulder, CO: Shambhala, 1992.
Fingarette, Herbert. *Self-Deception.* Berkeley: University of California Press, 2000[1969].

―――. *The Self in Transformation: Psychoanalysis, Philosophy, and the Life of the Spirit.* New York: Basic Books, 1963.
Flanagan, Owen. *Varieties of Moral Personality: Ethics and Psychological Realism.* Cambridge, MA: Harvard University Press, 1991.
Flexner, Stuart Berg, ed. *The Random House Dictionary.* Classic edition. New York: Random House, 1983.
Frank, Jerome D., and Julia B. Frank. *Persuasion and Healing: A Comparative Study of Psychotherapy.* Third edition. Baltimore, MD: Johns Hopkins University Press, 1991.
Frankfurt, Harry G. *The Importance of What We Care about: Philosophical Essays.* New York: Cambridge University Press, 1988.
Fredrickson, Barbara. *Love 2.0: Creating Happiness and Health in Moments of Connection.* New York: Plume, 2014.
―――. *Positivity.* New York: Crown Publishers, 2009.
Freeman, Judith. *The Latter Days: A Memoir.* New York: Anchor Books, 2016.
Freud, Sigmund. *An Autobiographical Study*, trans. James Strachey. New York: W. W. Norton, 1963[1935].
―――. *Civilization and Its Discontents*, trans. James Strachey. New York: W. W. Norton, 1989[1930].
Fuchs, Daniel. "Bellow and Freud," 27–50 in *Saul Bellow in the 1980s.* Edited by Gloria L. Cronin and L. H. Goldman. East Lansing: Michigan State University Press, 1989.
Gardner, Howard. *Creating Minds.* New York: Basic Books, 1993.
―――. *Frames of Mind: The Theory of Multiple Intelligences.* New York: Basic Books, 1983.
Garland, Eric L., and Barbara L. Fredrickson. "Mindfulness Broadens Awareness and Builds Meaning at the Attention-Emotion Interface," 30–67 in *Mindfulness, Acceptance, and Positive Psychology: The Seven Foundations of Well-Being.* Edited by Todd B. Kashdan and Joseph Ciarrochi. Oakland, CA: Context Press, 2013.
Gelles, David. *Mindful Work: How Meditation Is Changing Business from the Inside Out.* Boston, MA: Houghton Mifflin Harcourt, 2016.
Gethin, Rupert. "On Some Definitions of Mindfulness," 263–79 in *Mindfulness: Diverse Perspectives on Its Meaning, Origins and Applications.* Edited by Mark G. Williams and Jon Kabat-Zinn. New York: Routledge, 2013.
Gewirth, Alan. *Self-Fulfillment.* Princeton, NJ: Princeton University Press, 1998.
Ghiselin, Brewster. "Introduction," 11–31 in *The Creative Process: A Symposium.* Edited by Brewster Ghiselin. New York: Mentor Books, 1952.
Gilbert, Paul, and Choden. *Mindful Compassion.* Oakland, CA: New Harbinger Publications, 2014.
Goethe, J. W. *Italian Journey*, trans. W. H. Auden and Elizabeth Mayer. New York: Penguin, 1970.
Goleman, Daniel. *Focus: The Hidden Driver of Excellence.* New York: HarperCollins, 2013.
―――. *The Meditative Mind: The Varieties of Meditative Experience.* New York: G. P. Putnam's Sons, 1988.
Goodrich, Chauncey A., ed., *Merriam-Webster's Collegiate Dictionary.* Eleventh edition. Springfield, MA: Merriam-Webster, 2014.
Gordon, Mary. "Putting Pen to Paper, but Not Just Any Pen or Just Any Paper," 78–83 in *Writers on Writing.* Edited by John Darnton. New York: Henry Holt and Company, 2001.
Gottman, John M., with Nan Silver. *The Seven Principles for Making Marriage Work.* New York: Three Rivers Press, 1999.
Goyal, Madhav, et al., "Meditation Programs for Psychological Stress and Well-Being: A Systematic Review and Meta-Analysis." *JAMA Internal Medicine* 174:3 (March 2014): 357–68.
Gunatillake, Rohan. *Modern Mindfulness: How to Be More Relaxed, Focused, and Kind While Living in a Fast, Digital, Always-On World.* New York: St. Martin's Griffin, 2017.
Haack, Susan, ed. *Pragmatism, Old and New: Selected Writings.* Amherst, NY: Prometheus Books, 2006.
Hadot, Pierre. *The Inner Citadel:* The Meditations *of Marcus Aurelius*, trans. Michael Chase. Cambridge, MA: Harvard University Press, 1998.

———. *Philosophy as a Way of Life: Spiritual Exercises from Socrates to Foucault*, trans. Michael Chase. Edited by Arnold L. Davidson. Oxford: Blackwell, 1995.
Haidt, Jonathan. *The Happiness Hypothesis: Finding Modern Truth in Ancient Wisdom*. New York: Basic Books, 2006.
———. *The Righteous Mind: Why Good People Are Divided by Politics and Religion*. New York: Pantheon Books, 2012.
Hanh, Thich Nhat. *The Miracle of Mindfulness: An Introduction to the Practice of Meditation*. Boston, MA: Beacon Press, 1987[1975].
Hanson, Rick, with Richard Mendius. *Buddha's Brain: The Practical Neuroscience of Happiness, Love and Wisdom*. Oakland, CA: New Harbinger Publications, 2009.
Hanson, Rick, with Forrest Hanson. *Resilient: How to Grow an Unshakable Core of Calm, Strength, and Happiness*. New York: Harmony Books, 2018.
Harari, Yuval Noah. *21 Lessons for the 21st Century*. New York: Spiegel and Grau, 2018.
Harrison, Eric. *The Foundations of Mindfulness: How to Cultivate Attention, Good Judgment, and Tranquility*. New York: The Experiment, 2017.
Haybron, Daniel M. *The Pursuit of Unhappiness*. New York: Oxford University Press, 2008.
Heffernan, Virginia. "The Muddied Meaning of 'Mindfulness.'" *New York Times Magazine*. (April 14, 2015). https://www.nytimes.com https://www.nytimes.com/2015/04/19/magazine/the-muddied-meaning-of-mindfulness.html. Accessed 6/25/2017.
Heilbroner, Robert L. *The Worldly Philosophers: The Lives, Times, and Ideas of the Great Economic Thinkers*. Revised Seventh edition. New York: Simon and Schuster, 1999.
Hickman, Larry A. *John Dewey's Pragmatic Technology*. Bloomington: Indiana University Press, 1990.
Holt, Nathalia. *Rise of the Rocket Girls: The Women Who Propelled Us, from Missiles to the Moon to Mars*. New York: Little, Brown and Company, 2016.
Huang, Peter H. "Meta-Mindfulness: A New Hope." *Richmond Journal of Law and the Public Interest* XIX:iv (2016): 303–24.
Hunter, James Davison, and Paul Nedelisky. *Science and the Good: The Tragic Quest for the Foundations of Morality*. New Haven, CT: Yale University Press, 2018.
Ie, Amanda, Christelle T. Ngnoumen, and Ellen. J. Langer, eds. *The Wiley Blackwell Handbook of Mindfulness*, 2 vols. Chichester, England: John Wiley and Sons, 2014.
Ignatieff, Michael. *The Ordinary Virtues: Moral Order in a Divided World*. Cambridge, MA: Harvard University Press, 2017.
Irvine, William B. *A Guide to the Good Life: The Ancient Art of Stoic Joy*. New York: Oxford University Press, 2009.
Isaacson, Walter. *The Innovators*. New York: Simon and Schuster, 2014.
Ivtzan, Itai. "Mindfulness in Positive Psychology: An Introduction," 1–12 in *Mindfulness in Positive Psychology: The Science of Meditation and Well-Being*. Edited by Itai Ivtzan and Tim Lomas. New York: Routledge, 2016.
Jackson, Phil, and Hugh Delehanty. *Eleven Rings: The Soul of Success*. New York: Penguin Books, 2014.
Jackson, Sue. "Flowing with Mindfulness: Investigating the Relationship Between Flow and Mindfulness," 141–55 in *Mindfulness in Positive Psychology: The Science of Meditation and Well-Being*. Edited by Itai Ivtzan and Tim Lomas. New York: Routledge, 2016.
James, William. *The Principles of Psychology*, vol. 1. New York: Dover Publications, 1918[1890].
———. *Psychology: Briefer Course*. New York: Collier Books, 1962.
———. *The Varieties of Religious Experience*. New York: Modern Library, 1902.
Janning, Finn. *A Philosophy of Mindfulness: A Journey with Deleuze*. Buffalo, NY: NFB/Amelia Press, 2017.
———. "Compassion: Toward an Ethics of Mindfulness." *Mindfulness and Compassion* 3:1 (2018): 25–46.
John-Steiner, Vera. *Creative Collaboration*. New York: Oxford University Press, 2000.
Joiner, Thomas. *Mindlessness: The Corruption of Mindfulness in a Culture of Narcissism*. New York: Oxford University Press, 2017.

Kabat-Zinn, Jon. *Coming to Our Senses: Healing Ourselves and the World through Mindfulness*. New York: Hyperion, 2005.

———. *Full Catastrophe Living: Using the Wisdom of Your Body and Mind to Face Stress, Pain, and Illness*. Revised edition. New York: Bantam Books, 2013.

———. *Meditation Is Not What You Think: Mindfulness and Why It Is So Important*. Book One. New York: Hachette Books, 2018.

———. *Mindfulness for Beginners: Reclaiming the Present Moment—and Your Life*. Boulder, CO: Sounds True, 2016.

———. "Mindfulness-Based Interventions in Context: Past, Present, and Future." *Clinical Psychology: Science and Practice* 10:2 (2003): 144–56.

———. "Some Reflections on the Origins of MBSR, Skillful Means, and the Trouble with Maps," 281–306 in *Mindfulness: Diverse Perspectives on Its Meaning, Origins and Applications*. Edited by J. M. G. Williams and J. Kabat-Zinn. New York: Routledge, 2013.

———. *Wherever You Go, There You Are: Mindfulness Meditation in Everyday Life*. Tenth Anniversary Edition. New York: Hachette Books, 2014.

Kabat-Zinn, J., L. Lipworth, and R. Burney. "The Clinical Use of Mindfulness Meditation for the Self-Regulation of Chronic Pain." *Journal of Behavioral Medicine* 8 (1985): 163–90.

Kahneman, Daniel. "Objective Happiness," 3–25 in *Well-Being*. Edited by Daniel Kahneman, Ed Diener, and Norbert Schwarz. New York: Russell Sage Foundation, 1999.

———. *Thinking, Fast and Slow*. New York: Farrar, Straus and Giroux, 2011.

Kiernan, Robert F. *Saul Bellow*. New York: Continuum, 1989.

Kremer, S. Lillian. "Seize the Day: Intimations of Anti-Hasidic Satire," 157–67 in *Small Planets: Saul Bellow and the Art of Short Fiction*. Edited by Gerhard Bach and Gloria L. Cronin. East Lansing: Michigan State University Press, 2000.

Kronman, Anthony T. *Confessions of a Born-Again Pagan*. New Haven, CT: Yale University Press, 2016.

Lakshmi, Padma. *Love, Loss, and What We Ate*. New York: HarperCollins, 2016.

Landman, Janet. *Regret: The Persistence of the Possible*. New York: Oxford University Press, 1993.

Langer, Ellen J. *Counterclockwise: Mindful Health and Power of Possibility*. New York: Ballantine Books, 2009.

———. *Mindfulness*. Twenty-fifth Anniversary edition. Boston, MA: Da Capo Press, 2014.

———. "Mindfulness versus Positive Evaluation," 279–93 in *Oxford Handbook of Positive Psychology*. Second edition. Edited by C. R. Snyder and Shane J. Lopez. New York: Oxford University Press, 2009.

———. *On Becoming an Artist: Reinventing Yourself Through Mindful Creativity*. New York: Random House, 2006.

———. *The Power of Mindful Learning*. Second edition. Boston, MA: Da Capo Press, 2016.

Langer, E., A. Blank, and B. Chanowitz. "The Mindlessness of Ostensibly Thoughtful Action: The Role of Placebic Information in Interpersonal Interaction." *Journal of Personality and Social Psychology* 36 (1978): 635–42.

Langer, E., M. Cohen, and M. Djikic. "Mindfulness as a Psychological Attractor: The Effect on Children." *Journal of Applied Social Psychology* 42:5 (2012): 1114–22.

Layard, Richard. *Happiness: Lessons from a New Science*. New York: Penguin Press, 2005.

Leader, Zachary. *The Life of Saul Bellow: To Fame and Fortune, 1915–1964*. New York: Alfred A. Knopf, 2015.

Leigh, Mike. Screenplay for *Happy-Go-Lucky*, Miramax, 2008.

Levine, Robert. *A Geography of Time: The Temporal Misadventures of a Social Psychologist, or How Every Culture Keeps Time Just a Little Bit Differently*. New York: Basic Books, 1997.

Levitin, Daniel J. *The Organized Mind: Thinking Straight in the Age of Information Overload*. New York: Plume, 2015.

Levy, David M. *Mindful Tech: How to Bring Balance to Our Digital Lives*. New Haven, CT: Yale University Press, 2016.

Lin, Yanli, Megan E. Fisher, Sean M. M. Roberts, and Jason S. Moser. "Deconstructing the Emotion Regulatory Properties of Mindfulness: An Electrophysiological Investigation.

Frontiers in Human Neuroscience 10 (2016). http://journal.frontiersin.org/article/10.3389/fnhum.2016.00451/full.

Loomis, Carol. "The Inside Story of Warren Buffett," 62–75 in *Tap Dancing to Work: Warren Buffett on Practically Everything, 1966–2012*. Edited by Carol Loomis. New York: Portfolio/Penguin, 2012.

Lowenstein, Roger. *Buffett: The Making of an American Capitalist*. New York: Random House, 2008.

Luper, Steven. *Invulnerability: On Securing Happiness*. Chicago, IL: Open Court, 1996.

Lyubomirsky, Sonja. *The How of Happiness: A Scientific Approach to Getting the Life You Want*. New York: Penguin, 2007.

Mann, Thomas. *The Magic Mountain*, trans. H. T. Lowe-Porter. New York: Vintage Books, 1969.

Marianetti, Oberdan, and Jonathan Passmore. "Mindfulness at Work: Paying Attention to Enhance Well-Being and Performance," 189–200 in *Oxford Handbook of Positive Psychology and Work*. Edited by P. Alex Linley, Susan Harrington, and Nicola Garcea. New York: Oxford University Press, 2010.

Martin, Jonathan. "Mindful of Midterm Elections, Republicans Are Divided on How to Proceed." A-20 in *New York Times*. March 29, 2017.

Martin, Mike W. *Albert Schweitzer's Reverence for Life: Ethical Idealism and Self-Realization*. Aldershot, UK: Ashgate Publishing, 2007; and New York: Routledge, 2017.

———. "Balancing Work and Leisure," 7–24 in *The Value of Time and Leisure in a World of Work*. Edited by Mitchell R. Haney and A. David Kline. Lanham, MD: Lexington Books, 2010.

———. *Creativity: Ethics and Excellence in Science*. Lanham, MD: Lexington Books, 2007.

———. *Everyday Morality: An Introduction to Applied Ethics*. Fourth edition. Belmont, CA: Thomson, 2007.

———. *From Morality to Mental Health: Virtue and Vice in a Therapeutic Culture*. New York: Oxford University Press, 2006.

———. *Happiness and the Good Life*. New York: Oxford University Press, 2012.

———. "Happiness and Virtue in Positive Psychology." *Journal for the Theory of Social Behaviour* 37:1 (2007): 89–103.

———. *Love's Virtues*. Lawrence: University Press of Kansas, 1996.

———. *Meaningful Work: Rethinking Professional Ethics*. New York: Oxford University Press, 2000.

———. *Memoir Ethics: Good Lives and the Virtues*. Lanham, MD: Lexington Books, 2016.

———. "Mindful Technology," in *Science, Technology and the Good Life: Perspectives on Virtue in Modern Science and Technology*. Edited by Emanuele Ratti and Thomas A. Stapleford. New York: Oxford University Press, forthcoming.

———. *Of Mottos and Morals: Simple Words for Complex Virtues*. Lanham, MD: Rowman & Littlefield Publishers, 2013.

———. "Paradoxes of Happiness." *Journal of Happiness Studies* 9:2 (2008): 171–84. Reprinted, 31–46 in *The Exploration of Happiness: Present and Future Perspectives*. Edited by Antonella Delle Fave. New York: Springer, 2013.

———. *Self-Deception and Morality*. Lawrence: University Press of Kansas, 1986.

———, ed. *Self-Deception and Self-Understanding: New Essays in Philosophy and Psychology*. Lawrence: University Press of Kansas, 1985.

———. *Virtuous Giving: Philanthropy, Voluntary Service, and Caring*. Bloomington: Indiana University Press, 1994.

Martin, Mike W., and Roland Schinzinger. *Ethics in Engineering*. Fourth edition. Boston, MA: McGraw Hill, 2005.

McCloskey, Deirdre N. *The Bourgeois Virtues: Ethics for an Age of Commerce*. Chicago, IL: University of Chicago Press, 2006.

McCulloch, Jeanne. Interview with Leon Edel, 25–72 in *Writers at Work: The Paris Interviews, Eighth Series*. Edited by George Plimpton. New York: Penguin, 1988.

McKibben, Bill, ed. *American Earth: Environmental Writing since Thoreau*. New York: Penguin Putnam, 2008.

Mele, Alfred R. *Self-Deception Unmasked*. Princeton, NJ: Princeton University Press, 2001.
Memmert, Daniel. "The Effects of Eye Movements, Age, and Expertise on Inattentional Blindness." *Consciousness and Cognition* 15 (2006): 620–27.
Michaelis, David. *Schulz and Peanuts: A Biography*. New York: HarperCollins, 2007.
Michener, James A. *The Covenant*. New York: Random House, 1980.
———. *The World Is My Home: A Memoir*. New York: Random House, 1992.
Midgley, Mary. *Beast and Man: The Roots of Human Nature*. Revised edition. New York: Routledge, 1995.
Mill, John Stuart. *Autobiography*. New York: Penguin, 1989.
———. *Utilitarianism*. Indianapolis, IN: Hackett Publishing, 1979.
Monteiro, Lynette M., Jane F. Compson, and Frank Musten, eds., *Practioner's Guide to Ethics and Mindfulness-Based Interventions*. Cham, Switzerland: Springer International Publishing, 2017.
Morahg, Gilead. "The Art of Dr. Tamkin," 147–59 in *Modern Critical Views: Saul Bellow*. Edited by Harold Bloom. New York: Chelsea House Publishers, 1986.
Murphy, Arthur Edward. *The Theory of Practical Reason*. Edited by A. I. Melden. La Salle, IL: Open Court Publishing, 1964.
Nadelhoffer, Thomas, Eddy Nahmias, and Shaun Nichols, eds. *Moral Psychology: Historical and Contemporary Readings*. Malden, MA: Wiley-Blackwell, 2010.
Nagel, Thomas. *Mind and Cosmos*. New York: Oxford University Press, 2012.
Nasar, Sylvia. *A Beautiful Mind: The Life of Mathematical Genius and Nobel Laureate John Nash*. New York: Simon and Schuster, 2001.
Ngnoumen, Christelle T., and Ellen J. Langer. "Mindfulness: The Essence of Well-Being and Happiness," 97–107 in *Mindfulness in Positive Psychology: The Science of Meditation and Well-Being*. Edited by Itai Ivtzan and Tim Lomas. New York: Routledge, 2016.
Niemiec, Ryan, and Judith Lissing. "Mindfulness-Based Strengths Practice (MBSP) for Enhancing Well-Being, Managing Problems, and Boosting Positive Relationships," 15–36 in *Mindfulness in Positive Psychology: The Science of Meditation and Well-Being*. Edited by Itai Ivtzan and Tim Lomas. New York: Routledge, 2016.
Nobre, Anna C., and Sabine Kastner, eds. *The Oxford Handbook of Attention*. New York: Oxford University Press, 2014.
Nozick, Robert. *The Examined Life: Philosophical Meditations*. New York: Simon and Schuster, 1989.
Nussbaum, Martha C. *The Therapy of Desire: Theory and Practice in Hellenistic Ethics*. Princeton, NJ: Princeton University Press, 1994.
Oppenheimer, Mark. "Tweet Fatigue," *Los Angeles Times* (June 6, 2017): A-11.
O'Toole, James. *The Enlightened Capitalists: Cautionary Tales of Business Pioneers Who Tried to Do Well by Doing Good*. New York: HarperCollins, 2019.
Oxford University Press. *The Compact Edition of the Oxford English Dictionary*. New York: Oxford University Press, 1971.
Parini, Jay. *Promised Land: Thirteen Books That Changed America*. New York: Doubleday, 2008.
Penman, Danny. *Mindfulness for Creativity: Adapt, Create and Thrive in a Frantic World*. London: Piatkus, 2015.
Perkins, David N. "The Engine of Folly," 64–85 in *Why Smart People Can Be So Stupid*. Edited by Robert J. Sternberg. New Haven, CT: Yale University Press, 2002.
Peterson, Christopher. *A Primer in Positive Psychology*. New York: Oxford University Press, 2006.
Peterson, Christopher, and Martin E. P. Seligman, eds. *Character Strengths and Virtues: A Handbook and Classification*. Washington, DC: American Psychological Association, and New York: Oxford University Press, 2004.
Pickert, Kate. "The Art of Being Present," 71–79 in *The Science of Happiness*. New York: Time Books, 2016.
Pifer, Ellen. *Saul Bellow against the Grain*. Philadelphia: University of Pennsylvania Press, 1990.

Purser, Ron, and David Loy. "Beyond McMindfulness." Blog post, *Huffington Post*, July 1, 2013. www.huffingtonpost.com/ron-purser/beyond-mcmindfulness_b_3519289.html.
Ram Dass. *Be Here Now*. San Cristobal, NM: Lama Foundation, 1971.
Rieff, Philip. *The Triumph of the Therapeutic*. Chicago, IL: University of Chicago, 1987[1966].
Rooney, Kathleen. *Lillian Boxfish Takes a Walk*. New York: Picador, 2016.
Rosenbaum, Robert Meikyo, and Barry Magid. "Introduction," 1–10 in *What's Wrong with Mindfulness (and What Isn't): Zen Perspectives*. Edited by Robert Meikyo Rosenbaum and Barry Magid. Somerville, MA: Wisdom Publications, 2016.
Roth, Philip. "'I Got a Scheme!': The Words of Saul Bellow." Interview with Saul Bellow. *The New Yorker*, April 25, 2005.
Rottenberg, Josh, and Daniel Miller. "Hollywood's Director Shuffle," *Los Angeles Times* (September 13, 2017): A-1 and A-10.
Rubin, Gretchen. *The Happiness Project*. New York: HarperCollins, 2009.
Ruedy, Nicole E., and Maurice E. Schweitzer. "In the Moment: The Effect of Mindfulness on Ethical Decision Making." *Journal of Business Ethics*, 2011.
Ryle, Gilbert. *The Concept of Mind*. New York: Barnes and Noble, 1949.
Sartre, Jean-Paul. *Being and Nothingness*, trans. Hazel E. Barnes. New York: Washington Square Press, 1966.
Sattelmeyer, Robert. "The Remaking of *Walden*," 53–78 in *Writing the American Classics*. Edited by James Barbour and Tom Quirk. Chapel Hill: University of North Carolina Press, 1990.
Scanlon, T. M. *What We Owe to Each Other*. Cambridge, MA: Harvard University Press, 1998.
Schroeder, Alice. *The Snowball: Warren Buffett and the Business of Life*, updated version. New York: Bantam Books, 2009.
Schumpeter, Joseph A. *Capitalism, Socialism and Democracy*. New York: Harper and Brothers, 1947.
Seligman, Martin E. P. *Authentic Happiness: Using the New Positive Psychology to Realize Your Potential for Lasting Fulfillment*. New York: Free Press, 2002.
———. *Flourish: A Visionary New Understanding of Happiness and Well-Being*. New York: Free Press, 2011.
———. *Learned Optimism*. New York: Alfred A. Knopf, 1991.
———. "Positive Psychology, Positive Prevention, and Positive Therapy," 3–9 in *Handbook of Positive Psychology*. Edited by C. R. Snyder and Shane J. Lopez. New York: Oxford University Press, 2002.
Seligman, Martin E. P., and Ann Marie Roepke. "Prospection Gone Awry: Depression," 281–304 in *Homo Prospectus*. Edited by Martin E. P. Seligman, Peter Railton, Roy F. Baumeister, and Chandra Sripada. New York: Oxford University Press, 2016.
Seligman, Martin E. P., and John Tierney. "We Aren't Built to Live in the Moment." *New York Times* (May 21, 2017): 1, 6
Shapiro, Rebecca. "Oscars Ballot Counters: We Blew It, Warren Beatty Given Wrong Envelope." http://www.huffingtonpost.com. Accessed 2/27/2017.
Sharf, Robert H. "Buddhist Modernism and the Rhetoric of Meditative Experience." *Numen* 42 (1995): 228–83
———. "Is Mindfulness Buddhist? (and Why It Matters)," 139–51 in *What's Wrong with Mindfulness (and What Isn't): Zen Perspectives*. Edited by Robert Meikyo Rosenbaum and Barry Magid. Somerville, MA: Wisdom Publications, 2016.
Shonin, Edo, William Van Gordon, and Nirbhay N. Singh, eds. *Buddhist Foundations of Mindfulness*. New York: Springer, 2015.
Siegel, Daniel J. *Aware: The Science and Practice of Presence*. New York: Penguin Random House, 2018.
———. *The Mindful Brain: Reflection and Attunement in the Cultivation of Well-Being*. New York: W. W. Norton and Company, 2007.
Siegel, Ronald D. *The Mindfulness Solution: Everyday Practices for Everyday Problems*. New York: The Guilford Press, 2010.
Sifton, Elisabeth. *The Serenity Prayer*. New York: W. W. Norton, 2003.
Slote, Michael. *Goods and Virtues*. Oxford: Clarendon Press, 1983.

Slovic, Scott. "*Walden* and Awakening: Thoreau in a Sophomore American Literature Survey Course," 105–12 in *Approaches to Teaching Thoreau's Walden and Other Works*. Edited by Richard J. Schneider. New York: The Modern Language Association of America, 1996.
Smith, John E. *The Spirit of American Philosophy*. New York: Oxford University Press, 1966.
Snyder, C. R., Shane J. Lopez, and Jennifer Teramoto Pedrotti. *Positive Psychology*. Second edition. Los Angeles, CA: Sage, 2011.
Solomon, Robert C. *The Passions: The Myth and Nature of Human Emotion*. Notre Dame, IN: University of Notre Dame Press, 1983.
Spiller, Robert E., Willard Thorp, Thomas H. Johnson, Henry Seidel Canby, and Richard M. Ludwig. *Literary History of the United States*. Third edition revised. New York: Macmillan Company, 1963.
Statman, Daniel, ed. *Moral Luck*. Albany: State University of New York Press, 1993.
Steger, Michael F., and Eve Ekman. "Working It: Making Meaning with Workplace Mindfulness," 228–42 in *Mindfulness in Positive Psychology: The Science of Meditation and Well-Being*. Edited by Itai Ivtzan and Tim Lomas. New York: Routledge, 2016.
Sternberg, Robert J. *Successful Intelligence*. New York: Plume, 1997.
Stout, Jeffrey. *Ethics after Babel: The Languages of Morals and Their Discontents*. Princeton, NJ: Princeton University Press, 2001.
Strawson, Galen. "Against Narrativity." *Ratio*, XVII (2004): 428–52.
Sullivan, Paul. "Why the Wealthy Should Keep a Budget," B-6 in *New York Times*. January 12, 2019.
———. "Frugal When They Don't Have to Be," *New York Times* (June 6, 2015): B-5.
Talisse, Robert B., and Scott F. Aikin, eds. *The Pragmatism Reader: From Peirce through the Present*. Princeton, NJ: Princeton University Press, 2011.
Taylor, Charles. *The Ethics of Authenticity*. Cambridge, MA: Harvard University Press, 1992.
Thaler, Richard H., and Cass R. Sunstein. *Nudge: Improving Decisions about Health, Wealth, and Happiness*. New Haven, CT: Yale University Press, 2008.
Thera, Nyanaponika. *The Heart of Buddhist Meditation*. San Francisco, CA: Weiser, 1962.
Thoreau, Henry David. *Walden*. Princeton, NJ: Princeton University Press, 2004.
Tiberius, Valerie. *The Reflective Life: Living Wisely with Our Limits*. New York: Oxford University Press, 2008.
Tomas, Vincent. "Creativity in Art," 97–107 in *Creativity in the Arts*. Edited by Vincent Tomas. Englewood Cliffs, NY: Prentice-Hall, 1964.
Trainor, Kevin. *Buddhism: The Illustrated Guide*. New York: Oxford University Press, 2001.
Tyler, Anne. *A Spool of Blue Thread*. New York: Alfred A. Knopf, 2015.
Ueland, Brenda. *If You Want to Write*. Second edition. Saint Paul, MN: Graywolf Press, 1987[1938].
———. *Me: A Memoir*. Duluth, MN: Holy Cow! Press, 2016.
Van Hooft, Stan, ed. *The Handbook of Virtue Ethics*. Bristol, CT: Acumen Publishing, 2014.
Walker, Alice. "Metta to Muriel and Other Marvels: A Poet's Experience of Meditation," 246–50 in *Writers on Writing*. Edited by John Darnton. New York: Henry Holt and Company, 2001.
Wallace, James D. *Moral Relevance and Moral Conflict*. Ithaca, NY: Cornell University Press, 1988.
Walzer, Michael. *The Company of Critics: Social Criticism and Political Commitment in the Twentieth Century*. Second edition. New York: Basic Books, 2002.
Wansink, Brian. *Mindless Eating: Why We Eat More Than We Think*. New York: Bantam, 2006.
Warren, Robert Penn. *John Brown: The Making of a Martyr*. Nashville, TN: J. S. Sanders, 1993.
Watkins, Philip C. "Gratitude and Subjective Well-Being," 167–92 in *The Psychology of Gratitude*. Edited by Robert A. Emmons and Michael E. McCullough. New York: Oxford University Press, 2004.
Watson, Gay. *Attention: Beyond Mindfulness*. London: Reaktion Books, 2017.

Weinstein, Netta, Kirk W. Brown, and Richard M. Ryan. "A Multi-Method Examination of the Effects of Mindfulness on Stress Attribution, Coping, and Emotional Well-Being." *Journal of Research in Personality*, 43 (2009): 374–85.

Weisberg, Robert W. *Creativity: Understanding Innovation in Problem Solving, Science, Invention, and the Arts*. Hoboken, NJ: John Wiley and Sons, 2006.

Weiss, Leah. *How We Work: Live Your Purpose, Reclaim Your Sanity, and Embrace the Daily Grind*. New York: HarperCollins, 2018.

West, Michael A. "The Practice of Mindfulness," 3–25 in *The Psychology of Meditation: Research and Practice*. Edited by Michael A. West. New York: Oxford University Press, 2016.

White, A. R. *Attention*. Oxford: Basil Blackwell, 1964.

Williams, Bernard. *Ethics and the Limits of Philosophy*. Cambridge, MA: Harvard University Press, 1985.

Williams, Mark G., and Jon Kabat-Zinn, eds. *Mindfulness: Diverse Perspectives on Its Meaning, Origins and Applications*. New York: Routledge, 2013.

Williams, Mark, John Teasdale, Zindel Segal, and Jon Kabat-Zinn. *The Mindful Way through Depression: Freeing Yourself from Chronic Unhappiness*. New York: Guilford Press, 2007.

Wittgenstein, Ludwig. *Philosophical Investigations*. Third edition, trans. G. E. M. Anscombe. New York: Macmillan Company, 1958.

———. *Zettel*, trans. G. E. M. Anscombe. Edited by G. E. M. Anscombe and G. H. von Wright. Berkeley: University of California Press, 1967.

Wolenstein, E. V. *Psychoanalytic Marxism*. London: Free Association, Books, 1993.

Wood, James. *How Fiction Works*. New York: Farrar, Straus and Giroux, 2008.

World Health Organization. "Preamble to the Constitution of the World Health Organization." *Official Record of the World Health Organization*. Volume 2. Geneva: World Health Organization, 1946.

Wright, Robert. *Why Buddhism Is True: The Science and Philosophy of Meditation and Enlightenment*. New York: Simon and Schuster, 2017.

Wu, Wayne. *Attention*. New York: Routledge, 2014.

Young, Tarli. "Additional Mechanisms of Mindfulness: How Does Mindfulness Increase Well-Being?" 156–72 in *Mindfulness In Positive Psychology: The Science of Meditation and Well-Being*. Edited by Itai Ivtzan and Tim Lomas. New York: Routledge, 2016.

Zagzebski, Linda Trinkaus. *Virtues of the Mind: An Inquiry into the Nature of Virtue and Ethical Foundations of Knowledge*. New York: Cambridge University Press, 1996.

Zimbardo, Philip, and John Boyd. *The Time Paradox: The New Psychology of Time That Will Change Your Life*. New York: Free Press, 2009.

Zimbardo, Philip G., and Rosemary K. M. Sword. *Living and Loving Better with Time Perspective Therapy: Healing from the Past, Embracing the Present, Creating an Ideal Future*. Jefferson, NC: Exposit, 2017.

———. "Unbridled and Extreme Present Hedonism: How the Leader of the Free World Has Proven Time and Again He Is Unfit for Duty," 25–50 in *The Dangerous Case of Donald Trump: 27 Psychiatrists and Mental Health Experts Assess a President*. Edited by Bandy X. Lee. New York: St. Martin's Press, 2017.

Index

Academy Awards ceremony, 13, 26
Acceptance and Commitment Therapy (ACT), 117–119, 122
addiction, 122, 152
aesthetic values, 31–40
Alidina, Shamash, 3, 176, 177
Alter, Adam, 152
André, Christophe, 39–40, 54, 176, 177
anxiety, 117–118, 124. *See also* Kabat-Zinn, Jon; stress; Thoreau, Henry D.
appreciation, 25, 26, 33, 47, 64, 78, 137
Aristotle, 22
Armstrong, John, 37
attending, 47–59
attention: bare, 91–92; and bearing in mind, 4, 52, 89; careful, 15, 49, 175; direction of, 54–56; and fast and slow thinking, 56–57; general, 51; illusion of, 48; and meditation, 79; as mental muscle, 6, 15; meta-, 55–56, 59, 60n25; modes of, 6, 26, 47; and noticing, 57; scope of, 50; selective, 51; and skill, 57–59, 153; in stoicism, 120; strength of, 52; task, 53–54, 152; as value-guided, 3, 15, 49, 64, 79; versus wandering-mind, 50, 79, 89
Aurelius, Marcus, 119, 123
Austin, J. L., 28n2
authentic mindfulness, 180–185
authenticity, 8, 20, 176; as a hybrid virtue, 170–171; Marianetti and Passmore on, 156–157; and *Seize the Day*, 161–172n1; Thoreau on, 65–66; Ueland on, 33
autonomy, 170
awareness: in defining mindfulness, 3, 78, 79, 84; versus selective attention, 51

balance, 20; diachronic versus synchronic, 150; in lives, 150–153; money-, 151; of optimism and truthfulness, 138–144; tech-, 152–153; work-family, 150
Batchelor, Martine, 91
Baumeister, Roy, 40
Beatty, Warren, 13
Bellow, Saul, 8, 168, 170, 176
Berkshire Hathaway, 148, 150
bigotry, 99
Bin Laden, Osama, 97
Bishop, Scott, 84
Bodhi, Bhikkhu, 9n7, 14, 90, 181
bracketing, 113
Brown, John, 71
Buddhism, 1, 3, 5, 7, 18, 184; and criticism of mindfulness movement, 8, 180–185; Four Noble Truths of, 90, 154; influence on Kabat-Zinn, 77, 81, 88; and Phil Jackson, 154; on right-mindfulness, 1, 2–3, 4, 86–92, 176, 177
Buffett, Warren, 147–149, 150
Bundy, Ted, 97
Butler, Joseph, 58

Callahan, David, 28n11, 159n7
Cameron, Laurie J., 8n1
Carel, Havi, 111–114, 122
Carnegie, Dale, 148
Chabris, Christopher, and Daniel Simons, 48–50, 51
Ciarrochi, Joseph, 145n2
climate change, 20
cognitive behavioral therapy, 7, 41, 114–119
cognitive reappraisal, 135–136
Cohen, Elliot D., 123–124, 176, 177
Collingwood, R. G., 58
compassion, 77, 87, 89, 90–91, 100
contexts of "mindfulness", 14, 25–26, 34, 86, 106
control, personal, 31, 36, 47, 56, 80, 111–112, 119, 135; Epictetus on, 120–123; Mill on, 137
Conway, Jill Ker, 20
coping statements, 115. See also mottos
Cowley, Malcolm, 94n39
creativity, 57, 60n10, 97, 105
Csikszentmihalyi, Mihaly, 3, 44n4, 109n13, 133–134, 158, 175, 176, 177, 178

Dalai Lama, 181
Darley, John, and Dan Batson, 35
Davids, T. W. Rhys, 18, 64, 89
death, 113, 120, 121, 123, 139
deliberateness, 65
dependent virtues, 19
Dewey, John, 5, 7, 18, 104–108; on creativity, 105; on deliberation, 106; on education, 107–108; on habits, 105–106; on intelligence, 104–108, 176, 177; on the present, 34, 105, 107; on reflective thought, 106
DeYoe, Jonathan K., 151
Dillon, Robin, 73n11
discernment, 82, 83, 102
Doris, John M., 29n30
Dunaway, Faye, 13

eating: mindfully, 24; mindlessly, 103
Edel, Leon, 71
Ellis, Albert, 5, 7; on blaming, 116–117; on cognitive reappraisal, 135–136; on coping statements, 115; on mindful valuing, 3, 111–119, 123, 176, 177; on values, 116
Emerson, Ralph Waldo, 71
emotion regulation, 135–136
emotional intelligence, 135, 136
environmental mindfulness, 20, 25, 63, 67–68, 70
envy, 137. See also gratitude
Epictetus, 5, 119–122
Epicurus, 113, 119
Epstein, Ronald, 58–59, 158n1, 176, 177
equality, 21
ethical pluralism, 5, 24, 66, 72, 107, 179
ethical relativism, 24, 104
ethical subjectivism, 24, 65, 101, 143, 180
experience machine, 140

Fairlie, Henry, 137
Feinberg, Joel, 29n34, 73n7
Fields, Rick, 63
Fingarette, Herbert, 44n3, 61n31
flexibility-mindfulness, 7, 96–100, 177. See also Langer, Ellen J.
flow, 32, 55, 133–134, 158, 177. See also Csikszentmihalyi, Mihaly
focus, 148. See also attention
Frankfurt, Harry, 29n28, 29n32
Fredrickson, Barbara L., 118–119, 135, 176, 177
freedom, 21, 112. See also control, personal
Freeman, Judith, 16
Flanagan, Owen, 126n39
Freud, Sigmund: on free association, 114, 176, 177; on neurotic guilt, 69, 166; on the past, 41; on traditional morality, 94n38, 183

Gardner, Howard, 110n42
Garland, Eric L., 118–119, 176, 177
Gates, Bill, 148, 149
Gelles, David, 155–156, 176, 177
Gethin, Rupert, 94n42
Gewirth, Alan, 29n34
Ghiselin, Brewster, 109n11
Goethe, 5, 37–38
Goleman, Daniel, 59n2, 60n22, 60n27

good judgment, 4, 19, 20–21, 38, 57, 91, 107, 141, 144; and balance, 150; and Langer, 97; and *Seize the Day*, 163–164, 167, 170
good lives, 4, 24, 31, 80, 179; Goethe on, 37, 42; happiness in, 131; Thoreau on, 63–72
Gordon, Mary, 27
Gottman, John M., 135
gratitude, 16, 34, 64, 71, 119, 137–138
Gunatillake, Rohan, 152

habits: Dewey on, 105–106; Langer on, 103–104; and love, 135; Thoreau on, 67–68
Hadot, Pierre, 120, 123
Haidt, Jonathan, 136
Hanh, Thich Nhat, 154
Hanson, Rick, 28n8, 50
happiness, 7, 37, 102, 129–144; and caring relationships, 135; definitions of, 131; and emotion-regulation, 135–136; and flow, 133–134; and money, 151; paradox of, 141–144; and savoring, 133; as subjective well-being, 131; Thoreau on, 70; and virtues, 136–141
Harari, Yuval Noah, 93n11
Harrison, Eric, 4, 30n42, 56, 93n29, 176, 178, 184–185
Hawkins, Sally, 129
Haybron, Daniel M., 145n10
healthy-mindedness, 139
Heffernan, Virginia, 28n3
Hillel the Elder, 17
Huang, Peter H., 60n25
Hunter, James Davison, and Paul Nedelisky, 45n45, 145n25

Ie, Amanda, 108n6
intelligence, 104–108
Invisible Gorilla Experiment, 48–50, 51, 57
Ivtzan, Itai, 8n3, 144n1

Jackson, Phil, 153–154, 176, 177
Janus (Roman god), 36, 67
James, William, 50, 131, 139
Joiner, Thomas, 8, 178, 181–184

Kabat-Zinn, Jon, 3–4, 5, 178; influence of, 155, 156; on inward focus, 54; on nonjudgmental, 78–84; on personal vision, 80–81; on Thoreau, 63, 83; on values, 78–84
Kahneman, Daniel, 56–57, 87, 145n9
Kronman, Anthony T., 114

Lakshmi, Padma, 29n27
Langer, Ellen J., 3, 5, 7, 157–158; on creativity, 97; on definition of mindfulness, 96, 176, 177, 178–179; on habits, 57, 103, 109n38; on happiness, 139; on outward focus, 54, 95, 182
Leigh, Mike, 129–130
Levy, David M., 54, 60n13, 152–153, 176, 177
Lyubomirsky, Sonja, 73n12, 131; on mindful decision-making, 95–104; on morality, 101–102

Madoff, Bernard, 97
Mann, Thomas, 35
Marianett, Oberdan, and Jonathan Passmore, 156–158, 176, 177
Maslow, Abraham, 132
McFerrin, Bobby, 138
McMindfulness, 181
meaningful lives, 23
medicine, 58–59, 77
meditation, 6, 26, 53, 148; aesthetic, 39–40; aspects of, 88; Buddhist, 88; as contributing to happiness, 133; loving-kindness, 83; mindfulness-based, 77–83; and slowing down, 57; and sports, 153; and technology, 152; and turning inward, 54, 55; and work, 153–156
Mele, Alfred R., 61n31
mental health, 3, 15, 43, 88, 137, 144, 178; Ellis on, 111, 116, 117, 179; in holistic definitions, 25; in *Seize the Day*, 166, 171; and technology, 152–153; in Thoreau, 69; and work, 147, 150
Mercer, Johnny, 138
#MeToo Movement, 20
Michener, James A., 16
microscopic truthfulness, 33, 177
Midgley, Mary, 176

Milgram, Stanley, 99–100
Mill, John Stuart, 141–142
mindfulness: as attending to what matters, 2, 5, 13, 17; cultivating, 67–68; defined in *Merriam-Webster's Collegiate Dictionary*, 3, 84; flexibility-, 7, 96–101, 177; flow-, 134, 177; meta-, 60n25; movement, 1, 4–5, 175–185; as multifaceted, 25; multiple meanings of, 14, 15, 155, 176; ordinariness of, 2; Oxford English Dictionary illustrations of, 16–17; personal-, 2, 14, 19; true, 8, 14, 175, 180; types of, 25–27, 118; value-based, 2, 5, 14, 19, 25, 177; value perspectives on, 18, 63; value-suspending, 4, 77, 153, 178; virtue-, 2, 4, 14, 18–19, 153
Mindfulness-Based Stress Reduction (MBSR), 77, 156
mindfulness movement, 1, 8, 175, 180; critics of, 175–185
mindlessness, 13, 20, 27, 49, 92, 181
Monet, Claude, 39
money, 16, 36, 69, 70, 147–149, 151; in *Seize the Day*, 162, 165
Monteiro, Lynette M., 93n16
morality, 23
mottos, 17, 115, 153
multitasking, 20–21, 53
Munger, Charlie, 148
Murphy, Arthur, 96
music, 32, 122
mysticism, 35, 44n3, 169, 172n9

narcissism, 43, 55, 71, 182
Ngnoumen, Christell T., 8n3
Niemiec, Ryan M., and Judith Lessing, 138
Nobre, Anna C., and Sabine Kastner, 59n2
non-judgmental: confusing different senses of, 3–4, 82–83, 84–86, 156–158; in Kabat-Zinn, 77–78, 178; in Langer, 101, 102; senses of, 78, 156–158; in Thomas Joiner, 181–183
nostalgia, 33, 42
Nozick, Robert, 49, 139–141
Nussbaum, Martha C., 112

optimism, 33, 132, 138–144
O'Toole, James, 149

performance anxiety, 32, 117, 122, 148
personal-mindfulness, 2, 14, 19, 31
Peterson, Christopher, 138
phenomenology, 113
philanthropy, 15, 70–71, 149, 150
philosophical counseling, 124
Pickert, Kate, 9n6
positive psychology, 3, 7, 118, 129, 132–141, 178, 179, 180
pragmatism, 107
present, ix, 8, 20, 26, 31–43; as ambiguous, 34; Brenda Ueland on, 31–33; buffered versus broadened, 36–37, 79; mindful valuing in, 115; in *Seize the Day*, 161, 164–167, 170; Stoics' focus on, 120, 122, 123; Thoreau on, 66–67
PricewaterhouseCoopers, 13, 19
Princeton seminary experiment, 35
pro-social emotions, 154–155
prospective hindsight, 36
psychoanalysis, 41, 114, 176, 177
public speaking, 117, 122, 148
Purser, Ron, and David Loy, 181

Ram Dass, 44n1
Rational Emotive Behavior Therapy (REBT), 7, 114, 122
regrets, 41, 42, 102, 131, 132
Reich, Wilhelm, 168
religion, 3. *See also* Buddhism
Rieff, Philip, 94n38, 168, 172n5, 185n17
Rogers, Carl, 132
Rosenbaum, Meikro, and Barry Magrid, 28n4
Rousseau, Jean-Jacques, 166
Rubin, Gretchen, 142–143
Ryle, Gilbert, 17, 53

Sartre, Jean-Paul, 60n24
sati, 18, 64, 89, 185
savoring, 112, 133, 145n16
Schumpeter, Joseph, 156
Schweitzer, Albert, 23
Seize the Day, 4, 161–172
self-deception, 33, 58, 109n38–110n39, 131, 170
self-esteem movement, 183
self-expression, 31–32, 37, 38, 55
self-forgiveness, 171–172

self-fulfillment, 23
self-respect: and authenticity, 171; and meditation, 80; Thoreau on, 65, 69–70
Seligman, Martin E. P., 3, 41–42, 132, 138
Serenity Prayer, 122, 125n32
Sharf, Robert H., 92
Siegel, Daniel J., 108n3
Siegel, Ronald D., 9n5, 85–86
Slote, Michael, 19
Smith, Adam, 51
Smith, John E., 38
Solomon, Robert, 23
spectators versus participants, 53–54, 79
Steger, Michael F., and Eve Edman, 154–155, 177
Sternberg, Robert J., 110n39
Stoics, 7, 119–123, 142, 177, 183
Stone, Emma, 13
stress, 1, 79, 136, 137, 154, 155, 157, 180. *See also* Kabat-Zinn, Jon
Suffering, 113; Thoreau on, 69

Dr. Tamkin (in *Seize the Day*), 161, 177
Thales, 51, 87
Thayer, Richard H., and Cass R. Sunstein, 103
Thera, Nyanaponika, 91
therapeutic trend in ethics, 4, 168
thinking, fast versus slow, 56–57
Thoreau, Henry D., 5, 6, 18, 63–72, 112; critiques of his value perspective, 70–72; on cultivating mindfulness, 67–68; on health and suffering, 69–70; Kabat-Zinn on, 83; on living in the present, 66–67, 133; on mindfulness as wakefulness, 63–72, 176, 177, 179; on self-respect, 69
Tiberius, Valerie, 29n23
time: objective versus subjective, 34–35, 66; and psychotherapy, 40–43. *See also* present
Trump, Donald, 43
truthfulness, 13, 97, 104; and authenticity, 170; Carel on, 112–113; and optimism, 170; and self-deception, 58; Thoreau on, 65; Ueland on, 33
Tyler, Anne, 35

Ueland, Brenda, 31–33, 34, 39, 55, 133, 176, 177

value-based mindfulness, 2, 14, 19, 49, 57, 177; *sati* as, 89
value-suspending mindfulness, 4, 77–87, 92, 118, 133, 153; as promoting value-based mindfulness, 81, 119, 138; and slide to value-based mindfulness, 154
values, 23, 24; disagreements about, 18, 21, 71–72; moral and non-moral, 24; sound, 2, 14, 18, 19, 24
valuing, 23, 111–124
virtues: dependent, 19, 64; and happiness, 129, 136–141; in philosophical counseling, 124; as traits and in actions, 22. *See also* authenticity; compassion; gratitude; self-respect; wisdom
virtue-mindfulness, 4, 22, 33, 77, 95, 176; defined, 2, 4, 14; disagreements concerning, 20–21

wakefulness, 63–66
walking, 32, 67, 87, 103
Wallace, James D., 110n43
Wansink, Brian, 103
Watkins, Philip C., 137
Watson, Gay, 9n8
Weinstein, Netta, 145n24
Weiss, Leah, 9n13
West, Michael W., 8n2, 85
White, A. R., 60n18, 61n30, 93n6
Williams, Bernard, 29n36
wisdom, 19, 77, 129, 138
Wittgenstein, Ludwig, 14, 49, 51, 54
work, mindful, 7, 58–59, 147–158
writing, 27, 31–32, 56, 68, 93n10, 123
Wu, Wayne, 59n2

Zagzebski, Linda Trinkaus, 29n31, 110n51
Zimbardo, Philip G., 42–43

About the Author

Mike W. Martin is professor emeritus of Philosophy at Chapman University (Orange, California). His fifteen books include *Memoir Ethics* (2016), *Happiness and the Good Life* (2012), *From Morality to Mental Health* (2006), *Meaningful Work* (2000), and *Love's Virtues* (1996).

www.ingramcontent.com/pod-product-compliance
Lightning Source LLC
Chambersburg PA
CBHW021547020526
44115CB00038B/893